Michael White is the author of 3  international bestselling novels *Equin* and non-fiction titles *Stephen Hawki* John Gribbin), *Leonardo: The First Scientist*, *Tolkein: A Biography* and *The Science of the X-Files*. He was awarded the 1998 Bookman Prize for best popular science book in the US for his biography of Isaac Newton. In 2002 his book *Rivals* was shortlisted for the prestigious Aventis Prize and in 2006 his *Fruits of War* was longlisted for the same award.

He has been a newspaper columnist, science editor for *GQ* magazine and a series consultant for the Discovery Channel's *The Science of the Inevitable*. In 2001 he was awarded a Distinguished Talent visa by the Australian government and now lives in Sydney with his wife and four children. For more information visit his website at www.michaelwhite.com.au.

By Michael White

Fiction

Equinox
The Medici Secret

Non-Fiction

Coffee with Newton
Galileo Antichrist
Isaac Asimov: A Life of the Grand Master of Science Fiction
C. S. Lewis: A Life
A Teaspoon and an Open Mind: The Science of Doctor Who
Machiavelli: A Man Misunderstood
The Fruits of War
A Chronicle of the 21st Century (with Gentry Lee)
Rivals: Conflict as the Fuel of Science
Tolkein: A Biography
Leonardo: The First Scientist
The Pope and the Heretic
Isaac Newton: The Last Sorcerer
Stephen Hawking: A Life in Science
Einstein: A Life in Science
Darwin: A Life in Science
Breakthrough (with Kevin Davies)
Thompson Twin: An 80s Memoir
Asimov: The Unauthorised Life
The Science of the X-Files
Life Out There
Mind and Matter (for younger readers)
Alien Life Forms (for younger readers)
Super Science
Weird Science
Mozart (for younger readers)
John Lennon (for younger readers)

Galileo
Antichrist

A Biography

Michael White

Phoenix

A PHOENIX PAPERBACK

First published in Great Britain in 2007
by Weidenfeld & Nicolson
This paperback edition published in 2009
by Phoenix,
an imprint of Orion Books Ltd,
Orion House, 5 Upper St Martin's Lane,
London WC2H 9EA

An Hachette UK company

3 5 7 9 10 8 6 4 2

A CIP catalogue record for this book
is available from the British Library.

ISBN 978-0-7538-2210-4

Printed and bound in Great Britain by Clays Ltd, St Ives plc

The Orion Publishing Group's policy is to use papers that
are natural, renewable and recyclable products and
made from wood grown in sustainable forests. The logging
and manufacturing processes are expected to conform to
the environmental regulations of the country of origin.

www.orionbooks.co.uk

For David, in celebration of chats at Brew-Ha

Contents

Illustrations

I do not feel obliged to believe that the same God who has endowed us with sense, reason, and intellect has intended us to forgo their use.

Galileo Galilei

Introduction

[That] the sun is the centre of the world and completely
immovable of local motion is foolish and absurd in
philosophy, and formally heretical, inasmuch as it expressly
contradicts the doctrine of the Holy Scripture in many
passages, both in their literal meaning and according to the
interpretation of the Fathers and Doctors.

Declaration of the Committee of the Holy Office,
19 February 1616

Along with Michelangelo, Napoleon, Jesus and a small cadre of others,
Galileo is one of the few people in history to whom we refer habitually
by their Christian name alone. A great scientist, he was a man we may
bracket with Newton, Einstein and Darwin. Yet there was much more
to this man than his science.

If they stop to think of Galileo at all, most people remember two
things about him from school – the Leaning Tower and his trial before
the Inquisition. However, in the four hundred years since he walked the
Earth, some of the facts of his life have become obfuscated. This is
particularly true of the period between 1615 and 1642, when his scientific
work was at odds with Church doctrine. This loss of clarity has come
about because there are as many opinions and theories about the facts
surrounding Galileo's trial as there were enemies of the man ready and
waiting to strike him down. Indeed, even amongst scholars there is no
consensus about the causes of Galileo's troubles with the Church. Each
historian who studies and writes about this subject seems to have a
different take on it.

In his book *The Sleepwalkers* the popular historian Arthur Koestler
placed much of the blame for the clash between the cardinals and

Galileo at the door of the scientist, and many books and papers have been written by Catholic apologists about the ideological battle at the heart of the Galileo affair. Many of these concur with Koestler's view; but, at the same time, Galileo's fight has made him a popular mascot for radical Protestants, a questionable honour that would have utterly confused the man himself (not to mention the founding fathers of Protestantism).

Any biography of Galileo is, at its core, the story of the man's life and his astonishing scientific achievements, but from the moment his ideology began to clash with that of the Church of Rome his life acquired a far greater resonance. Even during his lifetime Galileo was perceived by some as a martyr, and it was not just Protestants with a vested interest who sided with him against papal bullying: many otherwise devout and orthodox Catholics believed that the Church was behaving irrationally over the affair. Because his ideas clashed so terribly with the Church, this has made Galileo a symbol of the differences between religion and science, which today seem just as great as they ever were during centuries past.

As I hope to make clear in this book, the clash between Galileo and the authorities in Rome that forced him to recant his scientific views and them to place him under house arrest came about because of a number of different factors. Some of these were prosaic, others deeply rooted in a conflict of world-views. Galileo was a tough character, determined and often overconfident. He had a powerful ego and a great sense of self-importance. He was also impatient with those who disagreed with him over scientific issues and he was quick to mock and to ridicule. Therefore, he had many enemies, some of whom were powerful and influential and eventually brought him down.

Galileo was also unfortunate enough to be in the wrong place at the wrong time to expose his radical scientific ideas – in Italy at the height of the Counter-Reformation, when Catholic paranoia was at its most intense. To make things worse, just as Galileo was putting forward his unorthodox theories, Europe was in the grip of a sprawling military conflict, the Thirty Years War, which was in part at least a war that had begun as a clash between Catholics and Protestants.

Beyond this is the fact that Galileo's radical opinions struck at the very heart of human vanity and ego. The Copernican model, which Galileo supported and for which he provided supporting evidence, placed the Sun at the centre of the universe and described the Earth as being just one of several planets in orbit about the Sun. Christian dogma stated that the Earth was the centre of all things. This was an ancient claim supported most significantly by Aristotle. To accommodate Copernicus and to reject Aristotle required an acceptance that the Earth was not the centre of the universe, that humans were not central to existence, that the universe might not have been made by God merely for the satisfaction of humanity.

It is hard for us, living in the twenty-first century, to understand why this should be such a problem for those of Galileo's time; but this is in large part thanks to men such as Galileo and the scientific advances that have been made during the past four centuries. In fact, since the seventeenth century and the Galilean/Copernican revolution, science has taken us through another revolution, another diminishing of the image of humankind. Darwin's theory of evolution via natural selection took us another step forward in our thinking. Not only is the Earth an insignificant rock orbiting an unremarkable star, but human beings are no different from other animals and have evolved from simpler forms: there is no need for God. As the Nobel laureate Steven Weinberg has commented recently: 'One of the great achievements of science has been, if not to make it impossible for intelligent people to be religious, then at least to make it possible for them not to be religious.'

Today many people are left completely unimpressed by orthodox Christianity and perceive many of its teachings as having been an insidious influence on the history of our civilisation: Christianity is anti-intellectual and anti-progressive, and many object strongly to the way in which popes and other influential figures have used their power.

Christian apologists are quick to claim that the evil-doing of some bad apples should not diminish the value of Christianity. Others declare that the mistakes of the Church are all in the past, that we should forget about the Inquisition and the thousands of innocents who died at their hands, that we should ignore the way in which the Catholic Church in particular held back intellectual and scientific development in past centuries. Such people argue these things could never happen now.

This is difficult to accept. Indeed, there may be much in the claim that the controllers of Christian doctrine have learned nothing from the mistakes of the past and it is merely the targets that have changed. Thanks to social and scientific development outside the limits of the Church, the world has moved on. The Roman Inquisition, which still exists as the Sacred Congregation for the Doctrine of the Faith (and was headed by Cardinal Joseph Ratzinger before he was elected as pope in 2005) cannot torture and burn people any more. Instead, the Church forbids women from becoming priests, outlaws homosexual clerics and rails against the use of contraceptives in Third World nations, where millions die annually from AIDS-related illness.

Yet even these arguments play only a peripheral role in the story of Galileo's conflict with the Church, for all that we know about the battle may have been nothing but a smokescreen. According to orthodox history, Galileo was put on trial before the Inquisition because he disobeyed a ruling which stipulated that he should only discuss, teach or write about Copernicanism as a hypothesis. He then wrote a book called *Dialogue Concerning the Two Chief World Systems*, in which he espoused the Copernican model *as fact*.

But recent evidence shows that Galileo had actually stumbled upon a far more dangerous scientific theory, one that, if proved, would have threatened doctrine during a time in which the men who ran the Church were feeling particularly vulnerable. Galileo had written about this theory in some detail in a book called *The Assayer*, which was published in October 1623. The new concept it contained had such potential to damage that when the extent of the danger was realised by Pope Urban and his cardinals they quickly concluded that no hint of the idea should be allowed to go beyond the Vatican.

What were they to do? Should they kill Galileo? It was certainly one possible answer to the problem, and the Church had no qualms about murdering innocent people; but it might raise suspicions. Should they instead let him go after making him promise never to discuss or write about his radical ideas again? Should they simply ban his books and burn as many copies as possible? This they considered too risky. There was, though, a third course the Church authorities could follow: they could strike a deal with the scientist. He would stand trial for the lesser heresy of proselytising Copernicanism, accept imprisonment and never teach again or publish anything. In return, they would not torture and burn him.

This then is the story of Galileo's life, but it is also a tale of intrigue and conflict – the story of one man whose intellect and radicalism were attacked by Rome in an act of self-preservation, a story in which our hero was defeated by the power of the Church but has been proven right posthumously. Galileo's life was wonderfully rich and filled with triumph and agony, but thanks to the pivotal event of his old age – his persecution by the Church – he has become a symbol of the struggle for freedom of thought, the epitome of the enlightened individual facing down institutionalised ignorance, and winning . . . eventually.

Like Father, Like Son

Arcetri, near Florence, Winter 1641

The blind old man, white hair falling to his shoulders, leans back in his chair and pulls the rough woollen blanket closer around his neck. In the chill room with him, seated at the desk close to the door, is his amanuensis, the promising young scientist Vincenzio Viviani, who has been living with him for several months now.

The 77-year-old Galileo Galilei cannot see the room, but he knows where everything is – the sturdy desk, the wooden chair, the doorway into his bedchamber. Now, as he dictates what will be his final notes, his last thoughts on the science that has obsessed him almost his entire life, he can visualise in his mind the cascade of events that have shaped his existence. He sees again the grandiose towers of the University of Pisa. Then before him lies the gorgeous vista of the Grand Canal in Venice, viewed from a small boat in which he sits wondering about the movement of water and the true meaning of the tides that sweep the lagoon. Next come the faces of all the dead: his mistress Marina Gamba; his beloved daughter, christened Virginia, who became Sister Maria Celeste and died so young. There, next in the procession, are his parents; his adored friends, Filippo Salviati, Gianfrancesco Sagredo, Paulo Sarpi and Prince Cesi. After they fade, he sees his reviled enemies, Pope Paul V, Cardinal Bellarmine, Orazio Grassi and the viperous Father Michelangelo Seghizzi.

More than most men, Galileo has cause to feel bitter, to be suffused with hatred for the Catholic Church, for this institution destroyed his career and placed him under house arrest. His bitterness is ever present, but he has gradually become resigned to his fate; the pain and the bile have drained away; he waits to die. Perhaps Galileo knows that one day the world will learn who was right and who was wrong in the dispute that has characterised his life. Perhaps he knows that one day the whole truth will be revealed about why he was tried before the Inquisition and persecuted by the Holy See. Then, he realises, the guilty and the ignorant shall be unmasked.

When the 42-year-old bachelor Vincenzo Galilei, a musician of some small renown, first arrived in Pisa early in 1562, he found a tiny city with a population of less than nine thousand. Coming from Pisa's far larger neighbour Florence, Vincenzo must have felt that he was moving to a tiny country town a long way from the glamour and excitement of the Tuscan capital he was used to.

Pisa had suffered something of a miserable history and this was in no small part thanks to the Florentines, and in particular the Medici family, who had controlled the region for generations. A succession of bloody wars had fractured the centuries-old relationship between Pisa and Florence, and on one occasion, in 1504, the larger city state had laid siege to Pisa in an attempt to starve it into submission. But the Pisans were a hardy people and patriotic in the extreme, so that Florence, for all its wealth and relative military strength, had never succeeded in properly subjugating the city. By Galileo's day, Pisans and Florentines worked together and pooled their resources under the banner of the latest Medici ruler, Cosimo de' Medici, the Grand Duke of Tuscany.

The Medici family had grown in power in Tuscany since the time of the first Cosimo de' Medici, who, during the first half of the fifteenth century, was regarded as the first citizen of Florence but never officially ruled the state. Between the times of the two Cosimos, the Medici family had become the wealthiest clan in Europe and Cosimo I's grandson, Lorenzo the Magnificent, had brought previously unimagined stability and social development to the region. As great patrons of the arts, drivers of humanism and men inspired by the new ideas of natural philosophers, the Medici not only embodied the Renaissance, they played a significant role in sustaining it. The Medici court provided fertile ground for any creative individuals who had done enough to get themselves noticed and here such figures as Michelangelo, Brunelleschi, Leonardo Bruni and a raft of other artists and philosophers established themselves as the intellectual elite of their age.

Many of Vincenzo Galilei's antecendents had once been prominent members of the Florentine community and he could trace the family line back to the twelfth century. Over the years, no fewer than nineteen Galileis had been members of the ruling body in Florence, the Signoria, and they had provided a state leader (the gonfalonier) in 1446. This was the first Galileo Galilei, the elder brother of Vincenzo's great-grandfather. The politician Galileo Galilei accrued great wealth and public honour for the family but died young in 1450. He was the most illustrious Galilei until a hundred and fifty years later, when his namesake revolutionised the world of science.

By Vincenzo's time, the Galilei family had fallen upon hard times. Only thirty-five years after a Galilei had presided over the government in the city, the gonfalonier's brother was forced to sell his properties in Florence and move his family to the village of Santa Maria a Monte, where, in 1478, Vincenzo's grandfather, Michelangelo, was born and where a major part of the family remained for generations. The reasons for the rapid social and financial decline of the Galileis remain something of a mystery, but it would not be unreasonable to assume that they were in some way linked with politics and that for reasons now lost to history the Galileis had clashed with the powerful Medici. Lorenzo de' Medici had come to power in Florence in 1469, and the very year the Galileis moved out of the city, 1478, the Florentine ruler had survived an assassination attempt which had been instigated in part by great rivals of the Medici, the wealthy and powerful Pazzi family. Although there is no record of any official link between the Pazzi and the Galileis, it is possible the latter fell out of favour with the Medici because of some loose connection with this attack on Lorenzo.

Little is known of Vincenzo's childhood. Born some time in 1520 (the exact date is not recorded) in Santa Maria a Monte, his musical talent was realised early and he was probably taught in Florence. His education, though, was exceptionally narrow. He knew little Latin and no Greek. This almost certainly proved a hindrance to his career because, although his musical gifts earned him respect, his modest education limited his chances of preferment and he never truly fulfilled his potential.

After basic schooling in Florence, Vincenzo had been trained in Venice under the master Gioseffo Zarlino, but before long they had had a bruising disagreement and a parting of ways over music theory. Seemingly undeterred, Vincenzo had gone on to dedicate his life to music. At first, he had performed the role of the orthodox musician, working for wealthy patrons, including Bernardetto de' Medici. But perhaps the most important figure in Vincenzo's early life had been the wealthy patron Giovanni Bardi, who also later became a great supporter of Galileo's. It was Bardi who had financed the young Vincenzo's training in Venice and he had also provided the funds for the young musician to travel to Turkey and the Near East.

What Vincenzo learned on these journeys was enormously influential in shaping his musical ideas and this experience led him to abandon many conventional musical strictures. Most importantly, he began to experiment with single-line melodies and rejected the fashion for word-painting and madrigal style. He also held strong views concerning the rigid system of dissonances adhered to by most composers and he argued for a relaxing of the rules.

In 1562, soon after arriving in Pisa, Vincenzo began taking in pupils, teaching the lute and the organ to make ends meet. We can imagine him living a rather free and easy existence at this time. He was always short of cash, but his life was filled with the music he loved and he had a large circle of friends. Within a few months of settling in the city he met and fell in love with a woman called Giulia Ammananti, who came from a noble family that had also, like the Galileis, fallen on hard times.

Giulia was justly proud of her heritage and claimed that she was a distant cousin of a well-known cardinal. The Galileis and the Ammanantis had more in common than crumbled dreams: some eighty years earlier their paths had intersected when a sister of Vincenzo's grandfather, a woman named Lisabetta Galilei, had married into the Ammananti family. It is therefore quite possible that within what was after all a rather small community, Vincenzo knew Giulia many years before arriving in Pisa. Whatever the origins of their romance, it obviously blossomed quickly, because by the summer of 1563 Giulia was pregnant and, as a consequence, Vincenzo's life was forced to change radically.

The couple were married on 5 July and four days later, on the ninth, Vincenzo rented a space for use as a small music school. His landlord was an acquaintance, Colonel Giuseppe Bocca, who recorded the event in his diary: 'Rented our house situated in Chiaso di Mercanti for 12 golden scudi to the Pisan Vincenzo Galilei, a Florentine maestro of music.'

After the wedding, Vincenzo received a dowry of 100 gold scudi from Giulia's brother Leon, but even with this and a tiny income from the music school he was always in financial difficulty and quite unable to keep his wife in the style to which she aspired. Within a few weeks, the 'Florentine maestro of music' was forced to accept a position in the wool-trading company run by Giulia's brother Leon, and the newly-weds rented a room in a large house on Via Giusti, which they shared with members of the Ammananti family, including Giulia's mother Lucrezia and sister Dorotea. This is where the Galileis' first child, a boy they named Galileo, was born on 15 February 1564. Today the spot is commemorated by a plaque on a café called Settimelli, which declares that Galileo Galilei was born on the floor above.

There is some confusion over the exact date of Galileo's birth. During the sixteenth century there was no legal requirement to record a birth date and the only accurate signifier comes from the date of baptism, which did have to be recorded by local Church officials. Galileo was christened on 19 February in the baptistery of the cathedral at Pisa. His date of birth has been placed variously as 15, 16 or 18 February, depending on which authority you believe. The University of Padua has long insisted it was 18 February, but during the 1590s, when Galileo was preparing an astrological chart for himself, he made a note that he was born at 4 p.m. on 15 February 1564. This information was only revealed in 1908 when the historian Antonio Favaro found the date in Galileo's copious collection of notes in a bundle that Favaro later described as some of Galileo's 'astrological mess'.[2]

Galileo was born into an era of great religious intolerance, and this provided a harsh backdrop to his early life. For Galileo, religious conflict and the corrosive power of the Roman Church were simply facts of life, part of the fabric of his world and as much an influence in shaping his thinking as were his interest in science and his great skills as an analytical thinker and mathematician.

Profoundly important as these things were, the influence of Galileo's father in shaping his son's mindset cannot be overlooked. Vincenzo Galilei was something of an innovator, a man keen to push the boundaries within his own field, who refused to blindly accept the status quo. 'It seems to me,' he wrote in his best known work, *Dialogo della musica antica e della moderna*, 'that those who try to prove an assertion by relying simply on the weight of authority act very absurdly'[3] – an attitude that was to rub off on Galileo.

As well as espousing unorthodox musical ideas, Vincenzo was also quite unconventional when it came to matters of religion. He conformed for the sake of appearances, but he was at best sceptical of some of the central tenets of the Faith. This manifested itself most clearly in his dislike for religious music. He resented the fact that all music revolved around the Church, that this great art form was perceived as worthless unless it was devotional.

Vincenzo had an overwhelming desire to change this view, and he believed the best way to do it was to take music back to pre-Christian times, when it had existed for its own sake. As well as this, fuelled by what he had gained from his travels, he was excited and inspired by ancient music and wished to fuse Greek and other pagan musical ideas with modern melodic and harmonic forms.

It was this approach that had lain behind Vincenzo's falling out with his old teacher and was perhaps part of the reason why he was to find gainful employment as a musician and composer increasingly difficult as the years went by. Vincenzo was an argumentative and difficult man who continues to frustrate historians. '[His] crookedness, inconsistency, and evasion', one critic has written '[are] not only annoying for us, but also unfortunate; for he was an original thinker and a widely experienced musician – he claimed to have collected and entabulated over 14,000 pieces of music, and he had some very interesting things to say, but his line of thought is constantly side-tracked and distorted.'[4]

Making a living as a musician in sixteenth-century Italy was difficult enough, but for a musician who had little time for orthodox religious music and held extreme views about musical form it was more or less impossible, and he was forced to devote more time than he would have liked to his brother-in-law's wool business. But, in 1572, when Galileo was eight, Vincenzo took the brave step of accepting a position as court musician in Florence, and there he began to develop new and exciting forms of music. His compositions were almost totally ignored at the time but were later perceived as a key element in the development of modern Western musical form. He also wrote a collection of books (most significantly his *Dialogo della musica antica e della moderna*) in which he vociferously attacked the elaborate polyphonic vocal style of the era. Many of Vincenzo's revolutionary ideas shaped the music of the next century, including the *recitativo* at the heart of opera.

Galileo's mother was in almost all ways the very opposite of Vincenzo. She seems to have received a poor education and the main focus of her thinking was to move the family up through the social order as best she could. She came from a noble and once-wealthy family who were still considerably better off than the branch of the Galileis into which her husband had been born. According to surviving letters and diaries, Giulia was something of a moaner, who was constantly dissatisfied with her husband's efforts to improve their lot. She appears to have had absolutely no interest in music and actively resented Vincenzo's obsession, mocking his efforts and complaining about the fact that he wasted his time on what she perceived to be valueless, commercially futile efforts.

In spite of this, Giulia did her duty: during the first fifteen years of marriage she bore Vincenzo seven children. Except for their names, little is known of three of these: Benedetto (born soon after Galileo), Anna (born around 1574) and Lena, who arrived some five years later at the end of the 1570s. It is likely all three died very young.

Galileo had three other siblings, who all survived to adulthood. Closest in age to him was his sister Virginia who was nine years his junior. She married in 1591 and had four children. Two years younger than Virginia was Michelangelo, born on 18 December 1575. Michelangelo turned out to be a ne'er-do-well, a rather unsuccessful musician who spent his life relying on his brother for money and support. His long-suffering wife Anna Chiari Bandinelli bore him nine children and died with four of them – Mechilde, Cosimo, Anna Maria and Maria Fulvia – in 1634 when plague struck Italy. Galileo's youngest sibling was a sister, Livia, who was thirteen years younger. She married at the age of 22 and had four children, one of whom died within hours of birth.

Galileo's earliest years were quite solitary ones and the Galilei house only began to fill with his siblings when he was 9 or 10 years old. Up to this time he was taught by a succession of private tutors, some of whom appear to have been very capable. According to his first biographer, his assistant Vincenzo Viviani (who admittedly had a penchant for elaboration), Galileo showed early promise. 'He began to show his intellect's brightness during the first years of adolescence,' Viviani wrote. 'During his spare time, he constructed himself several instruments and little machines, imitating and reproducing in small size every artificial construction he saw, such as mills, jails, and any other vulgar machines as well. In case a construction lacked of a necessary part, he supplied it by inventing it himself, using whale bones instead of iron springs, or other things: when he needed something, he used his brain in order to make the construction work and he never left anything imperfect.'[5]

This is quite possibly an accurate description of Galileo's personality as a child related to Viviani by Galileo himself during his final years, but it is striking how similar it is to a description of Isaac Newton as a child, reported by his first biographer, William Stukeley: 'He [Newton] penetrated beyond the superficial view of the thing . . . He obtained so exact a notion of the mechanism of it, that he made a true and perfect model of it in wood; and it was said to be as clean a piece of workmanship as the original.'[6] Intellectually, Galileo and Newton shared much, so it is perhaps not surprising that as children they should have viewed the world with similar perspectives.

In 1572, when Galileo was 8 years old, his father left to work in Florence under the patronage of Count Giovanni de Bardi, and the Galilei family remained in Pisa for the next two years, reuniting with Vincenzo during the autumn of 1574. Galileo was sent to the local school and taught by one of the instructors hired by the Commune di Pisa.

Some hints about the sort of education Galileo received there come from a set of official instructions given to one of the boy's teachers, Giacomo Marchesi of Piacenza, who taught at the school between May 1571 and May 1574: 'During working days, students are compelled to stay for three hours in the morning and three hours in the afternoon at least on Mondays, Tuesdays, Wednesdays, and Thursdays, plus an hour lecture,' the instructions recounted.

> On Saturdays, a student should lecture while others comment on, in order that any student lecture at least once. Moreover, at least three classes of students are needed: one composed of *epistolanti,* one of Latin scholars studying all the rules and one of beginners, which studies the concordances and the first rule. The class of *epistolanti* is compelled to present an epistle every day of the mentioned four. Two Latin texts are compulsory for Latin scholars. As for the beginners, it is the person who repeats that should remind the teacher to look after them and get him to prepare a general examination on Fridays. On Saturdays, beside the lecture, he should make them repeat some verses learned by heart.[7]

While his young son buckled down to the school regime in Pisa, Vincenzo was having a very exciting time in Florence. Although he received little respect from his materialistic wife, his ideas were highly regarded by many intellectuals and he became a prominent figure in a group calling itself the Florentine Camerata. Members of this group, intellectuals, writers and artists from across Tuscany, including the well-known composers Giulio Caccini and Jacopo Peri, met regularly at Count Bardi's home to discuss art, literature, music and other cerebral interests. According to Bardi's son Pietro, writing to his friend Monsignor Dini some seventy years later: 'My father's home was filled with the most famous men in the town.'[8]

Vincenzo probably felt a little out of his depth in such company. Except for his intimate knowledge of music, his education was limited.

He knew little of art or politics and his awareness of natural philosophy was restricted to a clear understanding of sound and acoustics, but nothing more. However, Vincenzo was a radical thinker. He possessed an enquiring mind and was not afraid to venture into unknown intellectual territory; indeed he relished such adventures, so that during the time he was a member of the Florentine Camerata he contributed much, as well as gaining from the broader knowledge of many of the other members. Crucially, Vincenzo's involvement with this influential group would later also offer benefits for his elder son.

The time when the family were split up is one of the few periods in Galileo's childhood that offers an intimate if short-lived glimpse of his life and the lives of his family. These snapshots come from a collection of letters exchanged between Vincenzo Galilei in Florence and a friend of the family, Muzio Teldaldi, a Pisan customs officer, a distant relative from the Ammananti side of the family, who later became godfather to Galileo's younger brother Michelangelo.

Sadly, only the letters from Muzio have survived, but they reveal something of the domestic lives of the Galileis of Pisa. On 13 January 1574 Muzio writes:

> I've received Galileo's *schizzatoio* and his ball, as well as the books for Sir Corvini. Everything will be carried as soon as possible, I gave Galileo five Liras to pay his teacher, regarding your Lady I'll do anything I can: if Lady Lucrezia wasn't sick, I'd like her staying in my house for a month. Anyway, there's no point in saying so. The child [Virginia] is so fantastic that she appears unbearable to those who are not used to her. Yet, I asked him [a mutual friend] to say what he needs, and I'll do what I can; since I'm always busy, I cannot do what my duty suggests, but I'll supply with my money.

In another letter, dated 9 February 1574, he reports: 'I think you won't receive any letter from Galileo during this trip, surely he won't write you before next Wednesday, since tomorrow is St William's celebration day. Anyway, I can assure you that everybody is healthy and happy, including the child [Virginia], except for your wife. Galileo is happy.'

It appears from both of these letters that Giulia was ill at this time. No clue has survived to shed light on the nature of the illness, but it eventually passed, because as spring approached, Teldaldi was able to write: 'Your wife and everybody else at home are fine and healthy.'

After the family left Pisa and joined Vincenzo in Florence, the two men continued to correspond, and from a letter written some three months after Giulia and the children left, we learn that all was well with the Galileis after they settled in the Tuscan capital. 'I received your letters together with one to the *rettore*,' Teldaldi writes. 'I'm glad to hear that your wife, you, your child, and the others are fine, that Galileo's talent for literature is improving, and that Virginia is growing up, because I love you all as I love myself, I see you as another myself. Your friend, Muzio Teldaldi.'[9]

During his first few months in Florence, Galileo was tutored by a highly regarded local teacher named Jacopo Borghini da Dicomano, who coached pupils in the basics of Latin, Greek and Rhetoric in his home on Via de Bardi. According to Nicolò de Gherardini, a confidant of Galileo's, Borghini da Dicomano was 'a rather ordinary man'. But Vincenzo Viviani was more upbeat about him and tells us:

> When he [Galileo] was a teenager, he spent a few years in human studies with a well-known teacher of Florence, since his father could not give him better comforts, having a big family and a scarce fortune. Even so, he would like him to go and live in a boarding school: he knew that Galileo's passion and intellect would drive him to do things out of ordinary progress in any profession he would start. Yet, being aware of his condition and wishing to overreach it, young Galileo decided to face the poverty of his destiny applying himself assiduously to his studies. Therefore, having studied the first class of Latin authors, he reached a deep erudition in humanities; of himself he studied Greek as well, and he learned it not so bad: he used it later, in his deeper studies.[10]

This teaching arrangement did not last long. For reasons that remain unclear, in 1575 it was decided that Galileo should leave private tuition and begin a course of study at the Monastery of St Mary of Vallombrosa just outside Florence.

Galileo spent over three years at the monastery school and appears for a while at least to have been attracted to the idea of joining the priesthood. When his father learned of his son's interest he was mortified and intervened immediately. Without warning he turned up at the monastery and took Galileo back home with him, forbidding his return. As a pretext, Vincenzo claimed that the monks were not looking after his son properly and that they had let him fall ill with an eye infection, which they had not taken the trouble to treat. The truth, though, was that Vincenzo was extremely sceptical of orthodox religion, and although at this time he had not realised the depth of Galileo's analytical and mathematical talents, a career in the Church would have been the last thing he would have wished for his son.

Interestingly, Galileo's first biographer Viviani played down Galileo's involvement with the monastery. 'He received lessons of Logic from a priest of Vallombrosa,' he wrote. 'But learning all these dialectic words, definitions, differences, as well as a great quantity of writings was boring, fruitless: his wonderful intellect was not gratified.'[11] He makes no mention of the fact that Galileo had been drawn towards the monastic life nor of the young man's interest in taking holy orders.

The archives of the monastery shed a little more light on the matter, recording that: 'Galileo Galilei was a famous man and an outstanding figure in mathematics: his name should not be forgotten. He was a novice in Vallombrosa, where he made his first intellectual practice.' The account then goes on to smooth over any conflict with Galileo's father. 'Pretending to see him to Florence in order to recover from a serious ophthalmy, his father kept him so long that he was diverted from religion.'[12]

Science will always be grateful for Vincenzo's decisiveness, for his anticlerical sentiments and for the fact that he was so conscientious about his son's education. From the monastery Galileo moved to the last stage of his education before entering university; he returned to Pisa, where he was taught at a boarding school.

Vincenzo's friend Teldaldi was supportive of the move away from the monastery. 'I see from your letter what you've decided about your son,' he wrote from Pisa on 29 April 1578. 'However, while you're waiting for accommodation in the boarding school of Sapienza, you can let Galileo start his studies: in case you don't succeed in obtaining a place, I'll offer my house, with no charge, I promise you.' In a later letter he added: 'I'm glad to know that Galileo is back with you, and that you'd like him to study here.'[13]

By this time the Galilei house was becoming almost unbearably crowded. To relieve the situation and to offer Galileo the best opportunity possible, it was decided he should move back to Pisa, where he would be looked after by the family of Vincenzo's cousin. There he would go to school in preparation for university, but he would also be taught about the wool trade, just in case his studies came to nothing. In the summer of 1578 Galileo entered the prestigious school of Sapienza, and two years later he had sailed through the entrance examinations to begin a degree in medicine at the University of Pisa. His true academic life was about to start.

2

Religion's Grip

Galileo was christened the day after the 89-year-old Michelangelo died in Rome and a little over two months before the birth of William Shakespeare. The Europe in which he grew up was a continent riven by religious conflict, a post-Renaissance world in which, for many people, religion was a constant, overbearing obsession, and the most important factor in their lives. In many respects, Europe in 1564 was in a state of ideological turmoil, and the Church of Rome in particular was facing some of the greatest challenges in its long history.

Until the sixteenth century the Catholic Church was all-powerful and any dissent was quickly and ruthlessly crushed. Heretics were hunted down, their work banned and their opinions silenced. The most famous example of this was the terrible fate of the philosopher and religious radical Giordano Bruno, who was burned at the stake in Rome in February 1600 after having endured seven years of imprisonment and torture in the dungeons of the Inquisition. Bruno's crimes had been to refute the notions of the Holy Trinity and the Immaculate Conception, to oppose Aristotelian science and to propose the idea that intelligent life might exist on planets far from Earth.

The meaning of 'heresy' is a broad one and interpreted with great flexibility by theologians and clerics. The term really refers to any ideas or opinions that contradict orthodox teachings. Many heretics were people who held views on religious detail that did not align well with official doctrine. Whole communities were exterminated by the Church for interpreting theology in a way different from the doctrine held by the majority. One example is the Cathars (or Albigensians), who lived peacefully in the South of France between the eleventh and early thirteenth centuries. They practised a variant of Christianity in which they greatly downplayed the importance of the physical realm: they were Gnostics, believing in the preeminence of personal spiritual development.

In 1208 the Church of Rome sent a crusading army to wipe out the Cathar communities. The town of Béziers was besieged in July 1209 by the army of the papal legate, the Abbot of Cîteaux, who, when asked how he could distinguish a Cathar from a Catholic, is reputed to have replied: 'Kill them all, the Lord will recognise His own.'[1] The town was razed; many thousands died there, including women and children. When it was over, Arnaud wrote to his master, Pope Innocent III, 'Today, Your Holiness, twenty thousand citizens were put to the sword, regardless of rank, age, or sex.'[2]

Those individuals and cults who held views that diverged significantly from orthodoxy were a very different sort of heretic. These were the mystics and occultists, Hermeticists and alchemists whose views challenged the power of the Church by offering the laity entirely new thought systems. We will encounter many of these people as they impinged on Galileo's life, and indeed, his own heresies could be placed into this category.

Heresy was not the only threat to the unity of the Medieval and Renaissance Church: different factions within the institution were constantly at loggerheads. Dominicans and Franciscans disagreed over points of faith, and the Jesuits, a society created by a former soldier, Father Ignatius, and given papal approval in a bull of 1540, were distrusted by both of the traditional divisions of cleric.

The creation of a united front against heretics and reformers attempting to debase the Faith lay behind the establishment of the Council of Trent. This was a regular gathering of churchmen in the city of Trent (now Trento) in Italy. The first meeting was held on 13 December 1545, and the last eighteen years later in 1563. From these sessions emerged a set of dogmas and decrees that offered strict guidelines to the practice of Catholicism, effectively outlawing any deviation or divergence from the word handed down by the gathered clerics. It is striking that almost a half a millennium after these rules were formulated, modern orthodox Catholics claim they are immutable and offer a sensible template for modern living. The online *Catholic Encyclopedia* says of the Council of Trent: 'Although unfortunately the council, through no fault of the fathers assembled, was not able to heal the religious differences of western Europe, yet the infallible Divine truth was clearly proclaimed in opposition to the false doctrines of the day, and in this way a firm foundation was laid for the overthrow of heresy and the carrying out of genuine internal reform in the Church.'

The Renaissance is a period in history usually associated with the reawakening of art and literature between the fourteenth and mid-sixteenth centuries and centred upon the cultural explosion that took place in Italy and a few other European states. But the evolution of philosophy and the broadening of intellectual horizons that went with this artistic and literary change should not be underestimated.

Around the end of the fourteenth century, almost two centuries before Galileo's birth, a small group of well-heeled Europeans seeking novelty, knowledge, and (it must not be ignored) coveting prestige and social kudos, actively sought out the literary and philosophical treasures of the ancients. Emissaries were sent far and wide to find lost manuscripts, Latin originals written by the semi-mythical figures of classical times.

The focus of all this activity was Florence, where the Medici and other wealthy noblemen nurtured a genuine appetite for knowledge and had the money and social impetus to pursue the often distant echoes of learning. What they collected came directly from Arabic and Turkish castles, obscure monasteries and ancient decaying libraries, treasures unearthed by hand-picked historians and linguists in their pay.

Some of the earliest classical Latin texts were found by Giovanni Boccaccio, Coluccio Salutati and Giovanni Conversini, who brought to Florence a raft of important works including Tacitus's *Histories*, Manilius's *Astronomica* and Cicero's radical work *Brutus*. Then, a short time later, Italian scholars (of whom Francesco Petrarch was pre-eminent) learned of a still older source for the ideas they had gleaned from Rome, and so the original ancient Greek manuscripts were slowly unearthed and taken to Italy, primarily to Florence. By the 1420s hundreds of texts lay in the hands of a few wealthy patrons and the job of translating these seminal works was begun. In this way the teachings of Aristotle, Plato, Pythagoras, Euclid, Hippocrates and Galen in their original form sparked a new era of humanism and reform and initiated a surge of interest in science, medicine and philosophy.

Humanism is an ancient philosophy and is based on the idea that human existence may be understood through rationality. Humanists claim not to need divine or inspired texts to guide their ideals, morals and ethics; they work on the principle that we are responsible individuals who are answerable to our own drives and do not need a godhead to answer to. Humanism was adopted enthusiastically by early Renaissance figures including influential men such as Cosimo de' Medici and Leonardo Bruni. These men were deeply religious and Catholics all; but, they held the view that an alternative thought system such as humanism could offer new ways to understand the human condition. It will become clear in the story of Galileo that his trial before the Inquisition was the greatest crisis to face humanism during the Renaissance, a clash between rationality, a thought system based upon observation and logic, and another that relied completely upon faith.

The discovery of ancient knowledge led to a fresh approach to ethics and assessment of the place of Mankind, but of equal importance was the way it opened up new vistas in the worlds of painting, sculpture and play-writing. It also offered fresh insights into scientific ideas, engineering, weapon-making and philosophy. And with these many-faceted shifts in the way people thought and did things came a new awareness. One aspect of this was the realisation that some of the premises upon which religious orthodoxy had been constructed could and should be questioned. All of this means that the Renaissance – what Engels called 'the greatest progressive revolution that mankind has so far experienced' – was not simply the springboard for an artistic revaluation: it also opened the minds of men.[3]

But the Renaissance was not energised only by the past. All the key figures of the period, from Leon Alberti to Machiavelli, were in one aspect creatures of a bygone age, each was infused with the ideals and thought systems of medieval Europe; but, from the mid-fifteenth century (the 'High Renaissance') onward, such pioneers lived in a different world, a world in which a new invention was beginning to change the face of learning. Little more than a century before Galileo's birth there had been fewer than thirty thousand books in existence, all of them written by hand; but Gutenberg's pioneering use of movable type made printing practicable. Gutenberg's famous 42-line Bible was produced around 1455; within three years there was a press in Strasbourg; twenty-five years later, in 1480, there were more than a dozen printers working in Rome; and by the end of the fifteenth century, an estimated 100 printers were employed in Venice. By then, some forty thousand titles had appeared in print. By 1564, the year of Galileo's birth, there was already a canon of some 50 million printed books.

This was fine for intellectual progress, but in almost all mundane ways the world of 1564 was little different from that of 1364. The average life expectancy was twenty-four years for a woman and perhaps twenty-seven years for a man. The majority of people were hungry and ill most of the time. The rich had some advantages – they ate better, did not have to work so hard and could afford to keep warm in winter and, although they were as vulnerable to plague and other diseases, they could also escape to country estates far from the cramped cities and their infestations.

Only the rich were literate, and most common people travelled no further than ten miles from their own homes during their entire lives. They were pathologically suspicious of strangers; because they were uneducated, most had no inkling of the year in which they lived, nor did they know anything of the world beyond their own village or town. Their religion, although outwardly Catholic, was composed of nine parts superstition and earth magic to one part Matthew, Mark, Luke and John; the form of Christianity they were force-fed was barely understood, enwrapped as it was in quasi-mystical terminology. Most importantly, the populace received its religious indoctrination in an ancient (and for most people) quite unintelligible language, Latin. For the fourteenth-century peasant religious education derived solely from the Bible and orthodox sacred works and it was largely a meaningless affair.

For common folk, everyday life was an agony and the society in which they lived was almost stagnant. Medics bled and smothered with leeches and alchemists in their hundreds nurtured avaricious dreams of transmuting base metal into gold. The waking world was controlled by bacteria carried by rats repeatedly laying waste great swathes of the population of Europe, and the wars of men took their terrible toll. Meanwhile, the power of fantasy and fear fuelled nightmares in which demons from an underworld stalked and slaughtered the unwary. Things only started to change with the advent of the Industrial Revolution, around 1780, one hundred and forty years after the death of Galileo.

Considerable responsibility for this sluggish progress must be laid at the door of one of the great institutions that had thrived at the core of Western civilisation for some thirteen hundred years, the Christian Church. For if the secular, humanist intellectual effort of the Renaissance represents human thought in the ascendant, the Christian Church was its negative twin, heading in precisely the opposite direction. And, most importantly, the Church completely dominated life in Italy and other parts of Europe. Indeed, there was no concept of the need to separate Church and State: ostensibly the two were one.

The philosophers of the Renaissance were nearly all faithful Catholics who for the most part kept their more radical thoughts to themselves. If they did publish, their work was read by only an elite few. The Roman Church muzzled the public expression of radical views with an abiding energy and it hunted down the authors of any anti-Catholic philosophies. Although they supported the proliferation of sanctioned theological knowledge among the privileged, educated classes, in a broader sense, the Church leaders were instinctively anti-intellectual and deliberately obscurist. For the cardinals who jealously guarded their privileged earthly existence, the less the laity knew, the better.

Few would doubt that the Christian faith had began in purity, but human desire had quickly unbalanced it: by Galileo's time the Church had sunk into a mire of corruption. The doctrine supplied by the Church's founding fathers provided a template for living only a very simple life, which was fine for the largely illiterate laity but quite inadequate for an inquisitive elite. As philosophers began to probe more deeply and inductive 'science' superseded deductive reasoning, and created a more sophisticated vision of how the universe operated, it became clear that orthodoxy provided inadequate models and paradigms that left more questions than answers.* By the late Renaissance, the intellectually curious were finding it difficult to reconcile what was clearly observable and quantifiable with the ancient theology offered by the Church.

At the same time, the stance adopted by the Church over worldly matters was also causing offence. Throughout the medieval period, the Church of Rome had become increasingly political and materialistic, merging the spiritual with the secular so that the pope had became as much a head of a sovereign state as a spiritual leader. To finance papal ambitions, the Church unstintingly compromised theology, and when its manufactured doctrine proved inadequate, the cardinals stretched interpretation of the Scriptures to breaking point.

Perhaps the most blatant expression of this was the increasing use of 'indulgences' to raise money for the papal coffers. Using this system, sinners could pay for absolution of their sins, and successive popes perverted the process so much that by the time of the Reformation this simple trick provided a major source of revenue for the Vatican. One Dominican friar, Johann Tetzel, was a sort of P. T. Barnum of his day

---

* Until the early eighteenth century science was usually referred to as 'natural philosophy'.

and travelled Europe selling indulgences to the populace from a stool set up in each town square he visited. He even sold indulgences absolving sins *before* they had been committed. By this contrivance, a murderer could gain absolution before committing the crime.

And not all the money acquired from this trade (which ran into many millions of sovereigns) was used to finance the political aspirations of popes; much of this 'sinner's gold', as it became known, replenished the papal coffers drained by the expense of orgiastic feasts, rare spices, fine silks and the services of specialist prostitutes. Thus the indulgences of the pope and his favoured cardinals in Rome were paid for by the indulgences of the peasantry, the whole sorry show apparently sanctioned by God.

As such wild hypocrisy escalated, Erasmus, a deeply sincere Catholic academic who yearned for papal purity, wrote a series of scathing, erudite attacks upon the clergy and highlighted the clear disparity between 'truth' and official doctrine. With his *Encomium Moriae* (*The Praise of Folly*, 1509), a book he wrote in England while staying with his friend Thomas More, Erasmus staggered Rome with his open attacks against the pope, Julius II. But what cut deepest was the fact that *Encomium Moriae* was such a popular book it was rapidly translated into no fewer than a dozen languages. This represented a terrible danger to Rome simply because the Holy See had sustained itself for so long by maintaining ignorance among the laity. All religious texts, including the Bible and the prayer book were available only in Latin; all religious services and all decrees were conducted only in Latin. This meant that the vast majority of people had no idea what they were reciting in Church or what they were committing their faith to. Suddenly, within Erasmus's prose, difficult questions were posed in the vernacular and with them suspicion towards all levels of the clergy began to ripen just as the cardinals had feared it would. Spurred on by intellectuals like Erasmus and lower clergy in the know (men like Luther and Calvin), it is not surprising that the laity began to question the Church and to demand clarification. Such was Erasmus's popularity that the Church failed initially to suppress his masterpiece. However, at the height of the Counter-Reformation, the Inquisition began collecting material in an effort to incriminate the great humanist author, an effort that continued even after he was dead. In 1544, eight years after Erasmus had died, the zealous Pope Paul IV took the extraordinary step of excommunicating him posthumously and then consigned all his works to the Index of Prohibited Books (*Index Librorum Prohibitorum*).*

However, radical as he was, Erasmus remained devoted to the essence of Catholicism; and, of course, until the Reformation orthodox Christianity *was* Catholicism. This only changed when the German cleric Martin Luther struck at the very heart of papal supremacy, catching it so wrong-footed it almost toppled. Grown lazy and over-confident, the papacy kept a wary eye on intellectual troublemakers but believed they could always effectively quash rebellion with little effort. It was only after Luther demonstrated his views publicly by pinning a notice on the door of the church in Wittenberg on 31 October 1517 declaring ninety-five points of disagreement with Rome (or 'Theses') that Julius' successor, Leo X, took any notice.

Leo issued a papal bull against the German priest called *Exsurge Domine*, in which he called for Luther to retract his objections. When he refused, the pope called a general assembly of the Church hierarchy, known as a 'diet', to bring him into line. This meeting, presided over by the Holy Roman Emperor Charles V, was named the Diet of Worms after the town of Worms (now in Germany) in which the council was held. Martin Luther attended the council but openly challenged the Roman Church. He was lucky to escape death by hiding in Wartburg Castle after a supporter, Prince Frederick, snatched him from the clutches of the Inquisition.

Luther went on to create a new religion – Protestantism – which had no affiliation to Rome and discarded the leadership of the pope. Almost contemporaneously King Henry VIII of England made an equally bold move against the Church. He had no high-minded ideas and almost nothing in common with Luther except that in his youth he had been a good and obedient Catholic. In 1528 he wanted to divorce his wife, Catherine of Aragon. The pope would not countenance the suggestion and so Henry broke ranks with Rome and within three years he had become the Supreme Head of the Church of England.

The combination of Luther and Henry turning against Rome and the introduction of printing into Europe around the middle of the fifteenth century together presented the Church with the greatest

*This list of books banned by the Church was first published in 1529. The body responsible for the creation of the list was the Sacred Congregation of the Inquisition of the Roman Catholic Church. The Index was regularly updated until 1948 and survived until the 1960s. This 32nd edition contained 4,000 titles including the works of Erasmus, Edward Gibbon, Giordano Bruno, Voltaire, Copernicus, Balzac and Jean-Paul Satre as well as a sex manual called *The Perfect Marriage*.

challenges to its dictatorship; they were threats that eventually pushed it into taking dramatic measures. In an attempt to re-educate the masses in the style of papal choosing, the Society of Jesus, or Jesuits, was formed by Ignatius Loyola in 1534. The Council of Trent was created a few years later, in 1545, and as we have seen this group of senior clerics met at irregular intervals to formulate papal policy designed to fend off theological attacks.

But perhaps the most controversial policy decision made to counter the growing tide of Protestantism, scientific thought and heresy was the creation of the Roman Inquisition established by Pope Paul III in 1542, twenty-two years before Galileo's birth. Modelled upon the Papal Inquisition which had been doing its bloody work since the thirteenth century, the sole aim of the Roman Inquisition was to seek out and eradicate all serious opposition to the Catholic Church, in whatever form it might be found. Its official duty was to investigate and to re-educate, to bring lost souls back to the mother church; but in reality the Inquisition was a weapon of revenge, a mechanism for murder, a sixteenth-century *Schutzstaffel*. This organisation exterminated more than one million men, women and children (1 in 200 people on Earth at that time). Typical of this group was the Inquisitor Conrad Tors, who once declared, 'I would burn a hundred innocents if there was one guilty amongst them.'

The original Inquisition, the Papal Inquisition, had been established by Pope Gregory IX in 1231. He had justified the methods of the Inquisition (including physical abuse and imprisonment) by calling upon the Augustinian interpretation of Luke 14:23. This reads: 'And the Lord said unto the servant, go out into the highways and hedges and compel them to come in, that my house may be filled.' Interpreting the word 'compel' as he saw fit, Gregory sanctioned extreme physical violence against all known heretics.

The Inquisition had flourished in Spain while falling into disfavour in early Renaissance Italy, but as the Reformation began to bite, Pope Paul III decided to resurrect the ancient institution. He gave it fresh and then increasingly draconian powers, and he again liberally stretched interpretation of the Scriptures to excuse a range of punishments, including confiscation of all lands and possessions, life imprisonment in solitary confinement, and almost any variety of mental and physical torture.

Groups of trained investigators travelled the kingdoms of Europe to unearth information about suspected heretics. Fear would precede them and they employed subtle psychological techniques to increase this fear. In the days before their arrival, notices were posted announcing the impending visit. The Inquisitor would enter the town in a solemn procession of hooded monks. Spies had already identified anyone with heretical leanings and these people would be rounded up to appear before the Inquisitor. With this example as a warning, the local populace was invited to confess their sins before they could be exposed by a secret source, and they were actively encouraged to report anyone they suspected of heresy. If a transgressor could bring in a dozen suspects, his own sins would be excused and he would be spared the stake.

According to surviving manuals written by one of the most abhorrent Inquisitor Generals, Bernard Gui, the Inquisition had two forms of general citation, the *inquisito generalis* and the *inquisito specialis*. The former was conducted in towns and cities and involved large numbers of heretics, sometimes entire populations; the latter was directed at individuals who had come to the attention of the Holy Office. Each was used without pity.

All that was required to bring a charge of heresy was the testimony of two informants. The suspect was imprisoned during questioning and the Inquisition was never in a hurry. Many innocent victims died while incarcerated waiting for the Inquisitor to assess their confessions. Others were tortured to death, desperate to confess to crimes of which they were actually innocent and about which they knew nothing. The informants were never identified and the statements they had made concerning the suspect were never revealed, so the accused had no information against which to defend themselves. Suspects were not allowed lawyers and – most insidious of all – the proceedings of the Inquisition were conducted in total secrecy; often the victims would simply disappear.

Of course, such despotism had a dramatic effect upon the political and social framework of the Western world. A particularly graphic illustration of this comes from the one hundred and fifty years between 1500 and 1650 during which an estimated thirty thousand women (and several hundred men and children) were murdered by the Inquisition. Their crime was really no crime at all; they were merely unlucky. According to official policy, these people had been suspected of practising witchcraft. If this was indeed the genuine belief of the Church authorities, it would have been a bitter irony indeed, for officially the Church rejected the notion of the occult yet condoned the murder of those they suspected of being witches. In fact, it has recently become clear through a close study of the records of the witch hunts that the murder of so many innocents was only superficially a matter of the righteous believing they were fighting an evil force in the guise of thousands of witches. It is now believed this horrendous process was a simple expression of misogyny energised by a few powerful men within the Church hierarchy.[4]

Even this abject cruelty was only one aspect of the way extreme religious zeal could become a destructive force. Extremists of all denominations murdered their fellow countrymen and religious inflexibility and paranoia propelled entire nations towards violent struggle, rebellion, and ultimately to genocide. As the Protestant religion became all-powerful in Germany, the rebellion of persecuted Protestant minorities in Catholic states escalated into all-out war.

Beginning in 1562, two years before Galileo's birth, a set of civil wars in France known as the Wars of Religion erupted into a pan-European conflict lasting some thirty-five years and drawing in German Protestants as well as Catholics from Italy and Spain. In Paris and other major cities, the French Calvinists, known as Huguenots, claimed persecution at the hands of the Catholic majority and organised themselves into a powerful political group. The friction between Huguenots and Catholics then sparked the tinder of the weak French monarchy. First Charles IX (who reigned 1560–74) and then his successor, Henry III (who was murdered by a religious fanatic in 1589), faced a succession of violent Huguenot uprisings supported by foreign Protestant armies. This conflict reached a bloody climax in the St Bartholomew's Day Massacre of 24 August 1572 when, during the course of three days, some seventy thousand Protestants were slaughtered. After this a group of moderate Catholics known as the Politiques came to political prominence through the powerful Montmorency family. But they were superseded by a rabidly anti-Protestant noble family, the House of Guise, who created a group calling itself the Holy League, violently opposed to any form of peaceful settlement with the Huguenots.

In 1589, when Galileo was twenty-five, it was a Guise who organised the murder of Henry III. This action served only to worsen the political turmoil and to escalate the violence for almost a decade. Indeed, it was not until the final years of the sixteenth century, in 1598, that a semblance of order was regained temporarily. Henry III's determined and courageous successor Henry IV created the Edict of Nantes, which declared liberty of conscience and equality of legal and educational rights for French Protestants and allowed them to hold government office.

*

The outward glorious reminder of the Renaissance lies with the great works of art we cherish still. But much more changed during this reawakening: humanism was rediscovered and with it came a transformation in the fundamental perception of the universe and the place of Mankind. Beyond this, an even more subtle metamorphosis was begun: a growing body of thinkers came to realise that orthodox religion was intellectually moribund and inadequate, that it was a thought system too immature to guide men through the blossoming new world. Some rare minds even began to see an alternative paradigm based on rationality, logic and mathematical rigour, a paradigm that would one day be called 'science'.

Science before Galileo

Science in one form or another is almost as old as civilisation itself. Ancient peoples applied fundamental principles to improve their lives, a system we can now see as a form of proto-technology. However, what we would define as 'theoretical science' – that is, the construction of guiding rules that may be applied in many varied situations – did not fully bloom until the time of the Greeks.

Two and a half thousand years ago Anaximander, Pythagoras, Anaxagoras and, most importantly, Archimedes and Euclid took quite vague ideas from what was known of Babylonian and Egyptian culture and began the process of quantifying, interpreting, imagining.

The foundations of natural philosophy were laid by two great mathematicians of the third and fourth centuries BC. The first of these was Euclid. So little is known of this mathematician that there is even some doubt that the name Euclid should apply to an individual. Some historians believe that the works left to posterity by Euclid were conceived by a team of mathematicians in Alexandria.

The body of work with which Euclid revolutionised mathematical thinking comes from about 300 BC. His most important collection is *The Elements*, in which the fundamental ideas of mathematics are defined and explained in thirteen books, covering plane geometry, number theory and three-dimensional geometry.

It is no exaggeration to say that this treatise is the bible of mathematics and that it has been essential to the development of science. Since it first appeared in printed form, in 1482, more than one thousand editions of *The Elements* have been published. According to one historian:

Almost from the time of its writing and lasting almost to the present,

The Elements has exerted a continuous and major influence on human affairs. It was the primary source of geometric reasoning, theorems, and methods at least until the advent of non-Euclidean geometry in the nineteenth century. It is sometimes said that, next to the Bible, *The Elements* may be the most translated, published, and studied of all the books produced in the Western world.'[1]

Euclid's writings offered the basic infrastructure of mathematics, but some fifty years after the writing of this book the mathematics of the age was pushed into new domains by Archimedes, a man who some consider to be the greatest mathematician who ever lived. Even if we refrain from such hyperbole, it is fair to say that Archimedes was the best, most far-sighted and innovative mathematician until Galileo and Newton.

Born in Syracuse in 287 BC, Archimedes was a dreamer who spent his entire time absorbed with mathematical and philosophical musings. Indeed, he was so obsessed that he spared no time to wash and barely allowed himself to stop working to eat. According to the Greek historian Plutarch (who lived some three centuries after Archimedes), the mathematician stank so badly his friends forced him to be washed. But even then:

> Oftimes Archimedes' servants got him against his will to the baths, to wash and anoint him, and yet being there, he would ever be drawing out geometrical figures, even in the very embers of the chimney. And while they were anointing him with oils and sweet savours, with his fingers he drew lines upon his naked body, so far was he taken from himself, and brought into ecstasy or trance, with the delight he had in the study of geometry.

And such dedication produced wonders. It is one of the great tragedies of history that what is thought to be only a modest part of the great thinker's legacy has survived; but even from this, it is clear Archimedes achieved a great deal. He derived a very accurate value for pi, invented a system to express large numbers using the notion of powers of ten, and he devised an early version of the calculus rediscovered twenty centuries later by Newton and Leibniz.

As well as being an unworldly mathematical prodigy, Archimedes was a brilliant writer who explained his ideas with great clarity. Plutarch enthused about the work of the ancient mathematician, claiming:

It is not possible to find in all geometry more difficult and intricate questions, or more simple and lucid explanations. Some ascribe this to his natural genius; while others think that incredible effort and toil produced these, to all appearances, easy and unlaboured results. No amount of investigation of yours would succeed in attaining the proof, and yet, once seen, you immediately believe you would have discovered it; by so smooth and so rapid a path he leads you to the conclusion required.

Archimedes was killed in 212 BC when his home of Syracuse was invaded by a Roman army. According to legend, he was murdered by a soldier because he was so absorbed in trying to solve a mathematical problem he did not hear a command to stop what he was doing. Apparently, Archimedes' last words were: 'Do not disturb my circles.'

For Galileo, and for Newton after him, Euclid and Archimedes represented the two fundamentals of ancient mathematical wisdom and their work had not been improved upon or substantially developed since ancient times. Although their ideas were almost two thousand years old when Galileo was entering science, they remained the most accurate and significant set of mathematical principles available, and today they remain immutable because these Greek thinkers were describing fundamental laws of the universe. Thanks to the discovery of the works of the Greeks during the Renaissance, Galileo was able to build his own ideas upon sturdy foundations; without Euclid and Archimedes he would have been rudderless.

But this abundance of riches that inspired Galileo did not include a great contribution from another Greek icon, Aristotle. The fourth-century BC philosopher Aristotle employed deductive reasoning, syllogistic logic, to draw conclusion C from ideas A and B, and this meant that his scientific work was fatally flawed. Aristotle and most other Greek thinkers shunned the concept of experiment but excelled in their thoughts of the fundamentals. They wondered what the universe might be made from, whether it might be a mere abstraction. Could the universe have been formed around a conceivable pattern? Were numbers repeated in its obvious glory?

Aristotle created a vast intellectual mosaic, an interpretation based upon what he saw and what he imagined, and through prominence and serendipity his philosophy lingered astonishingly long. For two thousand years Aristotelianism was taught in Oxford and Paris just as it had been celebrated and honoured in Macedonia, where the philosopher had taught.

Aristotle was born in 384 BC at Stagira, in Chalcidice. The son of the physician to Philip, King of Macedon, he later became the pupil of Plato and, in middle age, the teacher of Alexander the Great. He wrote a collection of tracts that not only were influential in his own time but whose rediscovery in an incomplete form by European scholars during the thirteenth century heralded a return to learning and the earliest emergence of the Renaissance. Those most relevant to his thoughts on natural philosophy were *On Generation and Corruption* and *Physical Discourse*, which concentrated upon ideas concerning matter, form, motion, time and the heavenly and earthly realms.

Aristotle is often credited with being the first to develop the idea of the four elements, but responsibility for this actually fell to a Sicilian philosopher named Empedocles, some half-century before Aristotle's birth. Aristotle did, though, refine the idea and make it popular. It is thought the concept first arose from watching the action of burning, and it is easy to see why. When green wood is burned, the fire is visible by its own light, the smoke vanishes into air, water boils from the wood, and the remaining ashes are clearly earth-like. This gave rise to the notion that everything in the universe is composed of different proportions of these four fundamental elements and it was an idea that became the foundation of Aristotle's work in natural philosophy, work that was then handed down to future generations.

To Aristotle, the earthly realm was composed of a blend of the four elements which, if left to settle, would form layers: water falling through air (or air moving up through water, as do bubbles), solid earth falling through water and air, and fire existing in the top layer because it moves up through air. Using this model, Aristotle would have explained the fall of an apple as being due to the earthy and watery parts of the solid apple trying to find their natural place in the universe, falling through air to reach the ground.

Aristotle's astronomical ideas seem quite alien to us. For example, although he correctly stated that the Earth was a sphere, it was for all the wrong reasons. He claimed the universe and the Earth itself were spherical because this was the most perfect shape. Another reason for this conclusion was that, according to Aristotle's unproven reasoning, all substances moved naturally towards the centre of the Earth; this must therefore lead to the planet being a perfect sphere. He also employed the reasonable argument that the Earth could not be flat because as one travelled north or south the stars that could be observed changed.

As well as popularising the idea of the four elements, Aristotle also pioneered the concept of the 'Unmoved Mover'. This is the name he gave to the omnipotent being who, he believed, maintained the movement of the heavens, keeping the Sun and the planets travelling around the Earth.

Apart from the fact that modern science has exploded many of the notions of Aristotle and we are now more knowledgeable about the true nature of the universe, the main reason these ideas seem so strange to us is that Aristotle made no distinction between physics and metaphysics – because he did not test ideas or conduct experiments, he simply stated what he believed to be facts.

Aristotle's work was encyclopedic in range, and he wrote on almost all subjects known at the time, covering logic, philosophy, biology, astronomy and physics. His strongest subjects were logic and, of the sciences, biology; his weakest was physics. Most significant for how Aristotle arrived at many of his scientific ideas was that use of syllogistic logic already referred to: the principle that a conclusion can be reached as a logical consequence of two preceding premises. An example of this is the collection of statements: 'All elephants are animals; all animals are living things; therefore all elephants are living things.'

Syllogisms are powerful tools in the study of logic, and were popular as a fundamental mathematical procedure until the nineteenth century, when they were superseded by more versatile ideas; but they offer a rather superficial way to conduct science, because, lacking the element of experiment, they are based entirely upon superficial observation or deductive reasoning.

Plato, Aristotle's teacher (and the man who established a school at the Academy in Athens that lasted nine centuries), actively disliked experiment and so it was never established as a guiding principle for Greek natural philosophy. Instead, Aristotle and the generations of Greek thinkers who followed him created a rigid set of rules based upon syllogistic logic only – rules which produced a grossly distorted picture of reality.

Because of Aristotle's stature, however, this limited approach became endowed with an aura of infallibility that persisted until the beginning of the modern era. The historian Charles Singer has said of this unfortunate process: 'The whole theory of science was so interpreted, and the whole of logic was so constructed, as to lead up to the ideal of demonstrative science [i.e. conclusions reached through reasoning alone], which in its turn rested on a false analogy which assimilated it to the dialectics of proof. Does not this mistake go far to account for the neglect of experience and the unprogressiveness of science for nearly 2,000 years after Aristotle?'[2]

In the same vein, the historian Sir William Dampier pointed out: 'Aristotle, while dealing skilfully with the theory of the passage from particular instances to general propositions, in practice often failed lamentably. Taking the available facts, he would rush at once to the wildest generalisations. Naturally he failed. Enough facts were not available, and there was no adequate scientific background into which they could be fitted.'[3]

The modern scientific method involves reasoning *and* experiment. To give a simple example: early on in a scientific investigation an idea is postulated – often based upon an inspired insight. This is then developed into a tentative hypothesis by means of pure reasoning – a process called the 'inductive method'. The practical consequences of this hypothesis must then be deduced mathematically and the idea is tested experimentally. If there are discrepancies between the hypothesis and the experimental results or observations, the hypothesis must be altered and the experiments repeated until there is either agreement between reasoning and observation or the original idea is discarded. If the reasoning and the practical verification eventually agree, the hypothesis is promoted to the status of a theory.

This can then be used to attempt to explain a more generalised scenario than the original concept, and it may hold for many years. But, crucially, it is still never considered to be the *only* theory that could fit the facts, and good science allows for new ideas to be introduced that may destroy the old theory or demand radical changes.

Aristotle became the best remembered philosopher of the Greek tradition, but he was not the best. Far more insightful, but almost overlooked until recent times, are the ideas of Democritus (*c*.460–370 BC). Democritus, brought to us in the writings of Lucretius (*c*.95–55 BC), describes a mechanical universe, a physical realm in which atoms form the most fundamental conglomerates and from their collisions create all movement and dynamism. Democritus and his followers applied *atomism to* every aspect of the observed world and even tried to explain human behaviour as a consequence of atomic collisions. 'This fright, this night of the mind, must be dispelled not by the rays of the sun, nor day's bright spears,' Lucretius wrote, '. . . but by the face of nature and her laws. And this is her first, from which we take our start: nothing was ever by miracle made from nothing.'[4]

Aristotle dismissed this notion by relying upon syllogisms that were founded upon inadequate knowledge. For example, he claimed that, if the atomic theory was true, matter would be heavy by nature and nothing would be light enough in itself to rise. A large mass of air or fire would then be heavier than a small mass of earth or water, so the earth or water would not sink (or the air and fire rise) and therefore the elements would not find their natural positions. This argument illustrates how Aristotle was not approaching the problem in the way a modern objective scientist would; he was unable to consider questioning his beliefs even when presented with a strong alternative theory.

A generation after Democritus, Plato (*c.*428–347 BC) had destroyed the atomic vision with his own semi-mystical interpretation of the universe. Within scientific development, Democritus had taken a leap forward and Plato moved the world two steps back. It has been said that: 'Plato was a great philosopher, but in the history of experimental science he must be counted a disaster.'[5]

Plato had taught an anthropocentric view of reality, in which everything was created and carefully controlled by a supreme being who held the interests of humanity paramount. For Plato, the purpose of planetary movement was simply to enable the marking of time, and he viewed the cosmos as a living organism with a body, a soul and reason. He also saw numerical relevance and meaning in all natural processes. But he abhorred experimental science, which, according to one historian, he 'roundly condemned as either impious or a base mechanical art'.[6]

Plato's greatest pupil, Aristotle, then took the world back another step, and unfortunately his ideas rose to the top of the pile. This is because in the fourth century BC they found immediate resonance; his comforting description of the four elements, his cosy ideologies and reassuring connections that placed humans immutably at the centre of things gave his followers a sense of meaning. Aristotle should be admired for at least trying to find answers in a world that had never enjoyed the illumination of science and it is easy to be overly critical of the great man's work; but it cannot be denied that it led the evolution of scientific reasoning down a blind alley. This false path grew from two great misfortunes associated with Aristotle's work.

The first was that his rejection of the experimental method led to some ridiculous conclusions. For example, he believed that we see because our eyes project particles that bounce off viewed objects, and he assumed that any object falls because it is trying to establish its rightful place in the universe. Aristotle also concluded that an object moves through the air because, as it does so, the displaced air in front of it flows behind it instantaneously and pushes it on.

The second unfortunate element linked to Aristotle's legacy (but not at all his fault) is that his ideas were placed above all others by future generations and his philosophies were hijacked by theologians for their own ends. Dogma turned to absolutism, and his teachings were passed on virtually unquestioned. This led astray later thinkers and pushed science towards a dead end.

By the time of Aristotle's death, in 322 BC, the Egyptian city of Alexandria was about to emerge as the intellectual centre of the world. At its heart was the great library that is said to have contained all human knowledge in an estimated four hundred thousand volumes and scrolls. From Alexandria learning spread eastwards with the conquests of Alexander the Great and westwards into Europe, where Greek philosophy, science and literature acted as the foundation for Roman culture. This was especially true of science: the Roman era could boast many great intellects – Pliny, who lived during the first century AD and wrote a thirty-seven-volume treatise, *Historica Naturalis*, and Plutarch, a thinker of the following generation, to name only two. But, in the tradition established by Aristotle, these men did little original science; instead they concentrated on refining and clarifying Greek teachings passed on to them.

Of the Greek science that survived through to the early Roman era, the works of Aristotle, Plato, Archimedes and Pythagoras were best preserved (although the ideas of Democritus were championed in obscurity by Lucretius). By the time Roman power was melting away and the library of Alexandria was decimated at the hands of the Christian bishop Theophilus around AD 390 (it was later sacked again by the Arabs during the seventh century), Aristotle's work was becoming temporarily unfashionable.

The reason for this lies in a shift from pure intellectual inquiry to a distrust of any learning beyond theological exegesis; this plunged most of civilisation into what has become known as the Dark Ages. In this era, as the Roman Empire was in rapid decline, education and learning became dominated by religious fanaticism. The disciples of a new movement, the Stoics, believed in the supreme importance of pure spirit over material existence and they shunned learning about the physical world as an end in itself. To them, Aristotle's work was too mechanistic, too embedded in physical reality. Plato's vision, they believed, held much greater relevance and was perfectly in tune with the new obsession with religious meaning.

And so, for Western civilisation, darkness. Some of the earliest human ideas that had flowed west to Greece as civilisation dawned now dispersed across the world, greatly modified. The Arabic culture that nurtured so many ingenious natural philosophers and mathematicians expanded the canon enormously: Rhazes (860–930), Alhazen (*c.*965–1038), Ibn-al-Haitam (965–1020), and the alchemists of Persia, who passed west through Alexandria, leaving their mark. In Europe, memory faded and the ideas of the classical tradition were only kept alive in the monasteries.

But in the monasteries all was not well. To maintain spiritual peace and earthly power the theologians and monks needed to find an amalgam of natural philosophy (the teachings of the heathen Greeks) and Christianity, a marriage of Aristotle and the Gospels. The intellectual fathers, holy men like Thomas Aquinas (1225–74) and Albertus Magnus (*c.*1200–1280) who looked at the world and wondered, facilitated a strange, short-lived compromise, a meld of Aristotelianism and Christianity they called Scholasticism.

Some time between 1200 and 1225, Aristotle's works, which had been saved in part by the Arabs and amalgamated with their own ideas, were discovered by European intellectuals and translated into Latin. From this point on, Aristotle's science returned to favour and took over from Platonic mysticism, gradually fusing with Christian theology.

Although this development may be viewed as an improvement upon the Dark Age mistrust of science and the Stoics' preoccupation with spirituality, it created a new obsession: a union of Aristotelian natural philosophy with Christian dogma. This meant that any attack upon Aristotle's science was also seen as an attack upon Christianity. Together the two doctrines formed a powerful alliance and created a world-view that was taught by rote almost unchallenged in every university in Europe for almost half a millennium from the thirteenth to the seventeenth century.

These twinned beliefs produced a self-contained picture of the universe: God created the world as described in the Scriptures and He guided all actions. All movement was not only set in motion by God but was supervised by divine power. Thus the Church's doctrine of divine omnipotence dovetailed perfectly with Aristotle's belief in the

Unmoved Mover – that no movement was possible unless initiated by an unseen hand. All matter consisted of the four elements and was not divisible into atoms as Democritus had proposed. To Aristotle, every material object was an individual complete entity, created by God and composed of a particular combination of the four elements. Each object possessed certain distinct and observable qualities, such as heaviness, colour, smell, coolness. These were seen as *solely* intrinsic aspects or properties of the object, and their observed nature had nothing to do with the perception of the observer.

To the thirteenth-century mind the notion that properties of an object such as smell, taste or texture were partly open to interpretation in the mind of the observer would have been totally alien. Every property of an object was intrinsic and the same for all observers. Furthermore, because Aristotle had rejected atomism, the concept that matter was composed of tiny, indivisible elements remained equally foreign to most intellectuals until at least the early eighteenth century. So, now that Aristotelian ideas were bound up inextricably with religion, any philosopher who openly challenged any aspect of accepted scientific ideology put his life in danger; and, as we shall see, this lay at the very heart of Galileo's conflict with Catholic doctrine.

But not everyone was deceived. Like Galileo, who lived some three and a half centuries after him, Roger Bacon (*c*.1220–92) was a man bigger than the myopic age in which he lived. Devout and pious, he was also a critical observer and did not always take the word of Aristotle as second only to that of God. As he watched, learned and gathered information, as he dipped a toe into forbidden alchemy and dared to question, he tried to loosen the taut bond between inherited wisdom and inherited faith. In a triumvirate of visionary books, *Opus Majus*, *Opus Minus* and *Opus Ertium*, he argued against elements of the Aristotelian creed (for creed is what it had become). Perhaps foolishly, he arranged for exquisitely bound editions of his books to be presented to the pope, Nicolas IV, who promptly had him arrested for heresy and imprisoned for twelve years.

Long before Bacon it must have become clear that the only way to discover truth, to probe deeper than the word of Aristotle and the word of God, was to keep outwardly silent but to shout loudly inside; and so, for a millennium, from the foundations laid by the Arabs of the seventh century until after Galileo brought analysis and mathematical rigour to natural philosophy, alchemists, who worked in secret and fled from prosecution across continents, carried the torch of investigation.

Alchemists – men who studied an early form of chemistry with philosophical and magical associations, the chief aims of which were to transform base metals into gold and to discover the elixir of perpetual youth – were misguided fantasists. But they were also intrepid individualists who consciously took a path less travelled. They were not true scientists, but they had imagination and determination and they did not accept the givens cherished by orthodox philosophers and theologians. The clashes between philosophy/science and religion that expressed themselves most viciously in the attempted intellectual assassination of Copernicus, Bruno, Galileo, Hobbes and Darwin had their origins in the scantly recorded tension between the dogmatists of the Church and the naïve experimenters who spent their lives at the cauldron risking the noose.

Alchemists had common goals: the elucidation of the twin pillars of the Hermetic tradition – the elixir of eternal life and the creation of the Philosophers' Stone – but each alchemist had his own agenda. Alchemists recorded their findings in coded form and, in order to ennoble and at the same time obfuscate their findings, they drew upon the rich culture of mysticism, from the Cabbala to the New Testament. This was not simply to keep their ideas from the eyes of the Church and the State, but it sealed discovery in a cocoon, removed it from interpretation, extrapolation and, most crucially, theft. So these men were pulled in two directions. The enemies of orthodoxy, driven to learn more than Aristotle or the theologians could offer them, risked everything to unveil what they perceived as truth. But while struggling to prise secrets from nature's clasp, they missed the chance to develop any truly profound understanding of the universe because they could never share their philosophies, could never communicate their findings, could never begin to build the edifice of science as later generations would do. As a consequence, they achieved little of lasting value.*

The scientific renaissance that accompanied its artistic twin marks a change in philosophical beliefs every bit as significant as the revolution in the arts. Leonardo da Vinci, who approached science from a practical standpoint, foreshadowed many of the ideas of Galileo, Kepler and Newton, but he did not write up his discoveries in any coherent form. The best we have is his collection of notebooks, which indicate the

---

*It should be noted that although alchemists contributed nothing of value to the theory of chemistry, their experimental fervour did lead them to develop sophisticated laboratory techniques and the invention of some very useful apparatus still used to this day, including fermentation and distillation equipment, methods for separating liquids and ways to control heat sources.

power and breadth of his studies and philosophies. In one sense, Leonardo was all experiment and his approach was the very opposite to that of the Greeks.

In the late fifteenth century Leonardo held a view of motion that was very different from Aristotle's. Aristotle had claimed that nothing moved unless it was made to do so by God, the 'Unmoved Mover'. Leonardo suggested the exact opposite, writing in his notebook, 'Nothing perceptible by the senses is able to move itself . . . every body has a weight in the direction of the movement.'[7] In other words, matter has an innate tendency to move in a certain direction unless stopped. This concept was explained and analysed by Galileo and then by Isaac Newton – the concept of 'inertia'.

Leonardo da Vinci was the first scientist, yet sadly he too suffered the alchemist's failing and could never bring himself to communicate his revelations. He was paranoid, but in part for good reason. There were those who wanted to plagiarise his ideas, rivals who planted assistants in his workshop to steal, and there were papal spies waiting for him to slip up. To counter these agents, Leonardo filled thirteen thousand pages of notebooks using mirror-writing (as a defence against the casual glance over his shoulder, perhaps) and he hid his discoveries from everyone save his most trusted disciples.

But defending himself against the prying eyes of the Holy See was far from easy. Leonardo spent most of his life in Milan and Florence during a period in the history of those cities when holy repression was at its least effective, but as soon as he left these regions he needed to be constantly aware of censure. Famed throughout Italy and revered by the powerful, Leonardo still had to tread carefully in pursuit of his more risqué interests.

According to Leonardo, one of his assistants 'hindered [him] in anatomy, denouncing it before the Pope'.[8] Leonardo offended few with his ideas for flying machines and he delighted his patrons with ingenious designs for weaponry, but the Church strongly objected to his nocturnal habits: for his deceitful assistant, horrified by the sight of his master up to the elbows in human viscera, dissection was a violation; and it was no less so for the cardinals.

Such censorship forced Leonardo into a peripatetic life keeping him barely one step ahead of his enemies until he was given protection by the young French king, Francis I at the chateau of Cloux, where, during his final years, da Vinci could do as he pleased.

As a scientist, Leonardo's greatest rival was the Catholic Church, and ideological conflict both spurred him to new heights of ingenuity and caused immense damage. He refused to be nailed to any cross and, while offering Rome every outward sign of respect, his only vision of God was a pantheistic one. Unusually for an intellectual of his time, he made almost no mention of the divine in anything he wrote. Facing the wrath of the Church, he was defensive but proud; any attempt at prohibition made him work harder, dig deeper and find more that would have shocked and infuriated, if only he had been able to speak out. But Leonardo published no treatise on natural philosophy (his *Treatise on Painting* is his only complete work, finally published in 1651), for much as he wanted to reveal truth, claiming: 'There is nothing more deceptive than to rely on your own opinion, without any other proof, as experience always proves to be the enemy of the alchemists, necromancers, and other ingenious simpletons,' he simply could not.⁹ Before he died, he entrusted his notes to his closest companion, Francesco Melzi, who spent the rest of his life attempting to catalogue and clarify the thousands of pages Leonardo had written. When Melzi died, his son, Orazio, a man with no interest in Leonardo, filed away the papers in an attic room on the family estate. There they remained for almost two centuries, lost to the world and the evolution of science. The Church may not have stopped Leonardo working, but they effectively cut out his tongue.

Leonardo was not the only hero. Three others from the pre-Newtonian era figure hugely in the struggle for reason. The most important of these is, of course, Galileo, but before him two others had made an enormous impact. Each of these men fought in his own way and was victimised by papal power, each became an enemy of ignorance.

Nicolaus Copernicus (1473–1543) was one of the Church's own, a Polish canon with a medical training and a fascination with astronomy. He knew well the power of his greatest opponents, the agonies they could inflict; and he could not face them. Writing in secret, he gathered astronomical observations and scribbled for thirty years before submitting his thoughts for publication – but only when he knew he was dying. He had no close family, no one Rome could persecute after his death, and he must have felt a swell of satisfaction as the first copy of his treatise was placed beside him on the bed in which he would soon die.

The year was 1543 and, though Copernicus could not have known it, science had won. For sure, the victory celebrations lay some time in the future and others would suffer, even die, for their knowledge before that day, but as *De Revolutionibus Orbium Coelestium* (*On the Revolutions of the Heavenly Spheres*) emerged from the press – the first great scientific work of the new age of printing and one of the most important – the cardinals, if only they had realised the true importance of the book, would have shivered. They had not yet noticed anything was wrong because of two things. First, Copernicus's publisher, a Lutheran minister, had, without the author's consent, included a Preface to *Revolutions* in which he declared that the treatise was merely an aid to calculation of planetary movement and not a statement of reality. Second, Copernicus had either deliberately or unintentionally confused his own message.

Copernicus had grown up believing that the universe was how the first-century Roman philosopher Claudius Ptolemy had described it. Ptolemy's was an interpretation of the cosmos based upon Aristotle's astronomical writings and sanctioned by theologians and successive popes. In this model, the Earth is placed at the centre of the cosmos. It is fixed in position and around it, in what Ptolemy called epicycles, move the stars (also fixed in the firmament), the planets, the Moon and the Sun. This was a great advance on Aristotle because, although his calculations were extremely inaccurate and led to a false conclusion about the nature of the universe, Ptolemy had formulated a mathematical description of his model to support his arguments: he had been guided by mathematical principles and observation rather than by supposition and guesswork.

Ptolemy laid down his theories in a book called *Almagest*, which is still considered one of the great works of science in the history of thought. 'As a didactic work,' one historian has written of the book, 'the *Almagest* is a masterpiece of clarity and method, superior to any ancient scientific textbook and with few peers from any period. But it is much more than that. Far from being a mere "systemisation" of earlier Greek astronomy, as it is sometimes described, it is in many respects an original work.'[10]

Through his own observations made during the first two decades of the sixteenth century, Copernicus had noticed that the stars and the planets moved in such a way that the Earth could not possibly lie at the centre of the universe, or 'heavenly spheres', but he still retained many classical ideas in the way he explained these observations. In *Revolutions* he began by boldly asserting that the Sun lay at the centre of the universe but then appeared to change his mind. After the first few pages, he went on to complicate his theory more and more with unnecessary refinements, finally placing the Sun slightly off centre. This prevarication makes the entire work almost unreadable and frequently contradictory. Running to 212 sheets in small folio, the heart of *Revolutions* may be found in the first twenty pages. These contain Copernicus's core innovations – the assertions that the Earth orbits the Sun, that the distance between the Earth and the Sun is almost insignificant compared to interstellar distances, that the revolution of the Earth on its axis accounts for the apparent daily rotation of the stars, and that the apparent annual cycle of movements of the Sun is caused by the fact that the Earth orbits the Sun – each wonderfully new, original and revolutionary.

As a result of the confusions in *Revolutions*, the book did not make the immediate scientific impact it should have done and its existence went unnoticed by the Church for seventy-three years, only finding its way on to the Index of Prohibited Books in 1616. (It was not removed until 1835.)

Even so, Copernicus had good reason for maintaining secrecy. In his treatise he had rejected the words that had for so long massaged the egos of men, the geocentric model taught since ancient times, the very essence of Aristotelianism and Ptolemaic astronomy: 'In the midst of all dwells the Sun,' he wrote in those crucial first twenty pages of *Revolutions*. 'Sitting on the royal throne, he rules the family of planets which turn around him . . . We thus find in this arrangement an admirable harmony of the world.'[11] This was absolute anathema to the enemy: and when Copernicus's heliocentric vision was eventually understood, it was, of course, immediately branded as contradicting Catholic doctrine.

By then it was all too late. The Church might have been slow to understand the radical nature of what had happened, but some intellectuals of the period had worked through the muddle that was *De Revolutionibus Orbium Coelestium*, and from it they had drawn their own rich conclusions.

Few choose to die in a way that changes all of history, but Giordano Bruno (1548–1600) was one, becoming the first and only genuine martyr to science. Late in January 1600, Bruno stood in chains before the Inquisition court of the Roman Church in the Vatican and was condemned to death by His Holiness Pope Clement VIII. Bruno's crime had been to publish heretical works: *The Ash Wednesday Supper*, *The Expulsion of the Triumphant Beast*, *On the Infinite Universe and its Worlds* – each based on Copernicanism blended with Bruno's own idiosyncratic vision of natural philosophy. Bruno had been persecuted for decades, his books banned, his ideas repressed; but, like Leonardo a century before him, he had always succeeded in keeping one step ahead of the Church and spent most of his life in liberal or Protestant states, in England and Germany. But in 1591 he received an offer to teach a Venetian nobleman named Giovanni Mocenigo and made the strange decision to return to his native Italy.

It was a trap: Mocenigo was working for the Inquisition. Bruno faced trial first in Venice and then in Rome, where he was incarcerated in a tiny cell for seven years, tortured, then burned alive. Bruno was everything the Church despised and feared: a thinker and populariser who offered an alternative vision of the universe. They did not burn him because of some pedantic detail of Catholic doctrine or transient political viewpoint, but because he possessed the power of communication, because people listened to him and read his inflammatory words.

Three-quarters of a century earlier, Martin Luther had shaken the roots of Catholicism by attacking the structure of the Church and lambasting the pope for his decadence. But Bruno, like Leonardo, like Copernicus, like Kepler, like all truth-seekers, attacked the givens, the philosophical foundations. While Lutherans and Calvinists merely proposed an alternative form of worship and argued over details, these rare men offered a completely fresh ideology.

The cardinals had tried to silence Bruno with edicts, proclamations, excommunications; but in the end they were forced to seal him in a room six feet square before piercing his tongue with a metal spike to stop him spreading his subversion to the crowds who flocked to see him burn in the Campo di Fiori.

Bruno died because he refused to accept orthodoxy, and he expressed his vision as an amalgam of the science of Copernicus (which the Church persecutors still did not understand fully) and a belief in a Catholic God. Bruno had never abandoned his faith in the divine and in some ways he was a traditional Catholic, but to the Holy See the man was an arch-heretic and therefore a terrible threat.

Unfortunately for Bruno, the world was not ready for a man who spoke as he did of life on other worlds, of a God that was more pantheistic than biblical, and of a natural philosophy that discarded almost everything Aristotle had taught. As early as the 1570s Bruno had become a champion of Democritus and the atomists and he had questioned openly what had long been cast in stone, asking: What is matter? What is energy? How could an infinite universe exist? If it did, what did it mean?

Bruno offered a poet's vision of these things. Like Leonardo, he had no maths. Only now, in a world explained by quantum mechanics and guided by relativistic insights can Bruno's world-view be appreciated. His model of a universe in which all things were interconnected on an atomic level bears comparison with ideas that sprang from superstring theory during the 1990s.

Although Bruno's ideas were visionary and other-worldly, they were also warm and personal; they touched both the poet and the analyst and they eventually influenced men such as Heisenberg and Einstein. But in the sixteenth century such philosophies sent a cold chill through the God-fearing cardinals. Bruno's questions were fundamental and they were the same questions as later haunted Galileo – questions that have occupied the thoughts of physicists from ancient times to the present day.

Our modern view of the universe is based upon the rather exotic world of quantum theory, but for most everyday purposes the way in which we manipulate matter and energy relies upon rules and systems dis-covered between Galileo's lifetime and the present century. For many historians of science, Galileo's ideas about how matter behaves and how energies and forces operate can be seen as a watershed in the develop-ment of physics. Indeed, it would be no exaggeration to say that Galileo's ideas and work acted as a bridge between the Renaissance (and all that went before it) and the Enlightenment. Galileo was the one who drew together the many threads that led from ancient times to modern empirical science (a study based upon mathematical analysis as well as experimental evidence).

Behind Galileo lay some two thousand years of changing ideas about the nature of the universe; his great achievement was to clarify and to bring together the individual breakthroughs of his antecedents, to begin to construct an overview that Newton and others later helped turn into contemporary science. Newton went on to create a set of laws and rules that has given modern physics a definite structure.

The story of Galileo's life is intimately connected with the history of the Church and in particular the way this ancient institution interlinked with the development of science before, during and after his time. When we consider the obstacles placed in the path of science by an uncompromising and misguided Church, it is difficult to imagine how any progress in rational thought in the West could have been made between the beginning of the Christian era and the time of Darwin. The fact that there was progress says a great deal for the persistence and devotion of men such as Galileo, Bruno, Descartes, Copernicus and many others. Indeed, it is pretty clear that Galileo fought a great cause throughout his career and that he was fully aware of the role he was to play in the history and development of thought. He believed that the Church was following a false trail in its resistance to scientific investigation and discovery. He abhorred the fact that much of the scientific work the Church actively supported was conducted purely to *disprove* the findings of secular scientists.

Ironically, though, quite by accident, the Church has actually done science a great service. There are two key reasons why science has flourished in western Europe. The first is the influence of the Greek philosophers, whose work provided the bedrock of the Renaissance. The second is the tradition of a monotheistic theology created by the founders of Christianity. This tradition provided a sense of order in the universe. It relied upon the idea that there is an all-powerful Creator who maintains the universe and breathes into it life, bringing order to all things.

The exclusively Christian thinkers who dedicated their lives to the development of science, from Roger Bacon to Newton, did so because they desired to unravel what for them was the ultimate truth. They sought out an understanding of the order of the universe so that they could bring themselves closer to their God. This was a powerful – perhaps *the* most powerful – stimulant for their efforts. So, by virtue of its rigorous traditions the Church unwittingly provided a cognitive framework for generations of scientists whose work eventually succeeded in undermining the very foundations of Christianity, replacing superstition with logic and reason.

4

Rebel with a Cause

Originally known as the Studium Generale, the University of Pisa was established some thirty years before the new learning arrived from the East to spark the earliest flowering of the Renaissance. Founded in 1321, it was not one of the first wave of universities established in Europe (that honour goes to Paris, Bologna and Oxford, which can trace their roots back to the early twelfth century); but by 1349 the Studium Generale of Pisa had acquired official recognition by the pope, Clement VI, who issued a Bull, *In Supremae Dignitatis*, giving the institution special privileges and elevating it to a level of importance shared by only a few of the most elite educational Establishments of the time. But the university suffered mixed fortunes, so that by the time Galileo enrolled there, more than two centuries later, it had diminished and was considered second-rate, academically weak and too much in thrall to the clergy who dominated its administration.

The curriculum at the university was much like any other of the period. All courses were built around Latin, Greek and Hebrew, classical history, art, scripture and some mathematics. Specialist subjects such as medicine were also studied. Although this curriculum covered a broad range, it was skewed towards the Arts, so that mathematics and natural philosophy were considered the least important subjects. This system remained almost unchanged until the early nineteenth century, when universities across Europe started to modernise, courses became more streamline and specialised, and the teaching of science began to be taken seriously.

The 17-year-old Galileo who entered the University of Pisa on 5 September 1581 was already a polymath, a young model for the image of the Renaissance man. Thanks to the teaching of his father, he was an accomplished musician, a virtuoso lutist who possessed a beautiful singing voice. He was also a remarkably good painter and had entertained rather vague ideas of pursuing a career as an artist.

Galileo was a well-built young man, almost beefy, and he had strong features, a broad face, large eyes and a powerful jaw. His most obvious characteristic, though, was his piercing intellect, a trait matched only by his strength of character and what many considered to be arrogance and excessive self-confidence. The boy was super-intelligent and he knew it. He had also been raised to be sceptical, taught to search and to probe. This was to make him the great scientist he became, but for many these talents also made him tiresome and difficult to get along with.

He must have been even harder to teach. Doubt of everything except oneself makes for a powerful personality, a man who achieves; but at the same time, within a climate of religious piety and an environment in which one was required to genuflect to long-dead heroes, Galileo was certain to clash with his elders and his far more conventional contemporaries.

Abiding by his father's wishes, he was enrolled to study medicine at the university, but the subject totally failed to inspire him. He attended lectures dutifully, but almost immediately he began to argue with his teachers over the material that had been handed down from generation to generation, from Galen and Aristotle – notions that had little, if any, experimental or practical foundation; and, when the arguments led from medicine to the physical laws as they were handed down from Aristotle's assumptions, unquestioned for almost two thousand years, Galileo found himself completely at odds with his lecturers. This stance quickly earned him the nickname 'the Wrangler'.

This epithet was not given with affection – far from it. Galileo may have been right, but his teachers and many of his contemporaries found him obnoxious. The Wrangler's healthy scepticism and probing spirit provided the backbone to his achievements, but it was also to cause him great trouble throughout his life.

An example comes from his first year in Pisa. During the winter of 1581, the city was struck by a powerful hailstorm, which had the entire town abuzz. In the lecture halls of the university the professors explained the storm using Aristotelian meteorology. This held that because heavier objects accelerated faster than smaller ones, larger hailstones arrived on the ground before smaller ones. However, when Galileo pointed out this was not what was actually observed, the story was changed subtly. The conventionalists admitted grudgingly that, yes, the stones did land at about the same time as each other, but this did not, they claimed, conflict with Aristotle's views, because the lighter ones fell from a part of the heaven that was closer to the surface of the Earth.

Faced with such arguments, it is perhaps easy to understand Galileo's impatience; but what is most striking about this story is that *we* can see the absurdity of the traditional argument thanks to the benefit of four centuries of science since that time. For Galileo, there was no such support structure; his thinking was not only original and completely at odds with the Establishment: it was visionary.

Galileo had first begun to appreciate mathematics before entering university. It had seeped into his mind through his familial immersion in music (which is, of course, a discipline rooted in mathematical rigour). Through this he had begun to understand the importance of proportion, of numeric repetition and number systems; but most importantly, from a relatively young age, music instilled in him an understanding that mathematics was not some nebulous or arbitrary concept but could be of enormous importance. Music took Galileo beyond the rather ethereal (but nevertheless accurate) notions of Plato that the universe is constructed around mathematical absolutes. He could also see that mathematics was a tool, an instrument that could be manipulated, and that with it, humankind could produce wonders.

During Galileo's first year at the University of Pisa, this interest in mathematics began to blossom thanks to the teacher, Filippo Fantoni, holder of the Chair of Mathematics. Fantoni was a capable and broad-minded man, and soon Galileo was skipping lectures in medicine to attend mathematics classes. While he should have been pawing over Galen, he was actually immersed in Euclid and Archimedes.

Fantoni had sparked Galileo's interest, but then, in 1582, the well-known academic Ostillio Ricci, who was employed by the Grand Duke of Tuscany as Court Mathematician, visited Pisa to deliver a series of private lectures to the wards of the duke, who were then studying at the university. Through Fantoni, Galileo heard about these and attended the first lecture uninvited, placing himself at the back of the lecture theatre.

Ricci quickly realised Galileo had a gift for mathematics. Indeed the two men – Ricci then 42 and the 18-year-old medical student – thought in similar ways. Ricci, a master of the ancient traditional mathematical techniques of his field, was also a man who understood, ahead of his time, the applicability of mathematics. This shared conviction drew them together, and Ricci began to take a special interest in Galileo, adopting him as a private pupil while he was in Pisa. The seed of interest that had been planted by Vincenzo Galileo through music and encouraged by Fantoni was fully nurtured by the grand duke's mathematician, and for Galileo this affirmed the fact he could not continue wasting his time with medicine. It was clear his future lay with mathematics and natural philosophy.

During a college vacation in the summer of 1583, back home in Florence where the Galilei family lived in a modest house in what is today called Piazza de Mozzi, Galileo told his father about the work he had been doing with his new friend and mentor Ostillio Ricci. His intention was to try to persuade his father to let him leave his medical course to pursue a degree in mathematics. Rather than dismiss this new interest of his son's, Vincenzo listened and agreed to at least discuss the matter with Ricci. He admired the mathematician, who was by then something of a celebrity academic, and the two men may have known each other from their involvement with the Tuscan court and through the Florentine Camerata. Chance would have it that Ricci was close by with the grand duke's court, who were spending the summer in Florence. Galileo arranged for Ricci to visit and the mathematician made a case for the young man to leave behind his medical studies.

Vincenzo was understandably doubtful, and he knew that Galileo's mother, Giulia, would be more sceptical still. Medicine offered a secure future and it was a highly regarded profession entirely suitable for Galileo, who was clearly a young man with talent. However, having the Court Mathematician tell Vincenzo his son was a prodigy must have had some influence; and so a compromise was reached. Galileo would continue with his official studies but pursue mathematics in his spare time; Ricci would take him under his wing and instruct him when he could.

Of course, Galileo interpreted this decision as he saw fit. He immediately stopped attending lectures in medicine, ignored his medical books and spent his entire time studying Nicolo Tartaglia's Italian translations of Euclid's *Elements* and the collected works of Archimedes. It was the second of these that probably started Galileo thinking about experiment and the value of practical science. Archimedes was a great mathematician, but he had also been a very practical man. He had designed weapons for this government – even winning a prize for one of his military machines – and he had considered a blend of mathematics and experiment, observation and experience to be the ideal combination with which to unravel the secrets of the universe. Later, we shall see how, in terms of his intellectual disposition and vision of science, Galileo was a man cut from the same cloth as Archimedes; the fact that the Greek philosopher had such a profound influence on Galileo is not surprising. Galileo viewed Archimedes as all that the natural philosopher should be – a light in the dark that Aristotle's work had created.

Like many things associated with the early life of Galileo, the truth concerning his first piece of real scientific work is mired in legend and half-truths. According to the biographer Vincenzo Viviani in his hyperbolic life of Galileo, during the autumn of 1583, soon after returning to the University of Pisa, the 19-year-old Galileo was attending a church service when, bored by an overlong sermon, he began to watch the movement of an oil lamp hanging from the ceiling as it was made to swing by air currents in the draughty church.

Absorbed, almost mesmerised by the swinging lamp, Galileo quickly noticed that when the draught made it swing through a longer arc, it moved more rapidly than when it followed a shorter arc. Using his own pulse as a measure of time, he found that the lamp took the same length of time to complete any arc.

Returning to his room at the university, he made a pendulum from a length of string and a metal bob. He repeated what he had seen in the church, changing the length of the string, making the bob move at different speeds and then swapping the bob for lighter and heavier ones. For each experiment he used his pulse as a timer, as this was then the only accurate method of timekeeping available to him.

After hours of experiment and writing up his findings in detail, he was able to formulate a set of rules to describe the motion of any pendulum. First, he confirmed that the time of a swing is independent of the length of the arc. He found that the longer the arc, the faster the bob travelled. He also found that the mass of the bob did not affect the path of the pendulum at all. Most importantly however, he discovered that the period of the oscillation *did* depend on the length of the string.

Although Galileo may have stumbled upon the impetus for this discovery, it is revealing that his first dabblings with experiment had strong links with his musical background. How else are different notes played on a lute than by varying the length of a string? A harpsichord, for example, is simply an instrument with a large range of notes that can be sounded by hammers hitting strings of different length. Even a woodwind or a brass instrument employs this principle; different notes are formed by resonance in a tube which may be altered in length. It is revealing that many years after performing his experiment with pendulums, during the early 1630s, when Galileo was a prisoner of the Church in Arcetri, he returned to the study of stringed instruments in an effort to verify a largely ignored theory his father had proposed as early as the 1560s. In a document published in Holland in 1638, four years before his death, Galileo broke off part-way through a discourse on pendulums to describe the mathematical relationship between the ratio of the length of a string and the harmonic intervals of the musical scale.

To a degree, this story illustrates how Galileo's mindset was that of the Renaissance thinker. Many of his forebears thought and wrote in a similar way – men such as Brunelleschi, Leonardo da Vinci, Giordano Bruno and Leon Alberti; like them, Galileo was enamoured of the concept of holism. To him the way the speed of a pendulum altered with length and the way a musical note could be varied by changing the length of a string were each a reflection of the same thing: they demonstrated the interconnectedness of very different aspects of nature.

As we shall see, Galileo was a man guided by mathematical truth, the beauty of mathematics. He was very different from the principal scientist who prefigured him, Leonardo da Vinci, a man who experimented endlessly but did not back up his theories with mathematical rigour. As I have said, Galileo bridged the gulf between the science of the end of the Renaissance and the form it was to adopt by the beginning of the Enlightenment. This is because, although he was born into the Renaissance and naturally adopted some of the thought patterns that defined this period, he expanded upon them enormously and made great intellectual leaps to formulate a 'new science'.

Another way in which Galileo was similar to Leonardo was in his abiding interest in the practicality of the things he discovered. Leonardo turned his imaginings into designs for aeroplanes, tanks and an aqualung, cars, steam engines and military defence systems (although none of these things was ever made during his lifetime). Galileo was more successful in adapting concepts and turning them into practical science, a discipline we might call proto-technology.*

The first time Galileo did this was immediately after completing his pendulum experiments. He had observed the regularity of the rhythm

---

* Leonardo was another great admirer of Archimedes and considered him the most original and visionary of the Greeks.

of the pendulum and how it could be altered by varying the length of the string and he quickly realised this could be made into a practical device for the measurement of a patient's pulse. He described this technique in a paper and made the prototype of a device which he called a *pulsilogium*. Following protocol, he submitted both the paper and the model to the authorities at the University of Pisa; and they had no compunction in immediately stealing the idea and attributing its invention to 'the Medical Faculty'.

Galileo's relationship with the university had never been a happy one. He had mocked and criticised both the lecturers who had been teaching there for decades and his fellow students, whom he accused of following the old ideas of Aristotle like sheep. Perhaps the snatching of Galileo's invention was nothing more than an act of vengeance; or maybe the authorities saw it as a way to bring the young man down a peg or two. There is no record of how Galileo reacted, but it marked the beginning of the end of his time studying at the university.

Towards the end of 1584 Galileo's father had fallen on particularly hard times. The Galilei home was filled to bursting with Galileo's siblings, and the wool trade was facing a downturn. Vincenzo knew he could not continue to support his elder son through his medical course and so he applied for one of forty special scholarships then being offered by the grand duke. Unfortunately, the award depended upon the support of the university and so Galileo was probably not too surprised when he learned that his father's application had been knocked back almost immediately by the good professors of the medical faculty. Galileo was cut adrift and left the university without completing his degree.

It was not uncommon for students to leave university before they had obtained their degrees, but it was clearly not desirable, nor was it helpful in securing a career, and in early 1585 Galileo's career opportunities were of paramount importance to the Galilei family. Vincenzo blamed his son for this latest disaster. The boy had ignored his official studies and followed his own path – a course of action that could not have endeared him to his masters. Then, of course, there was Galileo's cockiness and arrogance, the evident joy he took in mocking his elders and superiors. Vincenzo was himself hardly a model of orthodoxy, and he had played a significant role in shaping the attitudes of his eldest son, but Galileo's academic failure must have come as a severe blow.

One can only imagine the rows in the house, the accusations, the counter-accusations and the escalating resentments that were all triggered by this event. Vincenzo must have been bitterly disappointed, while Giulia was probably panic-stricken and furious. Galileo, though, simply shrugged it off; he was even then buoyed up by an unshakable sense of self-worth and a belief in his own destiny. Although his parents were not then aware of it, Galileo had found his muse, and he knew exactly what he wanted to do with his life. Those he considered fools – the authorities at the university – had simply made things temporarily a little awkward for him.

Through his father, Galileo followed up a few job contacts, but he was young and unproven, and with some justification many people considered him an upstart who was simply too full of himself. So he did one of the few things he could do and started to earn a little money from teaching mathematics to the children of wealthy locals.

Beginning in the spring of 1585, Galileo travelled between Florence and Siena and occasionally further afield to the large farms and country residences of Florentine merchants and bankers, where he taught young boys the basics of geometry and arithmetic in preparation for their university courses. It was work that was beneath him and he knew it, but he was able to temper his frustration with the knowledge that he had little choice, that he had messed up his university career and that he owed it to his parents to help pay the bills and return some of the money Vincenzo had wasted on him.

Of course, having the character he had, Galileo simultaneously kept his eye on bigger things. At home in 1586 he conducted a series of experiments with the object of producing an accurate balance, what he called *la bilanchetta* or 'little balance'. Making all the parts himself and carefully calibrating the device, he was able to construct what was certainly the most accurate weighing machine ever made up to that time. It consisted of a bar or 'wand' suspended from a fine wire. At one end were placed weights of known size and at the other end was a receptacle into which objects could be placed. To measure weights with a high degree of accuracy, Galileo produced a scale that was so fine it could not be read by the naked eye. Instead it was made from a wire with groves cut into it. By sliding a tiny crosspiece over the grooves and using the sense of touch an experimenter could feel how many grooves had been passed over and was able to judge the weight of the object under study. Galileo wrote a short document about the device called '*La Bilanchetta*' in which he described the construction of his machine and the best techniques for using it.

One of the first experiments Galileo conducted with his new

invention was an interpretation of Archimedes' famous displacement experiment. According to legend, the Greek philosopher had been in the bath when he stumbled upon the idea that the purity of a substance could be tested by the amount of water it displaced. Using this idea, he could tell whether or not a crown that had been offered to his master, King Hiero, was pure gold or a fake. By using his balance, Galileo could perform a similar experiment, but he was able to measure the weights and calculate the densities of a range of materials with far greater accuracy than Archimedes could have imagined.

The idea that he could better the work of one of the most respected thinkers of ancient times appealed to his ego enormously; but this work also served a practical purpose. He had quickly grown tired of teaching rich but often untalented children, and he was desperate to secure a university lectureship. The best way to achieve this was by attracting the attention of other scientists and academics. His 'little balance' offered him a perfect opportunity to do this.

Partly thanks to his paper on the balance and his experiments with the device, the following year (1587) Galileo had his first chance to change the course of his life and career. The Professor of Mathematics at the University of Bologna, a priest named Ignazio Danti, had died suddenly leaving the position vacant. Galileo heard about it and applied for the job immediately.

It was an uphill struggle just to get noticed by the university authorities. He had no degree, no experience and a personal manner that many found difficult to deal with. It is clear that his greatest assets were his sharp intellect, his imagination and his determination; but, perhaps just as importantly, he had begun to realise the importance of networking. If he was to have any chance of acquiring this newly vacant position he would have to gain the support of influential and respected people in the same field.

It is certain that Galileo's father played a significant role in this process. Although he had himself been in and out of favour with the most powerful men in Tuscany, and his relations with the Medici in particular had been haphazard, through his own lifetime of networking he was on good terms with many wealthy and powerful figures. It would have been only natural for him to pull as many strings as he could for his eldest son. After all, Vincenzo had been this way before, in his own often abortive efforts to succeed. He would have known just who to talk to and how to behave to help secure assistance.

Another guide was Galileo's friend Ricci, who managed to secure his young protégé an interview with one of the most famous mathematicians of the day, Christopher Clavius, the Jesuit mathematician who taught at the Collegio Romano in Rome. Clavius had acquired an impressive reputation amongst mathematicians across Europe – such that he was later referred to as 'the Euclid of the sixteenth century'.

No great revelation or career leg-up came from the encounter. The two men appear to have communicated on an instinctive intellectual level, and the acclaimed Clavius was magnanimous enough to participate in a brief exchange of letters with the young Florentine mathematician after his return to Tuscany, but he was unwilling to write a recommendation for Galileo which, had he done so, might have carried some weight with the authorities at the University of Bologna.

Not surprisingly, Galileo failed to get the position vacated by the death of Danti, but he did learn a great deal from the experience of trying. The first lesson was that in order to acquire a prestigious appointment at one of the important universities one had to have influential friends who could help ease you into such a position; talent was of secondary importance; originality and a spirit of adventure were considered negatives.

In 1587 Mary Queen of Scots was executed, Marlowe wrote his drama *Tamburlaine*, and in the world of music Monteverdi's first madrigals were performed. In Venice, construction of the Rialto had begun. During that year and into 1588 Galileo applied for four other positions, at the Universities of Siena, Padua, Pisa and Florence. He failed in all these attempts; but along the way he developed a few very important relationships. The most significant of these was with the Marquis Guidobaldo del Monte, who was himself a very capable mathematician and dabbled in experiments in his private laboratory.

Galileo and Guidobaldo shared many similar scientific opinions. Del Monte was sceptical of Aristotle and believed in the enormous value of experiment. In his mid-forties by the time he met the 23-year-old Galileo, he soon began to view the younger man as a protégé, and after Vincenzo and Ricci he was to become one of the first to really appreciate the depth of Galileo's talent.

Recognition was exactly what Galileo needed at this time. In 1587 the grand duke, Francis I, and his wife Bianca Capello died in mysterious circumstances within days of each other, and the grand duke's brother, Cardinal Ferdinand de' Medici, became the ruler of Tuscany. Ferdinand had a reputation for ruthlessness and he had so despised his sister-in-law Bianca that in some quarters he was suspected of having murdered the couple in order to grab the ducal crown. Whether or not this was true, Ferdinand's ascension spelt disaster for the Galilei family.

Thirteen years earlier, in 1574, Vincenzo Galilei had dedicated a book of madrigals to Bianca Capello. Ferdinand made it a priority to clear his court of all those who had admired or been in favour with his brother and sister-in-law. Although Vincenzo's connection with the former Grand Duchess was entirely marginal, the new ruler was a very thorough man and uncompromising in his methods. Within weeks of Francis and Bianca's deaths Vincenzo found himself unemployed at the Tuscan court.

Now aged 67, living under a new and hostile ruler, Vincenzo was not just unemployed, he was effectively unemployable as a musician or composer; and, at the same time, his share in the family wool trade was not earning him enough to support his large family. Virginia Galilei was 14, Michelangelo, 12 and Livia just 9: the family's only hope lay with Galileo.

Such pressure did nothing to help and Galileo was already trying his best. As well as applying for any suitable position that came to his attention he was campaigning hard to reinstate a Chair of Mathematics at the University of Florence. This had been created by Francis I's predecessor, Cosimo I, but had remained vacant since the mid-1570s.

The Marquis del Monte was a keen and conscientious supporter of Galileo's efforts and the younger man placed great hopes in his friend's ability to open doors for him. On 16 July 1588, after learning that his latest attempt to secure a position, this time in Pisa, had failed, he wrote to del Monte, declaring:

My wish regarding Pisa, about which I wrote your Lordship, will not work out. A certain monk, who lectured there formerly and who gave up the post to become general of his Order, has resigned his generalship and has taken to lecturing once again. His Highness, the grand duke, has already appointed him to be lecturer. But here in Florence, there was, in times past, a professorship of mathematics, which was instituted by the grand duke, Cosimo I, and which many nobles would willingly see revived. I have petitioned for it and hope to obtain it through your illustrious brother, to whom I have entrusted my petition. As there have been foreigners here with whom His Highness has been engaged, I have not been able to speak on the subject to him myself. Therefore I beg you to write again and mention my name.[1]

Del Monte was determined to find a position for Galileo and wrote to him: 'As you well know, if I can serve you, I am yours to command.'² Soon after this correspondence, the Marquis succeeded in arranging for his friend an audience with the grand duke, but it did little to help Galileo in his efforts to re-establish the Chair of Mathematics at the local university. Unlike his immediate predecessor, Francis, Ferdinand had no interest in academia. Beyond this, he might have look unfavourably upon the son of Vincenzo Galilei, the former court musician who had been so fond of Bianca Capello. Ferdinand had probably only agreed to see the young mathematician out of respect for the del Monte family.

During the latter half of 1588 Galileo hit rock bottom, and for a short time he seriously considered leaving Italy altogether to seek work abroad, in Turkey or beyond. He still had a few local teaching commitments to fulfil, but they were paying very little and taking him absolutely nowhere.

During this period he spent some time at home with his parents and kept himself busy helping his father conduct a series of experiments on the relationship between tension in strings and their pitch. This resulted in what is now regarded as Vincenzo's finest contribution to music theory, his *Dialogo*. In these experiments, Vincenzo and Galileo used different weights to change the tension of strings. They then found that the pitch produced when the string was stuck or plucked varied as the inverse square of the weight used (or the tension produced in the string), and not, as the Greeks had proposed, as a direct inverse of the weight (tension). It was while he was at home helping Vincenzo with these experiments that Galileo received an invitation that was to change his luck and open doors.

One of the most respected intellectual groups of the day was the Academy of Florence, which had been established during the early fifteenth century by Marsilio Ficino with the support and patronage of the ruling Medici. Viewed by many as the very epicentre of the Renaissance, where newly discovered classical works were first read to an audience and discussed, the Academy had inspired Cosimo de' Medici to finance further research and to establish other similar academies throughout Tuscany.

The Academy of Florence was a nexus for intellectuals and thinkers. Created by humanists and inspired by radical thinking, the members nevertheless modelled their academy on classical paradigms. This was never more evident than in the topics they chose for special, occasional lectures. One such was a problem that had preoccupied the members of the academy for some years. What, they wondered, were the dimensions and location of Dante's inferno as described by the great patriarch of Florentine literature some three centuries earlier?

During the 1580s the matter had been debated at length, and the academy had invited several high-profile clerics and literary figures to offer their opinion on the matter. But then, in 1588, the president of the academy, a Florentine senator named Baccio Valori, had the radical idea of asking a natural philosopher to deliver a discourse to the learned gathering in which an empirical scientific description could be offered.

Galileo, a very inexperienced and little-known natural philosopher, was approached by the illustrious Academy of Florence to deliver a talk describing what natural philosophy and mathematics could do to illuminate Dante's description. Quite why he was chosen is not immediately obvious and it must have puzzled him as much as it has historians. However, it is almost certain that the offer to appear before the academy was arranged by Galileo's friends, most particularly the ever-helpful del Monte. It would also be reasonable to assume that no one else would have wanted to take on such a task and that it fell to the determined and hungry Galileo almost by default.

The topic of this talk – a description of the size, shape and location of Hell as portrayed in Dante's *Inferno* – seems to us today completely absurd, but for the members of the Academy of Florence, and for most intellectuals of the sixteenth century, it was a question taken very seriously because it was believed that Dante had been writing about the real Hell, using information passed on to him directly from God. Many learned books had been written about the nature of Dante's Hell. The Florentine mathematician and architect Antonio Manetti, who lived a century before Galileo, had made a detailed study of its dimensions as described in the *Divine Comedy*; and fifty years after Manetti's death another Italian, the literary critic Alessandro Vellutello, had derided these claims and presented his own commentary.

In common with the academics of his age, to Galileo, the debate about Dante's Hell was a serious matter and he gave the subject his undivided attention. He considered Dante's description to be entirely literal and based on simple facts, and having studied the various opinions of his forebears on the subject, he concurred with Manetti's analysis, making this fifteenth-century work the centrepiece of his lecture.

The talk took place at the Medici Palace on Via Larga before an audience comprising many of the most important citizens of Tuscany; but Galileo took all this in his stride. He stepped up to the podium, immediately exuding his usual confidence, and went on to deliver a perfectly pitched and accomplished talk.

He began by estimating the size of Lucifer, using the concept of scaling to arrive at an answer. 'Let us speculate on the size of Lucifer,' he declared. 'There is a relation between the size of Dante and the size of the giant, Nimrod, in the pit of hell, and in turn, between Nimrod and the arm of Lucifer. Therefore if we know Dante's size, and Nimrod's size, we can deduce the size of Lucifer.'[3]

He found the numbers he needed from Dante's own detailed descriptions, clues from the *Inferno* indicating that Lucifer was forty-three times larger than a statue of a giant in St Peter's Square in Rome and that this statue was forty-three times taller than Dante himself. From this he calculated that Lucifer was close to two thousand yards tall. He then went on to use other mathematical relations to demonstrate that Hell was a cone-shaped domain taking up about one-twelfth of the mass of the Earth, with its vortex at the centre of the planet.

Galileo's lecture was received with great enthusiasm. He had not realised it at the time, but it had been a rather elaborate test of his character. Within nine months of his appearance at the Academy of Florence, the court of the grand duke offered him the post of Professor of Mathematics at the University of Pisa.

Debunking Aristotle

At the end of the sixteenth century the University of Pisa was very much a poor cousin in the family of colleges that had grown up in Europe over the past half-millennium. In 1589 the university had just six hundred students compared to the thirteen hundred or more at Bologna and an even larger number in Padua. Two-thirds of the students at the University of Pisa were studying law, but very few finished their degrees. Astonishingly, it bestowed fewer than forty degrees each year.

But for Galileo the offer of a post there as Professor of Mathematics could not be refused. The position, recently vacated by Galileo's former teacher Filippo Fantoni, came with very little prestige and a lamentable salary of just 60 crowns per annum (equivalent to about £5,000 in today's terms). To put this into some perspective, the Professor of Philosophy at the same university, Jacopo Mazzoni, earned a dozen times more, and almost a century earlier, in 1498, when the young Niccolò Machiavelli had first been appointed as Second Chancellor to the Florentine government, he drew a salary equivalent to what would today be about £90,000. As well as these negatives, there is also the fact that Galileo was returning to his alma mater and his experiences there had been, for the most part, unhappy ones.

Galileo began at the university late in 1589. He had accepted a three-year contract, which, considering that he had no degree and no experience as a lecturer, was surprisingly favourable; but in hindsight he was to view the following years spent in this position to be a rather tawdry part of his life, almost an extension of his threadbare student days. Mathematics was the least important subject on the university curriculum and very few students even bothered with it at all. As a consequence, Galileo was obliged to teach a handful of less-than-enthusiastic students and because maths was considered an unimportant subject, he was designated a dingy back room for his lectures. Impoverished as he was, his clothes were worn out and he took little interest in his appearance. Furthermore, he flatly refused to wear academic dress, even though the regulations of the university stipulated that all professors were required to dress in gowns at all times. To add insult to injury, he proclaimed that the gown of the academic was used simply to disguise intellectual inadequacies. Little surprise, then, that he made few friends amongst the teaching staff.

Galileo was required to adapt quickly to a rigid routine at the university. He taught every day except Sunday. This work took three forms: tutorials with small groups of students, conventional lectures and public lectures. The last of these were often quite grand affairs and the lecturer was required to prepare an address to students and other staff members on a specialist subject once each academic year. Like all teachers of the period, Galileo spent lectures standing at a raised lecturn and reading from translations of original texts of the Greek masters – in his case, Aristotle, Euclid and Archimedes. The students sat in silence and the keen ones made copious notes.

Galileo lived in a small apartment close to the university buildings, and he had a manservant provided by the university, who attended to his domestic needs. He ate all his meals in college, but he was also fond of the tavern and quickly discovered a fondness for gambling and whoring. His drives and interests differed little from those of the other young men who dominated the small city during term time, and Galileo (who was only a few years older than his students) preferred their company to that of his colleagues.

Even taking into account these distractions, in most ways the University of Pisa was entirely the wrong place for Galileo. It was a very traditional institution that encouraged the continuation of tried and tested teaching methods, and enthusiastically supported classical thinking and teaching. This approach was epitomised by the star academic in the city, a philosopher named Girolamo Borro, whom Galileo grew to despise.

Borro was an ultra-conservative and a vociferous supporter of Aristotelianism, a man who accepted and treated almost as gospel every word prescribed by the Greek philosopher. It was Borro who had proposed the idea that hailstones landing on Pisa in a storm originated from different levels of heaven according to their size, an idea the student Galileo had mocked openly.

Borro was extremely successful in his field. He had become well known on the strength of two highly regarded books, *On the Flux and the Reflux of the Sea* (1561) and *De Motu Gravium et Levium* (1575). He had an abiding interest in Aristotle's ideas on motion, and in particular the behaviour of bodies in free fall, and he had explored these subjects at length in his *De Motu*. Such was his reputation amongst fellow academics that this text was considered by fellow contemporary Aristotelians to be the last word on the subject.

Borro was a traditionalist, but he was also a serious thinker, and although he considered Aristotle's ideas to be the true basis of science and an accurate description of the way the universe functioned, he was different from many Aristotelians in that he also understood the value of experiment.

Some years before Galileo took up his position at Pisa, Borro had enlisted the help of some colleagues to test Aristotle's notion that objects fall at a speed according to their nature and their mass. Aristotle had claimed that 'a one-hundred-pound ball falling from a height of one hundred cubits (about 58 metres) reaches the ground before another of one pound has descended a distance of one cubit'. After dropping wooden and metal balls of different masses from the top window of a house, Borro reported in his treatise that the wooden ball had landed first. Then, after another set of experiments, he concluded that balls made from the same material landed at different times depending on their mass.

During the months immediately before starting at the university, Galileo had begun his own investigations into the motion of bodies in free fall and he knew Borro's conclusions to be nonsense; but, as a very junior faculty member, his views were not taken at all seriously. This must have irritated Galileo and made him more determined than ever to prove the traditionalists wrong. At this time (before Copernicus's vision had become familiar to a wide audience of intellectuals and theologians) it was Aristotle's theories of motion that lay at the heart of any dispute between classicists such as Borro and radical thinkers epitomised by the young Galileo. It was the battleground upon which Aristotle's credibility (as well as that of his opponents) could be tested.

Indeed, Galileo was was not the first to attack Aristotelian mechanics. The mathematician Simon Stevin and the sixteenth-century Italian natural philosopher Giovanni Benedetti, along with Giuseppe Moletti, who in the 1590s was Professor of Mathematics at the

University of Padua, had each offered alternative theories to Aristotle's; but Galileo was to go on to produce models far more radical than any of these men; and although his ideas were for the most part ignored by senior philosophers, Galileo was lucky enough to find the support of one close colleague who was also a highly regarded academic. This was Jacopo Mazzoni, a man whom Galileo respected enormously for the depth and the breadth of his intellect – a thinker who was almost as sceptical as Galileo about some aspects of Aristotelianism.

Mazzoni, who was fifty when Galileo arrived in Pisa, had made his name as a biographer and analyst of Dante. He was a modernist and a humanist who believed in the open discussion of controversial scientific and philosophical ideas. He had first noticed Galileo when the younger man had delivered his lecture on Dante at the Academy of Florence the previous year. After getting to know him, Mazzoni had quickly grown to admire Galileo's ambition, his unconventional approach (which chimed so well with his own) and his insouciance.

Mazzoni was a socialite as well as an academic, and he held regular dinners at his home to which he invited his friends and where discussion of science and philosophy was actively encouraged. By the end of 1589 Galileo was a member of Mazzoni's circle and a frequent guest at his dinner parties. Galileo's stance at this time was already anti-Aristotelian, but he had not yet embraced the revolutionary ideas of Copernicus, which then lay at the extreme end of what were considered acceptable, even for forward thinkers such as Mazzoni.

But Galileo was determined to prove Aristotle wrong about the physics of falling bodies. At the same time, he was vigorously opposed to the closed-mindedness of many of his contemporaries, who followed blindly the word of Aristotle. Most importantly, he was convinced that mathematics was an entirely undervalued subject and that it held the key to unlocking many of the secrets of science – that it could be forged into an amazingly versatile tool that would help mankind to properly interpret the universe.

One of the most famous stories about Galileo is that he conducted a set of experiments in which he dropped objects from the top of the Leaning Tower of Pisa in order to disprove Aristotle's depiction of free fall. This tale originated with Galileo's first biographer Viviani, who claimed that Galileo carried out these experiments sometime in 1590. In Viviani's version of the story the experiments created quite a spectacle. Taking heavy metal balls to the top of the tower was hard work and it required the help of several assistants, who also participated in synchronising the drops. By the time the experimenters were ready a large crowd had gathered to witness the spectacle. Galileo was apparently delighted by the attention because he wanted as many witnesses as possible to confirm how he had clearly debunked Aristotle.

Recently, some historians have suggested this demonstration never actually took place; but although we only have Viviani's word for it, there is actually no real reason why Galileo could not have conducted the experiment as his first biographer described it. One of Galileo's most pronounced and consistent characteristics was his love of drama and theatre; it was a thread that ran through his entire life, from his days of student rebelliousness to the spectacle of his defence before the Inquisition many decades later. The Leaning Tower experiment was also a very good way of demonstrating the concept of free fall under the influence of gravity and it was not so very different from Borro's more mundane and far less flashy experiment dropping balls from a high window of a friend's house.

Whether or not Galileo conducted free-fall experiments from the Leaning Tower of Pisa or merely gathered data in a more prosaic fashion, by 1590 he had acquired clear evidence to support his anti-Aristotelian stance, and he could show conclusively that all bodies fell at the same speed irrespective of their physical nature or their mass.

In the summer of 1590 Galileo wrote the short treatise entitled '*De Motu*' in which he described the findings from his free-fall experiments. With this work he not only offered a new and different perspective on the matter of falling bodies, but he also made a first attempt at an entirely original form of presenting his findings. Rather than offering his results cold, he utilised the literary device of creating characters who discussed the contrasting theories – in this case, the Aristotelian and the Galilean – and he then resolved the argument to show the falsity of the traditional argument.

This device came naturally to Galileo. He had been introduced to the value and beauty of literature by the monks of Vallombrosa and by his father, who was friends with many important writers of the period. It allowed him to present difficult ideas in a digestible way, and it was a style Galileo honed and perfected and used in almost every paper and book he ever wrote.

'*De Motu*' was a rather immature work, and Galileo knew it. His use of character and story in this first try-out was based on a rather scant tale about two friends, Alexander and Dominicus, who walk along the bank of the Arno and strike up a discussion about motion. In this account, Alexander takes Galileo's view and he successfully refutes the traditionalist ideas put into the mouth of Dominicus. In 1590, Galileo had still to find his literary voice – the voice that would become so well developed by the time he composed his master works, *The Assayer*, *Dialogue Concerning the Two Chief World Systems* and *The Discourses on Two New Sciences*.

But, aside from the weakness of his presentation, Galileo was not altogether happy with the scientific details of his treatise. He was clear about the experimental data supporting his anti-Aristotelian theory of falling bodies, but at the time he was unable to take these experiments as far as he would have liked. Also, in many places '*De Motu*' was contradictory and muddled, and no matter how much he reworked and revised it, he could not pull the book into shape.

Galileo had exacting standards. At the start of '*De Motu*' he had declared: 'In this treatise the method we shall follow will be always to make what is said depend on what is said before, and never, if possible, to assume as true that which requires proof. My teachers of mathematics taught me that.'[1] In taking this view Galileo was thinking in a very modern way and rejecting the traditionalist, classical approach of Aristotle as well as the haphazard methods employed by many medieval philosophers.

Indeed, this simple paragraph illustrates just how far apart Galileo and Borro were in their thinking. Borro followed what was (as Galileo put it) 'said before' by emulating Aristotle's syllogistic logic. Galileo followed the experimental inventiveness of Archimedes. Borro was trying to prove what he already believed to be true and was not above changing his observations to fit his beliefs. Galileo was also, of course, attempting to show that he was correct, but he placed supreme importance upon the truth of what he observed. The need never arose for Galileo to change what he observed, but it is very unlikely that he would have moulded his observations and experimental findings to suit his passionately held beliefs. It is this more than anything that separates Galileo from tradition and, most strikingly, it was also this stance of Galileo's that was later to set him at odds with the faith system of the theologians.

Men such as Leonardo and Roger Bacon had appreciated the value of experiment, and even ultra-conservative and backward-thinking men such as Girolamo Borro had come to realise its importance. Both Leonardo and Bacon had documented their experimental findings in detail and in the late fifteenth century Leonardo had conceived of the entirely original notion that if experiments showed a pattern of behaviour in a particular situation then that same behaviour might well describe a pattern behind a broader set of observations. An example of this is tucked away in Leonardo's copious scientific notes, in a passage concerning an optical experiment he had conducted. He first described his observations and then declared: 'and form your rule from that'. This was really the first declaration of the scientific method: Take an observation and create a rule to describe what you see. Then, do more experiments to see if your rule works in other situations.

Leonardo had been a very capable experimenter, but his great weakness was that he had little understanding of mathematics. Galileo was ostensibly a mathematician who appreciated early on that a marriage of experiment and mathematics would provide a new path for science. The big idea contained in '*De Motu*' was that experiment could be used to test a concept and then mathematics could be used to create a rule, which might subsequently be applied to any connected situation.

Galileo knew his approach was the right one and that the views of Borro and his supporters were anachronistic. 'These grand personages who set out to discover the great truth and never quite find it give me a pain,' he mocked. 'They can't find it because they are always looking in the wrong place.'[2]

Galileo was not content with what he had written in his '*De Motu*' and decided to withhold publication of this work. Instead, he chose to use the treatise as the basis for other books, culling the best parts for inclusion in later efforts.

An example of this comes from his final book, *The Discourses on Two New Sciences*, in which he revived his findings of half a century earlier and compared them with statements made by Aristotle: 'Aristotle says that a hundred-pound ball falling from a height of a hundred cubits hits the ground before a one-pound ball has fallen one cubit,' Galileo wrote. 'I say they arrive at the same time. You [my critics] find, on making the test, that the larger ball beats the smaller one by two inches. Now, behind those two inches you want to hide Aristotle's ninety-nine cubits, and speaking only of my tiny error, remain silent about his enormous mistake.'[3]

Galileo's decision not to publish '*De Motu*' and his reasons for making this decision offer us an important insight into Galileo's character. '*De Motu*' was far superior to any other work that had been published on the subject up to this time. It made Borro's efforts look antiquated and it proved that the older man's entire model was absurd. But Galileo had the maturity to wait until he had perfected his ideas before laying them before his peers. Many years later, he wrote: 'I am quite content to be last and to come forth with a correct idea, rather than get ahead of other people and later be compelled to retract what might indeed have been said sooner, but with less consideration.'[4]

Galileo could have gained preferment and recognition if he had sent '*De Motu*' to the presses. Having written a treatise that was a significant improvement on anything that had gone before it and coming as it did from such a young man working in a backwater institution like the University of Pisa, '*De Motu*' might well have attracted attention and helped him find a superior position in a more prestigious university. It is uncertain whether or not Galileo was aware of this at the time, but he did possess an entrepreneurial streak unusual in a philosopher of any era, and he certainly knew just how difficult it was to gain respect in the academic world. Therefore it is likely he did indeed know what he was giving up and chose to withhold his book regardless.

By the summer of 1591 Galileo's strong opinions and his radical scientific ideas were leading him into serious trouble with his fellow academics at the university. In his typically arrogant way he had ridiculed his senior colleagues over their slavish attachment to out-moded thought systems, but then he went too far and slipped into foolhardiness. In the formal surroundings of the lecture theatre and before his small band of students he quite brazenly denounced traditional ideas and placed great emphasis on the findings of his own experiments (which, of course, he had not published). It should not have surprised him, then, when conservative students (who had been planted in the lecture theatre by his enemies) began to heckle and disrupt his lectures.

Galileo realised that he was being persecuted, but there was little he could do about it. He simply awaited the backlash. 'There will be many,' he wrote at the time, 'who, after reading my writings, will turn their mind not to consider what I have said as true, but only to seek means of impugning my arguments, whether justly or unjustly.'[5]

Galileo's list of enemies within the academic community was growing long and many of them were powerful figures. Yet, ironically, the event that led to his departure from the University of Pisa came not from arguments over academic matters, but from his insistence on interfering in a matter that was actually no concern of his. In 1592 the grand duke gave his seal of approval to a major engineering project that would improve the harbour in the town of Livorno close to Pisa. To implement this plan, Ferdinand had also committed to using a machine invented by Giovanni de' Medici, an illegitimate son of his father, Cosimo I. Galileo believed that this machine would never work and, without thinking about the offence his comments might cause in high places, he decided to publicly criticise the invention (and, by association, the illustrious inventor).

Although Galileo turned out to be right about Giovanni de' Medici's machine, this incident epitomised the boorish mood he had adopted. His face just did not fit in Pisa, and this mistake was all the academics at the University of Pisa needed to finally rid themselves of the troublesome Galileo. Giovanni de' Medici was a powerful and influential figure and the university authorities were in thrall to the Medici family, who provided them financial support and gave the institution its official and legal validation. When Galileo's three-year contract came up for renewal in the autumn of 1592, he was shown the door.

Galileo was certainly a loudmouthed, opinionated and often arrogant man, but he was also astute and, for all his lack of social graces, he was perfectly aware he was skating on thin ice. The fact is, he had had no real desire to continue working at the University of Pisa and had been expending great effort behind the scenes to find a new and altogether more rewarding position elsewhere.

Having acquired a network of admirers and supporters during his time at the University of Pisa, he was certainly not too proud to rely on the support this network could offer him. He knew the way academic positions were acquired and that the more important the post, the greater the leverage one must bring to bear. He had acquired something of a reputation and was viewed as a man of great scientific ability – ambitious, but difficult and tenacious.

During the autumn of 1591 the Chair of Mathematics at the far larger and more prestigious University of Padua had become available, and by then Galileo knew the writing was on the wall at the University of Pisa.

He was almost sure that 1592 (the final academic year of his contract) would be his last in the Chair of Mathematics at Pisa and throughout late 1591 and into early 1592 he worked hard to acquire this newly available chair. Helping him in this was his friend and supporter, the Marquis Guidobaldo del Monte, a nexus for his network. Through del Monte, Galileo was introduced to three important men. The first was Paolo Sarpi, a leading political and intellectual figure. The second was another del Monte, general Francesco del Monte, who was one of the most powerful military commanders of the Republic of Venice and a man of considerable influence. Perhaps an even more valuable contact facilitated by del Monte was the third of the triumvirate, the wealthy and powerful intellectual Gianvincenzio Pinelli. A nobleman from Naples who had lived in Padua for many years, Pinelli, who was 56 when he met Galileo, was key to the intellectual life of the city. He lived in a palazzo on the fashionable Via del Santo and hosted regular gatherings of thinkers, not just from the local university and from Venice but from all parts of Europe.

At this time Galileo needed all the help he could get in order to secure the position at Padua. The post had been left vacant for almost four years and the previous incumbent had been Giuseppe Moletti, a respected intellectual and famous anti-Aristotelian. This fact worked in Galileo's favour, as the liberal authorities in Padua wished to continue the line of teaching and anti-Establishment rhetoric for which Moletti was renowned. But Galileo's path to the professorship was not as clear as he would have liked. He had a rival in the shape of Giovanni Antonio Magini, a capable and highly regarded anti-Aristotelian academic who had beaten Galileo to the Chair of Mathematics at Bologna four years earlier.

In June 1592 the Venetian senate met and voted by 149 votes to 8 to elect Galileo to the post of Professor of Mathematics at the University of Padua. The formal report hailed 'Domino Galileo Galilei, who lectured at Pisa with very great honour and success, and of whom it can be said, he is the most outstanding person in his field.'[6]

There could be no better illustration of the distance Galileo had travelled in just four years than his success in acquiring the chair at Padua; and it was a clear sign the man was set to achieve even greater things. For Magini, an older and more experienced academic with a far superior track record, Galileo's success came as a humiliation. Returning to Bologna, he seethed, his anger fermenting while he put on a brave public face. Some two decades later he would come out in the open as one of Galileo's most cunning enemies and vociferous critics.

But in 1592 Galileo had little need to worry about Magini's damaged pride. He had finally succeeded in manoeuvring himself into an important academic position, and it came with the bonus of being in a city in which he felt comfortable. Suddenly, the career path ahead of him seemed bejewelled.

6

A Fresh Start

Padua is an ancient city that can trace its origins to pre-Roman times and boast that it was one of the most prominent towns of the Caesars. Later, beginning in the twelfth century, it became a free commune and experienced a huge growth in economic and cultural importance. This was marked by architectural splendours, including the Palazzo della Ragione in the centre of the city, which has one of the largest hanging halls in the world. The nearby Scrovegni Chapel, built around the same time (early in the thirteenth century), is famed for its peerless Giotto frescos, which the Florentine artist produced between 1303 and 1305, when he lived in Padua.

By the time Galileo arrived to compete for the job at the university, the city had been governed by Venice for almost two centuries. Enjoying peace and prosperity, Padua had settled into a symbiotic relationship with the larger, grander city, but at the same time the university had acquired a reputation as one of the great academic centres of the world, a place students flocked to from all over Italy and even from abroad. It had established its enormous international reputation during the previous century largely thanks to the success of its medical faculty, which was regarded as the best in the world. Such important figures as Andreas Vesalius had taught there and this drew other famous scholars to lecture at the university. As early as the mid-fifteenth century, a hundred years before Vesalius and a century and a half before Galileo's arrival, the university had become so popular and successful that it was able to compel the Venetian government to pass ordinances forbidding all subjects of the Most Serene Republic to attend any *studium* other than that of Padua.

In 1592 Venice was a city only just awoken from a series of political and natural upheavals. Fifteen years earlier the plague had killed almost one-third of the population, including one of its most famous sons, the artist Titian. The people of Venice had seen four doges come and go during a mere one and a half decades and the state was treading a delicate path, acting as broker between the great powers of Europe – France, Spain and Rome.

Positioned uniquely, so that it gained cultural influence from the east, it cherished a long tradition of learning and was a crossroads for the adventurous traveller. Marco Polo set forth from here in 1271 and what he and other explorers took with them as emblems of Western culture was more than matched by the knowledge and influence that flowed from east to west, passing through San Marco and the Lido. In the many centuries during which Venice had maintained global prominence, such learning had altered the very look of the city and created a backdrop of cosmopolitanism and liberalism.

Uniquely for sixteenth-century Europe, Venice was governed by a twenty-six-member *collegio* selected by using a primitive form of democracy. Senators came exclusively from the wealthiest families (not necessarily the most ancient or noble), but the system contained sophisticated safeguards against the obvious corruption that endangered less enlightened states. The government was led by an elected 'chief executive', the doge (or duke) who, theoretically, held his elective office for life. In practice, a number of doges were forced by pressure from their political peers to resign the office and disappear from public service altogether when it was felt they had been discredited by political failure or scandal.

Directly answerable to the doge was the Council of Ten (or simply, the Ten) which was first created in the early fourteenth century. It consisted exclusively of noblemen and it acted as a form of 'second house' to the *collegio* of twenty-six senators. Again as a safeguard against corruption and abuse of the system, a member of the Ten could serve no more than two successive terms and no more than one member of any family could be elected for a particular session. The Ten were led by three *capi* elected from the main body of the council, and these were only allowed to serve a term of one month, during which they were required to live in isolation behind the walls of the Doge's Palace. The primary responsibility of the Ten was the security of the state, but it was also involved in internal legal issues and law enforcement, and it played an important part in diplomatic processes, including the monitoring of vice and gambling in the republic.

By the sixteenth century, the Venetian Republic had gloried in centuries of successful trade and had established itself as a world military power. A constant feature of this position for some six hundred years had been its disputes with the Turk – the Ottoman Empire. Venice was a Christian state and had contributed to crusade after crusade, but its people were motivated as much by money as by God, and through its struggles with the Ottoman Empire as well as with its European neighbours, Venice had sought always to expand its territories. Success and wealth had added splendour and beauty to an already glorious city state. Between 1588 and 1592 the aptly named Ponte brothers had constructed the Rialto Bridge as we see it today, and during the second half of the sixteenth century, the accommodation of the ducal palace was expanded enormously to include new prisons, apartments and government offices.

At the border where Venice's interest in money met with the faith of her people, the city's rulers inevitably walked a delicate tightrope. Successive popes had clashed with successive doges and efforts to compromise were often exhausting and expensive for everyone. The power of the Council of Trent, which had been created almost half a century earlier to counteract any theological rebellion, remained a potent force in Italy and other strongly Catholic states, and while Venice and Rome squabbled over disputed territories, as they had done for centuries, these differences were less significant than painful clashes over doctrine and ideological independence. The pope was ever suspicious that Venice (and indeed Padua) had become a happy hunting ground for a motley assortment of Calvinists, Lutherans, occultists and other heretics. More often than not, behind the scenes, diplomats smoothed arguments and each state awarded concessions to the other to avoid open conflict; it was in everyone's interest to affect a compromise whenever possible. Sometimes Venice won a dispute, sometimes Rome. Successive popes made it forcefully clear the Holy See was the spiritual guide of Venice, but the Venetian government won the right to allow its booksellers to trade in texts on the Index of Prohibited Books. At least two popes insisted the state finance the building of more churches; the Venetians gained the right to allow Calvinist literature to be freely published and distributed in the city. Such compromise allowed the Venetians to make a living and to reserve their plot in the world to come, while popes and cardinals kept face.

Venice and Padua were considered the most liberal southern European cities and they each welcomed unorthodox philosophers. The Venetians and Paduans had also long remained distrustful of the

Inquisition. For some fifty years after Pope Gregory IX had first founded the Inquisition in 1231, successive governments of the republic had refused even to allow Inquisition administrators to set foot in the city. This decision was only reversed when, in 1288, Pope Nicholas IV threatened the Venetian ruler, Doge Giovanni Dandolo, with excommunication unless he complied with the Vatican's wishes. Even then, the Venetian inquisitors remained uninterested in mirroring the rabid enthusiasm of their Roman counterparts.

As late as 1521, during the height of the Reformation, Venice quietly defied papal orders. It established its own Inquisition rules, which dictated that all trials must be conducted by two bishops and torture in any form was banned. For forty-two years, between 1552 and 1594, just 150 trials were held in which Venetian citizens were accused of magical incantations, witchcraft and sorcery; only six of these led to prosecution, and throughout the ignominious century and a half of the witch hunts not a single person was executed or severely tortured in Venice.

Such independence of spirit had chafed relations between Venice and Rome. When King Henry III of France was assassinated in 1589 (just three years before Galileo arrived in Padua), Venice gave political asylum to his rightful successor, the Protestant sympathiser Henry of Navarre. This had incensed the zealous House of Guise, angered Philip of Spain and infuriated Pope Sixtus V to the point where he considered excommunicating the entire state of Venice. Sixtus stayed his hand only after sensibly taking the advice of trusted cardinals, who pointed out that in the past the weapon of excommunicating Venice had merely energised revolt. The city had been struck by the ultimate papal threat four times during its history – by Martin IV in 1284, by Clement V in 1309, by Sixtus IV in 1483, and most recently by Julius II in 1508; each time the Vatican had been forced to back down and reinstate Venice to the Faith. The Venetian people would be forever influenced as much by worldly pursuits as by religious sentiment.

In Padua, the pope, through his mouthpiece the Council of Trent, had taken different action. Rome had established a Jesuit university in the city and the administrators and teachers of this institution did everything they could to gainsay public pronouncements made by the liberals across town at the ancient university.

This conflict became something of a public spectacle, with the citizens of Padua divided in their loyalties. At one point, soon after Galileo's arrival, a group of students from the University of Padua conducted a night raid on the Jesuit school, dragged dozens of novice priests naked from their beds and frog-marched them into the streets.

For Galileo, there was much to attract him to Padua. His salary was three times that in Pisa, and he was drawn to the liberal stance of the university. Another advantage was the presence in the city of the nobleman and intellectual Gianvincenzio Pinelli, the friend of del Monte who had been instrumental in securing Galileo the chair at Padua. Pinelli and Galileo enjoyed an almost instant rapport, and the new arrival began to spend a great deal of time at Pinelli's palazzo. As soon as Galileo had accepted the Chair at Padua, Pinelli insisted he take rooms in his sumptuous home on the Via del Santo.

This proved hugely beneficial to Galileo. During the final two decades of the sixteenth century Pinelli's palazzo was considered an intellectual crossroads and the group who gathered there have since been recognised as an embryonic scientific society. Pinelli was certainly fascinated with natural philosophy and the new ideas of experiment and investigation, but his interests extended much further so that he attracted to his gatherings mystics and occultists, leading Roman Catholic intellectuals, writers and artists, as well as men like Galileo with radical scientific opinions.

During the first evenings Galileo spent with Pinelli (as he was preparing for the campaign to secure the Chair of Mathematics during the spring of 1592), it is possible he met both Giordano Bruno and Robert Bellarmine. These two men held extremely contrasting views on theology and philosophy, but each of them was received warmly by Pinelli. Giordano Bruno was a famous heretic, reviled by the Vatican. Robert Bellarmine was a highly regarded intellectual and senior papal aide. He had been appointed to the position of Spiritual Director of the Collegio Romano by the newly elected pope, Clement VIII, who had taken the tiara a few months earlier, in January 1592. Both Bruno and Bellarmine were to play significant roles in Galileo's own future.

If Galileo did meet Bruno, it would have been a very brief encounter, and there is no surviving documented report of any such meeting. The maverick former priest and famed occultist was working at the University of Padua in the early part of 1592 and he had become famous across Europe as an anti-Establishment figure who lived danger-ously and espoused extreme views. This made him a perfect guest at Pinelli's table and in the discussion groups hosted by the wealthy aristocrat. Trained as a cleric, Bruno viewed himself as a devout

Catholic, but his anti-doctrinal opinions were considered extreme heresy by the Church. He had only recently returned to Italy after spending most of his life abroad, and by taking up residence in a Catholic state he had placed himself in an extremely precarious position.

It is possible (but by no means certain) that Bruno, Galileo and Bellarmine shared the same guest list at the Via del Santo on at least one occasion. What sort of exchanges took place across the dinner table on these evenings may only be imagined. Bellarmine was a very clever man, and ruthless. His loathing for heretics had earned him the nickname 'Hammer of Heretics', and he had a particular hatred for Giordano Bruno, whom he viewed as an evil influence, a corrupter of the Faith.

On 22 May 1592 Bruno had returned to Venice to put his affairs in order before leaving for Germany when he was arrested and thrown into the prison of the Inquisition close to the Doge's Palace. While Galileo prepared for his examination by the selection panel, who sat no more than a hundred yards from the prison, Bruno was confined to a two-metre-square dungeon and chained to the wall. Throughout that summer and into the autumn of 1592, as Galileo was accepted by the University of Padua and organised his first lectures there, Bruno was placed on trial, condemned by the Venetian court as a heretic and transported to the Vatican, where he was to spend a further seven years before being burned at the stake in the Campo di Fiori in February 1600.

It is certain that Galileo and Bruno were never friends, and if they met at all their paths only crossed briefly. It is quite possible that, if they did meet, Galileo would not have agreed with many of the mystic's convictions. But whether or not the two men knew each other personally, Galileo was certainly quite aware of Bruno and his ideas. Years later, after Giordano was executed, the spectre of his horrible fate hung heavily over all those living in Italy with anti-Aristotelian views.

Another frequent guest of Pinelli's and another figure who was to have a profound effect upon Galileo's thinking and intellectual growth was Paolo Sarpi. Galileo had been introduced to Sarpi by del Monte, but he only got to know him properly through the gatherings at Pinelli's home. The two men very quickly became friends. Sarpi was a member of the Servite Order, which had been created in the thirteenth century. This sect was dedicated to the service of the Virgin Mary and was accepted as an orthodox part of the Church. However, Sarpi possessed a mind that was far too flexible and open for him to be confined by convention. Born to a relatively poor family, thanks to his brilliance and innate ambition by 1592 he had risen to become the most important cleric in Venice.

A more prosaic part of Galileo's life was spent in the lecture theatres of the university. His inaugural lecture was held there on 7 December 1592. The contents of the speech have not survived, but we know that by tradition the lecture was a public one, attended by the majority of the university teaching staff, and it was always a discourse on the fundamental ideas of the lecturer's field of expertise. The speech was delivered in Latin, and Galileo spent weeks in preparation, committing the whole thing to memory and practising his delivery.

The lecture was a triumph and word soon spread that a great new talent had arrived in Padua. News of the event even reached the most famous astronomer of the day, Tycho Brahe, who was then working far away at his observatory in Denmark. When he heard about Galileo's lecture he is said to have responded: 'A new star has appeared in the heavens.' Another admirer, the medic Giolamo Mercuriale, told Galileo in person: 'The University of Padua is the natural home for your genius.'

Galileo's students at the university were of a far higher calibre than those he had taught at Pisa, but he thoroughly disliked teaching. He covered up his disinterest with a great effort of will and even gained a reputation as an inspiring lecturer, but teaching novices was something he could barely tolerate and his distaste for the profession increased as he grew older. Late in life he even went so far as to declare: 'You cannot teach a man anything; you can only help him to find it for himself.'

This dislike for teaching might at first seem to be at odds with what we know of his character. After all, he relished the attentions of an audience and was a fine and confident public speaker. But at the same time he resented having to teach to pay the bills, because every minute he spent in the lecture theatre was a minute away from his researches.

Compared with his time in Pisa, Galileo had little to complain about and his life in his new and vibrant home was certainly not all serious talk and academic commitments. He had always been a man who enjoyed life. After taking up the professorship in Pisa, he had often been confused for a student and he had spent as much time out on the town as he had in the lecture theatre. He liked to relax, and Venice was the perfect place for him.

Venice in the 1590s was a city renowned for its splendid architecture and its cultural influence, but it was also one of the most popular destinations for the pleasure-seeker and the libertine. As far back as 1358 the Grand Council of Venice declared that prostitution was 'absolutely indispensable to the world', and the Venetian way was to regulate and to furnish rules rather than to censor or to ban.[1] Courtesans were obliged to conform to a strict dress code and were only allowed to ply their trade in pre-designated parts of the city. In the same way, drinking and gambling were legal but controlled, except during the carnivals in February and August, when even the lax Venetian rules were largely forgotten.

Galileo, gregarious and fun-loving, had no shortage of companions who would travel with him by barge from Padua to the canals and waterways of Venice only twenty miles away. But amongst a large circle of associates one friend stood out. This was Gianfrancesco Sagredo, a man Galileo later immortalised as a character in one of his master-pieces, *Dialogue Concerning the Two Chief World Systems*, published in 1632, in which Sagredo takes the role of an intelligent layman who discusses astronomy with two other characters – Simplicio, a blinkered Aristotelian and Salviati, who represents Galileo's views.

Gianfrancesco Sagredo was a larger-than-life character. Living off an inherited fortune, he enjoyed the very best of everything in a vast palazzo close to the newly built Rialto Bridge. The palazzo was known as 'The Ark' and had acquired this name in part because of its shape, which resembled a ship's hull, but also because he filled the place with a menagerie of animals.

Sagredo was a playboy and a libertine who had a specially con-structed set of rooms on the top floor of his home in which he entertained courtesans; but he was also an intellectually precocious man with wide-ranging interests. Almost a decade younger than Galileo, he was drawn to the older man in part because of the mathe-matician's lively character but also because he knew he could learn much from him. Galileo liked Sagredo for his flamboyance, his verve and the exciting lifestyle the young aristocrat opened up for him.

Pinelli and Sagredo formed the twin hubs of Galileo's life in Padua and Venice for the best part of a decade. Pinelli, the eldest of the three, offered a solid pillar of intellectual exploration and a social network unmatched in Italy. He was sorely missed when he died in 1601 at the age of sixty-five. Sagredo, equally wealthy, equally flamboyant, more in the Lord Byron mould, perhaps, than Pinelli's paternal character, drew Galileo into a different social group, which included two future doges, the wealthy and ambitious Niccolo Contarini and Leonardo Dona.

Galileo had started to mix in refined circles; but at the same time he was more or less impoverished, living with increasing debts and with little hope of financial security. His professor's salary was generous compared with what he had earned at the University of Pisa and Pinelli treated him as an honoured guest, providing him with comfortable rooms and meals; but even so, he was struggling.

In July 1591 Galileo's father had died, aged 71. Vincenzo Galilei's life had been filled with difficulties, and in many ways he had not come close to fulfilling his potential; his talent had remained largely unappreciated. He also died leaving a legacy of financial problems for his large family.

Galileo was the elder son and the only one of Vincenzo's children earning a living, which meant that he was responsible for the well-being of the entire family; a fact that placed on him a terrible burden. To make things worse, just before he died Vincenzo had agreed a very generous dowry for Benedetto di Luca Landucci, who was to marry Galileo's sister, the 18-year-old Virginia. A hint of Galileo's frustration and anxiety over all this can be gleaned from a letter he sent to his mother as Virginia's wedding day approached, in which he talks of his gift to the couple and adds: 'Do not say a word to anyone, that it may come to her quite unexpectedly. I will bring it when I come home for the Carnival holidays, and as I said before, if you like I will bring her worked velvet and damask, stuff enough to make four or five handsome dresses.'[2]

The dowry agreement drawn up between Landucci and Vincenzo Galilei was a crippling one. The initial payment to Landucci was for 800 ducats, and this was to be followed by payments of 200 ducats each year for five years. While he was still teaching in Pisa (for more than a year after his father's death) Galileo's salary had barely been enough to feed him. Moving to Padua had boosted his earnings threefold but it was still only 128 ducats per year. To make matters worse, Virginia's husband-to-be was a tough and practical man and not the sort to let his relatives off lightly when it came to the regularity of his dowry payments.

As well as this, Galileo's younger brother Michelangelo, who was 17 when Galileo moved away from the family and settled in Padua, had little ambition but an unhealthy appetite for spending other people's money, especially Galileo's. Finally, to add still more pain, the years 1590 to 1610 were economically unstable ones for much of Italy, a time during which inflation rarely dipped below double figures and many cities, including Venice, experienced crippling trade deficits and vigorous foreign competition in traditional markets.

We can only assume that Galileo borrowed money to relieve the immediate financial burden. Although there is no surviving record of any such loan, it would seem likely that during the summer and autumn of 1591, one or other of his wealthy friends (most likely the ever helpful del Monte) came to his aid. Even so, Galileo was always late with his payments to Landucci and this became a source of embarrassment as he slipped further into the financial mire. In May 1593 he was several months late with his yearly payment to his brother-in-law. On the eve of his first visit home to Florence since leaving for Padua he received an urgent message from his mother: 'Come,' it said; 'but you should know that Benedetto wants his money now and is threatening to have you forcibly arrested when you arrive here. He is just the man to do it, so I warn you: it would grieve me much if anything of the kind were to happen.'³

Galileo worked hard to improve his finances. He took on private students, but this provided little and he quickly became aware that he could only make serious amounts of money outside the academic world. So he set his mind to invention and looked to the military as a source of extra income. He was perfectly placed to do this. His status as Professor of Mathematics at the university and the fact that he was on good terms with important members of the Venetian Establishment helped to open doors.

In many ways it was an obvious idea. Venice was famed for its military power and most especially its huge navy. The city's geographical position at the crossroads between East and West was part of the reason for its considerable wealth and trading power, but this also meant that it was surrounded by potential enemies and invaders. Being an island city afforded a level of protection envied by many other Italian states, but this was only as good as its defences and the prowess of its navy.

The Venetian government oversaw a large military budget for the era and most of this went into constantly improving the defences of the republic and the all-important navy. In 1590, two years before Galileo moved to Padua, the Venetian Republic employed 200 ships' carpenters, 450 caulkers (workmen who sealed the planks of ships' hulls) and 100 oarmakers. Each year, the shipyards produced eighteen large galleys and 118 small vessels. According to legend, during a visit by the French king, Henry III, in 1574, the doge ordered a galley to be built, armed and launched during the time he entertained the monarch over lunch.

Almost a century earlier, Leonardo da Vinci had tarried in Venice for a while and during his time there he had acted as a military adviser before moving on to become a consultant for Cesare Borgia during his campaigns in central Italy. Galileo shared with Leonardo a fascination for mechanical devices and ingenious military applications of scientific principles. Leonardo had acted as a precedent for innovators offering their services to a ruler and had proposed to the doge such wonders as the aqualung, the dinghy and designs for pontoons.

Galileo's thinking was not so diverse nor so adventurous as Leonardo's, but he had a far more sophisticated, mathematically led understanding of the basic principles of science. Most of his advice to the military involved ways to design better ships and more effective defensive walls. Galileo did a great deal to improve the design of Venetian war vessels by changing the positions in which oarsmen sat and having the oar holes moved to a better position so as to greatly increase efficiency. As well as these improvements, he suggested ways in which the battlements and bulwarks that acted as a final lines of defence for the city could be built faster and provide a stronger barrier. 'Defence can be achieved in two ways, and the commander must decide which is more useful,' he wrote. 'Either the thrusting type of shot or the grazing type. The grazing shot follows a line parallel to the wall. Its advantage is clear. When ladders are resting on the curtain walls, one shot can remove many ladders, while the thrusting shot can remove only one ladder at a time. But the thrusting shot has the advantage of neutralising a man with a pickaxe, which is the most important assault weapon.'[4]

Although such consultancy work was welcome, it did not pay enormously well, and this forced Galileo to explore other avenues. The first of these was a simple thermometer. He made a glass bulb with a long stem about two feet long and filled the bulb with water. He immersed this in a bowl of water and, warming up the bulb with his hand, watched as the level rose up the narrow tube.

In this form his thermometer was little more than a novelty; but later Galileo adapted the idea using alcohol instead of water in the bulb. This produced a more dramatic effect. Today, the Galileo thermometer is still sold as a toy, consisting of a sealed tube containing a collection of bulbs holding coloured liquids of different densities. As the temperature changes, these bulbs float to specific levels in the container and indicate the temperature. It is really a simple device based on Archimedes' principle: as the temperature changes, the density of the liquids alters and they find new levels within the sealed container of water.

This was fun to play with, but Galileo soon concluded it would never become a serious scientific instrument, nor would it provide a way in which he could make much money. So, some time in 1593 he transferred his attention to the development of an irrigation system and made a note to himself in which he reported: 'I have invented a device for raising water from the earth most easily, at little expense and great accommodation, which from the motion of one horse can spout water continuously through twenty mouths.'[5] But again, hopes of making a fortune were dashed and he managed to sell just one of his machines, purchased by the Contarini family (one of the wealthiest and most powerful in Italy), who used it to irrigate their lavish Venetian gardens.

Galileo was determined, but he seemed to keep hitting upon dead-end proposals. Then, in 1597, some eight years after arriving in Padua, he struck upon an idea that became his first commercial success. This was the military compass, which probably first came to him some time in 1596 through his associations with the Venice Arsenal and his consultancy work for the military.

Galileo's military compass should not be confused with the orthodox compass devised in ancient times to aid navigation. It comprised two arms pivoted by a disc, and joined at one end by a quadrant. Each of these parts was covered with carefully crafted scales and markings. In effect, it was a primitive slide rule that could be used to calculate almost any simple arithmetical problem from compound interest to the angle of inclination needed for a cannon.

The need for such a device had been much in the minds of strategists and commanders for many years, but it took a man of Galileo's particular talents (a knowledge of theory and an understanding of practical requirements) to make a usable device. But, crucially for Galileo, his invention could be used as a tool by a variety of professions, not just military men. Mathematicians, bankers and accountants quickly became enamoured of the device and it was to remain in common usage for some two centuries before it was superseded by the slide rule, and then, much later, by the electronic calculator and computer.

Galileo constructed the prototype himself, but after securing a few orders on the strength of this initial design he employed a craftsman, Marc'Antonio Mazzoleni, and between them they developed a production method that could make accurate and aesthetically pleasing devices at a cost that turned a good profit on each instrument.

For some years, Galileo had rented a small house in the Santa

Gaussian district of the city. When he and Mazzoleni set up in business together, Galileo put aside a room for manufacturing the military compass and also provided accommodation for the craftsman's family. Mazzoleni took two-thirds of the profits from the compass as well as a small fee for making each device. Although this might seem like a raw deal for Galileo, he had realised early on that the real money would not come from the sale of the device itself but through selling the knowledge of how to use his invention.

Starting in 1597, Galileo began to spend his free time giving tutorials to anyone interested in the compass, and by 1599 his customers and tutees included Prince John Frederick of Alsace, Archduke Ferdinand of Austria and the Duke of Mantua. His fee for a course of lessons was twenty scudi (while the compass sold for five), but he never charged aristocrats or famous figures, because he knew from them he would gain new business and valuable kudos. By 1600 he had published an instruction manual for the compass entitled *Le Operazioni del compasso Geometrico e Militare*, which he sold privately with each model purchased. This he dedicated to Cosimo de' Medici, the future Grand Duke of Tuscany, declaring: 'If, Most Serene Prince, I wished to set forth in this place all the praises due to your Highness's own merits and those of your distinguished family, I should be committed to such a lengthy discourse that this preface would far outrun the rest of the text, whence I shall refrain from even attempting that task, uncertain that I could finish half of it, let alone all.'[6]

At first it might seem strange that Galileo had decided to dedicate his invention to a foreign head of state and not the doge. But we have to remember that, as well as being a great scientist and a very practical man, Galileo was a capable entrepreneur who always kept an eye on the main chance. He relied on patronage, whether it was that provided by a university or the support of a rich statesman, and probably knew that he did not need to waste his dedications on an elected doge. To begin with, he was already established with the Venetian hierarchy and noted as an important scientist working for Venice and Padua. Secondly, even though he was happy in his position, Galileo would have known that this might not always be the case, and that, after the pope, the most powerful men in Italy were the Medici, who also happened to be the first family of his homeland.

By the turn of the century, after seven years in Padua, Galileo had made enough money from his military compass to clear his debts and buy a substantial three-storey house on the fashionable Via Vignali del Santo close to the palazzo of his friend Pinelli. Here he built a large workshop and provided more spacious accommodation for the Mazzoleni family.

In old age Galileo considered this to be the best period of his life. He was still enamoured of the city of Padua and he adored Venice; he had a network of friends, he had money and he was respected as a professor at the university as well as for his inventions. During the period when he was seeking financial rewards for his engineering ideas he had not lost interest in natural philosophy, but, for a while at least, theory had been forced to take a back seat. Now, after finding financial stability, he was able to return to his first love: mathematics. This renewed interest came just as, across Europe, forward-thinking scientists were beginning to realise the true importance of Copernicus's ideas. As the new century dawned, Galileo was about to enter a vibrant new and incredibly productive period of his life, during which he would establish himself as one of the most important natural philosophers in the world. Most importantly, he was now ready to speak openly of his controversial ideas.

Conflict

As Galileo approached his thirty-sixth birthday, he could feel satisfied that he had already achieved great things, and a lesser man might have been tempted to settle into contented middle age; but Galileo was not the type. He was an adventurer, a man who often flaunted convention both with his personal pursuits and within his intellectual life. He was a restless man who always wanted more, a man who actively sought out change, progress and, in some cases, conflict.

A perfect example of his alternative lifestyle may be seen in his relationship with the mother of his children, a woman named Marina Gamba. Marina had been a prostitute from the district of San Sofia, one of the poorest areas of Venice. It is probable that Galileo met her at the palace of his friend Sagredo when she was employed there as one of the entertainments. Unfortunately there are no surviving portraits of Marina, who was 21 when she met Galileo, nor are there any detailed accounts in which she plays a significant role; but from the few scraps of family correspondence that mention her at all, she appears to have been a feisty woman with a fiery temperament and determined to do well for herself.

The pair never married, nor did they ever share a home; but when, in late 1599, Marina fell pregnant, Galileo installed her in a small but comfortable house on the Ponte Corvo close to his own more substantial residence in Padua. On 13 August 1600 Marina gave birth to the first of their three children, Virginia, who was baptised a week later at the Church of San Lorenzo, in Padua. The church records declare that the baby was 'born of fornication'; Marina was named as the mother but no mention was made of Galileo Galilei.

The reason for this is clear. Galileo had no wish to marry Marina, but by fathering a child out of wedlock with her he was breaking social convention and he thought it wise to distance himself officially from Marina and the baby. Although having children outside of marriage was by no means uncommon, it was largely limited to the nobility and the poorest, the peasant class. In each of these social strata there was little stigma attached to either the child or the parents. Within the middle classes however, such behaviour was considered unseemly. Children of unmarried middle-class parents could not attend university or join a professional guild, and they were tainted by shame throughout their lives.

Just a year after the birth of Virginia, on 18 August, a second daughter was born to the couple and christened Livia on the twenty-seventh. Again, the registration document carries a blank space where the name of the father would have gone. By 1606, when the couple's third child – a boy they named Vincenzo – was born, Galileo could still not put his name to the birth certificate, but this time the document read: 'Vincenzo Andrea son of Madonna Marina, daughter of Andrea Gamba and an unknown father'. For Vincenzo, Galileo allowed his parents to be named as grandparents.

It was not common for scholars to marry, but it was also extremely uncommon for them to take a mistress with whom they sired a family; and in a strictly Catholic country during the first decade of the 1600s Galileo's was a remarkably unorthodox lifestyle choice. He was always an independent thinker and cared little for social conventions, but the fact that he did not take Marina as his wife even when they had a young family together shows an unusual resistance to the traditions of marriage and family. He provided for Marina and his children and they were given all the opportunities society would allow, but at no point did Galileo intend marrying, and when he finally left Padua, in 1610, he did not take Marina with him.

What Galileo's colleagues and superiors thought of the arrangement is unknown, but it seems the relationship was gradually accepted. Galileo was never secretive about his mistress, even if he could not make the relationship official on birth certificates. But one person who never did acknowledge Marina was Galileo's mother, Giulia. Always a haughty and difficult woman, a snob and social climber, she detested the fact that a woman of such low birth, a common tramp in her eyes, should live in a house that was actually better than her own, and that her son supported her in what she considered a lavish style. Giulia's hatred ran so deep she even paid Marina's servant to spy on his mistress, and on more than one occasion Galileo was called upon to break up a cat-fight between the two women outside the house on Ponte Corvo.

It is possible Galileo resisted marriage because of the financial burden it would bring. Although in many ways he treated Marina as a wife and never shirked his responsibilities as a supportive father, he knew that while his relationship with her was not officially sanctioned he did not *have* to provide for her, nor for any children they had together. This was probably only a vaguely conceived notion, but it was incubated by the financial pressures Galileo still felt even after finding commercial success with his military compass. For, although he had created a comfortable lifestyle for himself, he now needed to maintain it and, at the same time, his mother and siblings continued to be a tremendous burden.

Much to Giulia Galilei's disgust, Galileo's good-for-nothing brother Michelangelo was trying to forge a career as a court musician. Predictably, he was finding very little success and Galileo was constantly obliged to bail him out of financial trouble. Then, early in 1600, Michelangelo announced that a few weeks earlier he had married and that he was passing on to his brother the bills for the lavish wedding feast. 'You complain of me having spent a large sum on one feast,' Michelangelo retorted pointedly to Galileo's justifiable protests. 'The sum was large, yes, but it was my wedding. There were more than eighty guests present, among them were many gentlemen of importance. Present were no less than four ambassadors! If I had not followed the custom of the country, I should have been put to shame.'[1]

Unfortunately for Michelangelo, the illustrious guests he had tried to impress at his wedding did nothing for his career, which continued to languish. As a consequence, he was never to stop sponging off his hardworking and aspiring brother. Worse still, words of thanks from Michelangelo were rare indeed. 'I know you will say that I should have waited and thought of our sisters before taking a wife,' he wrote to the frazzled Galileo a short time after the wedding. 'But good heavens! The idea of toiling all one's life just to save a few farthings for one's sisters! This joke is too heavy and bitter.'[2]

Some joke. To rub salt into the wounds, in the summer of 1600, with Marina about to give birth to Galileo's first child, his younger sister Livia, then approaching 22, announced her wish to marry immediately. Understandably, Galileo was not pleased and wrote to his mother: 'It is impossible for me to consent to this arrangement just at present. Since she is determined to come out and partake of the miseries of the world, she must be patient. Tell her that there have been queens and great ladies who have not married until they were old enough to be her mother.'[3]

Livia, though, was insistent, and within weeks Galileo was forced to find her a suitor who would not demand too large a dowry. Rejecting Livia's own wish to marry a local bachelor she had been courting, he found for her a young Polish gentleman living in Pisa named Taddeo di Cesare Galletti and the two men agreed a dowry of 1800 crowns, which included 200 needed immediately for a trousseau and 600 in cash. The remaining thousand crowns were to be paid in equal instalments over five years. Although this was a bargain compared with the cost of Virginia's marriage to Benedetto di Luca Landucci a decade earlier, Galetti turned out to be even more aggressive in making sure he got what he was owed. When Galileo failed to make a yearly payment in 1602, the young man took legal action against his brother-in-law.

Michelangelo had promised to help his elder brother cover the cost of Livia's wedding, but of course he reneged at the last minute, prompting Galileo to write to him: 'If I had imagined that things were going to turn out in this manner I would not have given the child in marriage, or else I would have given her only such a dowry as I was able to pay myself. I seem destined to bear every burden alone.'[4]

The pressure Galileo was under may be seen clearly in his throw-away comment in the letter to his mother: 'Since she is determined to come out and partake of the miseries of the world . . .' By most standards Galileo was doing very well, but the demands of his family were also enormous and difficult to bear.

As the sixteenth turned into the seventeenth century, the usual turmoil of life rolled on. *Hamlet* opened, the future Charles I was born in England and the East India company was founded with an initial capital investment of £70,000. In Padua, Galileo turned again to pure research, and during this period he was concerned with two very different areas of science. The first of these was his interest in mechanics, which he had begun studying in Pisa. The other was a growing fascination for astronomy, and in particular the ideas of Copernicus.

With the experiments he conducted in Pisa more than a decade earlier, Galileo had shown that all objects fall equal distances in equal times, irrespective of their mass; but this work had told him nothing about how they fell or whether they changed speed during the descent.

The ancients had observed and described acceleration, but their explanation for it was convoluted. Aristotle believed acceleration was a punctuated process. In his view, an object in free fall speeded up in bursts. In other words, an object travelled at a constant speed before experiencing a spurt of acceleration that would take it to a new constant speed. Galileo doubted the veracity of this notion, but to create an experiment to illustrate a different mechanism was no easy matter.

One of the greatest hurdles he had to overcome in conducting any experiments to discover the true nature of acceleration was the fact that during the first years of the seventeenth century there were no accurate timepieces available to him. So unless an object was allowed to fall from an extremely high altitude, the time taken to cover the distance was too small to measure with any accuracy. The method Galileo had employed up to this time (using his own pulse as a guide) was far from satisfactory for such an investigation.

It is perhaps surprising that he did not at this point return to his pendulum experiments in order to create a reliable timing mechanism for his new venture. The most likely reason he did not is that he wanted to concentrate on the true nature of acceleration and not be distracted by the effort needed to create an accurate clock. Instead, he worked around the problem, designing a set of experiments using an inclined plane and a ball that was allowed to roll along the surface. As a timing device he sometimes used a musical pulse, or a water clock – a barrel with a small hole punched in the bottom. Collecting and measuring the volume of water from each experiment allowed him to produce a set of relative timings.

Inclining the plane was a crucial element of the experiment. Creating a slope with an inclination of about two degrees meant the balls travelled more slowly; but they still moved under the effect of gravity. If friction was ignored, the motion of the balls matched those dropped from the Leaning Tower of Pisa or any other elevated point.

The essence of the experiment was to measure how far the balls fell in different time periods. In the first experiment Galileo measured how far the ball travelled in the space of one pulse or beat. He found this was 8 feet. He then found how far the ball went in two pulses or beats. This was 18 feet. In three beats, the ball travelled a total of 32 feet along the slope.

The difference in distance between the first and second experiment was 10 feet (18 minus 8), yet the ball covered this last 10 feet in the time it took to travel just 8 feet in the first experiment (one time unit). In the third experiment the ball travelled 14 feet further than in the second experiment (32 minus 18), yet it did this in the same time as it took to travel 8 feet in the first experiment and 10 feet in the second experiment (one time unit). Galileo could conclude that the further the ball travelled, the greater its final speed. As it fell, the ball began to travel faster and faster; in other words, it was accelerating.

These were, in themselves, significant findings, but of greater importance was the method Galileo was employing to determine and compare his results. He understood that the central aspect of this process was the way in which he took accurate measurements and repeated the experiment using different initial parameters. He was combining experiment with mathematics and logic. He had done this before with his pendulum experiments, but this new set of experiments was far more elaborate. It was a revolutionary approach, which for some historians marks the beginnings of modern science, the point at which there was an intimate fusion of mathematics and experiment.

Galileo could see that there was a clear mathematical relationship between the distance an object falls and the speed at which it travels, but it was to take him three years of further experiment and careful measurement before he was able to create a law relating the two factors. This law, which he described in great detail in his later masterpiece *The Discourses on Two New Sciences*, published in 1638, four years before his death, showed that there is a squared relationship between the time taken for an object to fall and the distance it has fallen. This relationship is known as Galileo's law of falling bodies and it is considered to be one of his greatest achievements.

At the time Galileo was formulating his earliest laws of motion he became interested in an entirely different science. He had been fascinated with astronomy since his student days in Pisa, but it was only after he moved to Padua and began to be recognised on the intellectual stage that he tapped into the network of philosophers and astronomers across Europe who were beginning to conduct co-ordinated observations of the heavens and to question accepted wisdom and ancient dogma.

The two biggest names in the astronomy fraternity at the turn of the seventeenth century were the German Johannes Kepler and the Danish astronomer Tycho Brahe. In 1596 Kepler, then just 26, had published his first important treatise, *Mysterium Cosmographicum*. In this he lent support to the Copernican cosmic model, in which the Earth is not placed at the centre of the universe but is considered as simply one of the planets orbiting the Sun.

At the time Galileo was first working in Padua, Kepler was living in the city of Graz, which was part of the Holy Roman Empire. Raised as a Lutheran, he was naturally scathing of Roman interference in intellectual concerns, but unlike Galileo, who was living in a Catholic state, he enjoyed far greater freedom of expression.

During the following decade, Kepler's star rose remarkably quickly. He left Graz for Prague, where he became assistant to Tycho Brahe, one of the grandees of science. When Tycho died, in 1601, Kepler inherited his master's position as Imperial Mathematician and in this role he made some of the most important discoveries of the age, including what became known as Kepler's laws, which accurately describe the motion of planets.

The correspondence between Galileo and Kepler had begun in 1597 when the younger man sent to the University of Padua a copy of his recently published *Mysterium Cosmographicum*. Galileo had reservations about some of Kepler's ideas, but he immediately saw in him a kindred spirit, a man with views on Aristotle as daring as his own. With some envy he perceived how Kepler was in a much freer position than he was, but saw also how they could do much to help one another. 'It is really pitiful that so few seek the truth,' Galileo wrote to the astronomer. 'But this is not the place to mourn over the miseries of our times. I shall read your book with special pleasure, because I have been an adherent of the Copernican system for many years. It explains to me the appearances of nature which are quite unintelligible within the commonly accepted hypothesis.'[5]

This is Galileo's earliest documented claim in support of Copernicus, and it could only be safely made in a private letter to a fellow scientist of like mind. If Galileo had made such a statement in an official document or in a published work he would have received immediate ecclesiastical criticism. For this reason, Galileo was careful to keep very quiet on the matter of Copernicus beyond the limits of private discussion – though, of course, this did not stop him theorising and considering all aspects of the Copernican model.

If anything, Tycho Brahe was, just before his untimely death, a more important figure than Kepler. Born in 1546, he came from a noble family. After university, he had travelled widely around Europe, dabbled in alchemy and discovered his love for astronomy. At the age of 20 he had become involved in a duel and lost part of his nose. For the rest of his life he wore a metal insert to cover the missing part.

Tycho's contribution to astronomy is almost without peer. He was a meticulous observer and, through his familial connections in high places, King Frederick II of Denmark gave him the funding to build a state-of-the-art observatory on the tiny island of Hven, near Copenhagen. There he worked for over two decades observing and recording what he saw as well as training young astronomers.

Like Galileo, Tycho placed great importance on carefully reporting observations and building theoretical models in attempts to explain what he saw. In 1572 he noted the appearance of what he called 'a new star' and five years later he followed the course of a comet, calculating its orbit and postulating its origin and place in the universal scheme. Through these discoveries Tycho came to reject the Aristotelian concept that the heavens were perfect and unchanging. However, he never did accept the Copernican model of the universe and was unable to loosen his attachment to Aristotelianism so as to embrace the new astronomy.

Tycho had been dead three years by the time another great astronomical event stirred up the community of astronomers in a similar way to the 'new star' of 1572 and the comet of 1577. In September 1604, some seven years after Kepler and Galileo first made contact, another 'new star' appeared in the heavens.

It was noticed first by an amateur astronomer, a priest named Ilario Altobelli, who, from his nightly observations, had noticed the appearance of a dull smudge in the constellation of Sagittarius. He wrote to Galileo describing the observation, but within days of this letter arriving in Padua, many other observers across Europe had also begun to notice the strange new object, including Kepler in Prague and Michael Maestlin in Tübingen. Within a month Galileo had observed the object himself and declared: 'At one point it would contract its rays with a sudden and faint extinction paling before Mars's reddish glow.'[6]

Opinion concerning the object was wide-ranging. For many it was perceived as an ill omen; fear of any new celestial body was common and such things as a 'new star' had long been associated with portents of doom. The official line from the Church was that the object lay close to the Earth, within the 'Earthly sphere'. This was thanks to Aristotle, who had claimed some two millennia earlier that 'the heavens above (the sky, stars, Sun and Moon) are distinctly of a different nature from the things of Earth. Things on the Earth are subject to decay, as elements decay (fire, air, water, earth). But things above the Earth are perfect (even in their shape) and of a higher order (ether), divine (like gods)'.

The new star was obviously a blemish, so it could not reside within the 'heavenly sphere'.

Neither Galileo nor Kepler, nor indeed any astronomer of the day, knew what the light really was – a supernova, a star that had grown old and exploded – but they knew this new object was no 'celestial vapour' or 'meteor' 'beneath the Moon', as the papal astronomers would have it. These Vatican observers were convinced of the Aristotelian precept that the heavens were perfect and unchanging and therefore any blemish or visible change must come as a result of an alteration in the atmosphere or the void between the Earth and the Moon, a part of the cosmos that was not considered to be part of the heavenly sphere.

Galileo, Kepler and other anti-Aristotelians believed the 'new star' was an object that lay far from the Earth, amongst the most distant heavenly bodies. After observing the object for several months and watching it gradually fade, Galileo could see how the angle at which it could be seen from the Earth was altering. From this, he concluded that both the mysterious object and the Earth were moving.

By 1604 Galileo was already recognised as an accomplished teacher and his scientific opinion was sought after, especially when such an oddity as a 'new star' appeared in the heavens. Some people were simply curious and wanted to understand the true nature of the object. Many, though, were less rational and placed occult meanings on the new light in the sky. Some were fascinated but needed reassurances from an intellectual of great repute, a figure who could give a convincing explanation for this odd phenomenon.

To satisfy these interests and to stake a claim to understanding the 'new star', between December 1604 and January 1605, just as the new light was fading from view, Galileo gave three public lectures in Padua. Hundreds were turned away at the doors to the lecture theatre, and inside the audience was packed in with no standing room to spare.

The lectures were transcribed and have survived. Galileo told his audience,

> You are the witnesses, all of you young people who flock here to hear me discourse on this marvellous apparition. Some of you are terrified and excited by vain superstition. You came to learn whether some outstanding portent of ill omen is being foretold. Others wonder whether a true constellation of stars exists in the heavens or whether this new star is merely vapour near the Earth. By Hercules! That splendid desire of yours is worthy of the most superior intellects! Ah,

would that my slight intellect could serve the magnitude of the question and of your expectations![7]

Galileo had no idea of the true nature of the new star, but he was certain that it offered another piece of evidence with which to denounce Aristotle and papal dogma. At the same time, the fact that his observations showed that the Earth was moving lent support to his increasingly positive opinion of the Copernican model; but at this time, he could still say very little. Using obscure language, he described genuine vapours – the sort that sometimes filled the skies over Venice – and compared them with the new source of light, illustrating how they were quite different. But at no time could he come out and say that papal doctrine was erroneous, that the 'new star' was situated in the heavens, or that the heavenly sphere was anything but unchanging and perfect, as Aristotle had declared it to be.

However, even Galileo's subtle remarks were noticed and opposed. One of his friends in Padua was the philosopher Cesare Cremonini, a highly respected and honoured member of the faculty of the University of Padua. Cremonini was a great self-publicist, an academic who cherished the spotlight and was not afraid of controversy. He was no friend of Rome and was known to harbour strong anti-Jesuit sentiments, which later led to his opinions being investigated by the Inquisition. But Cremonini was a dyed-in-the-wool Aristotelian, and he did not wish to sit by and let Galileo trample all over his hero. In private the two men enjoyed a cordial relationship, but this did nothing to stop them denouncing each other's views at the lectern or in self-published pamphlets. Each of them wrote under a thinly disguised pseudonym, which allowed the eminent philosopher and the eminent scientist/mathematician to tear strips off each other. Cremonini went first with a tract entitled 'Discourse on the New Star'. Galileo countered with 'Dialogue Concerning the New Star', using the pseudonym Cecco di Ronchitti. In this pamphlet he employed his favoured technique of having characters take opposing stances on the question under debate.

It was a battle that served little higher purpose than to cement the views of those who had already taken sides on the matter; each man was preaching to the converted. Yet even though Galileo was treading with care along the line between scientific inquiry and what the Church would deem heresy, he was beginning to be perceived by Rome as a radical and a friend of radicals. This became apparent to him some six months after the appearance of the supernova and it was prompted by a fresh clash between Venice and Rome over their very different attitudes to what constituted heresy.

At the core of the dispute were two men whom Galileo knew well, the Venetian Paolo Sarpi and the pope's right-hand man Cardinal Robert Bellarmine, the man who had acted as Giordano Bruno's primary persecutor a few years earlier.

In the decade or more since Bellarmine had been a guest of Pinelli in Padua, when he first met Galileo, his career had gone into a sharp ascent no less vertiginous than Galileo's own. In 1592 he was made Rector of the Roman College, and in 1595 Provincial of Naples. In 1597 Pope Clement VIII made Bellarmine his Personal Theologian, Examiner of Bishops and Consultor of the Holy Office. Then, two years later, he was promoted to cardinal. So successful had he become that his name was already being mentioned in connection with the papal succession.

Bellarmine, though, was apparently never interested in the tiara. He was the sort of man who was most comfortable not as a figurehead but as a mover and shaker. He knew that he could shape the future of the Church far more effectively by working as puppet-master. In this he was very successful; he was ruthless, determined and focused. He believed that the survival of the Church in the form in which it had been created by Christ and his disciples was paramount – little else mattered. In pursuit of this ideal, Bellarmine sanctioned the scourging of all heresy and any form of ideological opposition to the Faith.

In many ways his opponent Paulo Sarpi was a match for Bellarmine. He was a polymath – an accomplished writer, a natural philosopher and experimenter and a theologian with an international reputation. A decade earlier Sarpi and Bellarmine had been on friendly terms, each respecting the other's sharp mind and probing intellect; but by the beginning of the seventeenth century their world-views had diverged so far that each considered the other a mortal enemy.

Sarpi was a devout Catholic, but he hated the way Rome operated. In this he shared many of the ideals of Giordano Bruno, a man whom he tried unsuccessfully to protect; and he may be compared closely with the great thinker of a century earlier, Erasmus. He was also a sincere patriot and he refused to allow Rome to dominate the spiritual life of Venice. This defiance made him enormously popular in Venice, and infuriated Rome.

The dispute was sparked by a change of leadership in both the

Vatican and Venice. Pope Leo XI died in April 1605 and his successor was the Italian cardinal Camillo Borghese, who took the name Paul V. A year later, a renowned anti-papal political activist Leonardo Dona became the doge. Few were surprised when doge and pope clashed almost immediately.

Paul V believed the head of the Catholic Church should also be a political figure. He was certainly not the first pope to hold this view, nor would he be the last. Most famously, Cesare Borgia's father (Rodrigo, who became Pope Alexander VI in 1492) and his immediate successor, Julius II (who was pope between 1503 and 1513) each declared himself to be a military leader as well as a spiritual guide. They seized the lands of neighbours and imposed their will by blackmail and bribery. Paul V had once been a lawyer specialising in ecclesiastical law. Those territories he could not grab by force of arms he managed to dominate by manipulation and by drawing upon popular fear of the Church. Almost as soon as he took the papal throne he set his sights on changing the way Venice was ruled and bringing to book those who believed they could maintain a liberal state under his very nose. But ironically, at the same time, just as the new doge took office, he and his closest allies in the Venetian government began to forge an even more liberal republic and implemented measures to loosen the shackles of Rome.

Initially the dispute was played out as a political game. This included arguments over territories, fights about taxation of Church buildings and other niggling matters, but gradually the row became more focused on ecclesiastical concerns. Soon the gloves were off and the fight came into the open as a serious clash of ideologies. It was at this point that the arguments between the two states shifted from the rulers, Paul V and the doge, to their closest representatives. On the Vatican side, Robert Bellarmine took up the baton, and on the other, his old sparing partner from Pinelli's Paduan palazzo, the theological counsellor to the doge, Paolo Sarpi.

During the spring of 1606, just a year into Paul V's papacy, relations between Venice and the Vatican had sunk to an all-time low. The Vatican loathed Sarpi. To the Church leaders this man represented the very worst of Venetian liberalism. In terms of intellectual clout Sarpi was an equal of Bellarmine, but his mind was very different from that of the papal stooge. Where Bellarmine's thought processes seemed to wheel along a single, very narrow-gauge track, to one side unquestioning adulation for the Faith, and on the other a psychotic hatred for anyone he considered a heretic, Paolo Sarpi was a genuine Renaissance man. He had studied anatomy, astronomy and mathematics, written widely on a range of subjects, and he was a powerful orator. Most importantly, he was a respecter of learning, a man who believed in broadening education, who questioned authority and often found it wanting. To the pope's fury, he had once gone so far as to declare that the Vatican's creation of the *Index Librorum Prohibitorum* was 'the first secret device religion ever invented to make men stupid'.[8]

From the lectern Sarpi sent his poisoned arrows, attacking the pope head on and declaring that he had no business interfering in politics, that it was the role of a pope to tend to the spiritual needs of the world, not to play the military leader or the egregious powerbroker. An incensed pope retaliated with the most extreme weapon in his armoury – a spiritual nuke of the day: he excommunicated the entire Venetian government, including the doge and Paolo Sarpi.

To the modern mind this action seems almost laughable, but to those living in the seventeenth century papal proclamations carried real weight and for many they were terrifying. For any devout Catholic excommunication was agonising because not only did it mean they would be consigned to Hell, it also meant they could not take communion, and for many ordinary people this was one of the few pleasures they could savour in a harsh and unforgiving world of grinding poverty, hunger and premature death.

Sarpi, though, was unimpressed and he and his superiors in the Venetian government simply refused to publish the interdict, thereby making it clear that the churches in the city must remain open. To ensure that this would happen they announced that any priest who refused to give communion would be imprisoned immediately.

By the early summer, with the Venetians simply refusing to acknowledge the actions of the Vatican, it looked as though the two states would soon be at war. Jesuits in Venice and Padua were compelled to leave or be forced to disobey the pope and ignore the interdict, and the two governments stooped to flinging veiled insults at each other through their respective diplomats. But then, perhaps realising that they had let things go too far, both sides began to calm down and bloodshed was avoided. A brief period of quiet ensued. Galileo was in Venice for most of that summer, trying to arrange an increase in his salary; but he found that the government was understandably distracted by the grave political climate and little interested in handing out pay rises. His third child, Vincenzo, was born in August and Galileo was, like much of the

Venetian and Paduan populations, little more than a bystander watching nervously as great matters of state and religion were argued over.

The lull in the clash between Rome and Venice did not last long. Early in 1607, Paolo Sarpi announced his intention to leave the government so that he could concentrate on scholarship, which had always been his first love. He planned to write a detailed account of the history of the Council of Trent, the papal committee established over forty years earlier as a direct challenge to the Reformation and the establishment of the Protestant Church in Northern Europe. To write this he would need to have full and unrestricted access to the archives of the government, including secret documents pertaining to the relationship between the Venetian state and the Vatican since the early 1560s. In this desire Sarpi was, of course, given the blessing of the government and the personal support of the doge, Leonardo Dona.

Whether or not this was a deliberately provocative move on Sarpi's part, it was without doubt a dangerous one. Within weeks of the news breaking, rumours began to circulate that the pope would spare no efforts in stopping the wayward cleric. At first, the Vatican made a rather sorry attempt at coercion, inviting Paolo Sarpi to Rome: 'Let the theologian come, and we shall embrace him,' the pope's representative declared in a letter to the Venetian government. 'He shall be caressed and well received.'

Sarpi was no fool and he realised precisely what this meant: that in Rome he would be caressed by the flames of the executioner's pyre – caressed just as Giordano Bruno and countless thousands of other innocents had been. Such unsubtle moves on the part of the pope merely insulted Sarpi, and he of course ignored the request. With this rebuttal the pope turned to violence.

Sarpi was probably alert to the possibility of a physical attack; after all, such things were not without precedent. In 1478 Pope Sixtus IV had instigated a plot to assassinate Lorenzo de' Medici. Lorenzo had escaped with his life, but his brother Giuliano had been murdered. However, when the attack came, Sarpi was caught completely off guard.

On the night of 7 October he was due at a meeting in the ducal palace. As he left home, a fire broke out in a neighbouring district and his bodyguards left to investigate. Sarpi decided to continue on his way with just a young servant and an elderly government official. It was a trap. A few moments after the guards had vanished, the three unarmed men were attacked by five assailants. The priest's two companions were dispatched quickly and Sarpi himself was stabbed no fewer than fifteen times. The most dangerous wound came from a stiletto that was thrust through his left ear; it smashed his upper jaw and exited through his right cheek.

The noise of the attack brought people out on to their balconies and into the street. Sarpi was taken to the ducal palace, and his and Galileo's mutual friend, the famed physician Fabricius of Acquapendente, was woken up and rushed to his bedside. Paolo Sarpi's life hung in the balance for three weeks, but miraculously he survived this terrible attack. Those who perpetrated the crime escaped Venice and headed straight for Rome. There they were received by a disappointed pope, who nevertheless put them on a pension as reward for their attempt to kill the Venetian.

The people of Venice were outraged by the attack on one of their most prominent and respected citizens, and Galileo was shaken by it. Sarpi was one of his closest friends and confidants; but, most poignantly, the two men shared very similar views on religion, science and philosophy. Because of this, the attack must have had a dramatic effect on Galileo's state of mind. Like any other educated person in Europe he had heard of the execution of Giordano Bruni some eight years earlier, and now the Church had reached into the very heart of another country to attempt assassination of a powerful figure who opposed them. If he had stopped to think about his own position he might have felt the first clear sense of anxiety about his intellectual journey, a sense that by challenging orthodox philosophy he was tugging the tail of a sleeping lion.

This incident certainly marked a turning point in Galileo's view of his own career and what he was trying to achieve in his life. It was the beginning of a period in which he became increasingly unhappy with his job in Padua. This was not helped by the fact that the winter of 1607–8 was the coldest in living memory. Snow covered the roofs and blocked the streets for months and the temperature rarely crept above freezing throughout January and February. In Padua and Venice people starved, while others froze to death in their houses. During that winter, Galileo started to think about his old home in Florence, and for the first time in well over a decade he began to entertain the thought of returning to his homeland and to consider seriously the possibility that he might do better for himself in the pay of the Medici.

Once he began to contemplate this idea, it took hold. Soon, he was coming to the conclusion that he had stayed in Padua long enough, that he needed some new source of stimulation, a change of scene perhaps, a fresh muse. Keeping himself warm by the fire in his house in the Via Vignali del Santo as the snow piled high outside, he could not have imagined how or from where such a change might come, but come it did.

8

The Crystal Moon

Within intellectual circles in the summer of 1609 news began to circulate of an amazing new device, a simple tube containing two lenses with which an observer could see faraway objects as though they were close by. Information about this invention was sketchy, but it seemed that a previously obscure experimenter and spectacle-maker from Middelburg, in Holland, named Hans Lippershey had been the first to make a practical telescope, which, according to some reports, could magnify up to eight times. This device went under a variety of names – 'lookers', 'Dutch trunks' and 'cylinders' – and it became popular with hunters and sailors. Other reports told of spyglasses that could magnify an object up to three times being sold as novelties and toys in Parisian markets. By June 1609 news had reached Venice of the observations of an English astronomer called Thomas Harriot, who had turned one of these 'toys' towards the Moon and noted what he'd seen.

For the breadth and depth of his researches Harriot could justifiably be called the 'English Galileo', and he was once described as 'the greatest mathematician that Oxford University has produced'.[1] His was an extraordinary life: he travelled to America with Walter Raleigh, with whom he enjoyed a close friendship for the rest of his life. Somehow he acquired a reputation as an atheist and when Queen Elizabeth died, in 1603, succeeded by James I, Harriot lost favour at court. Later he was even implicated in the Gunpowder Plot and was lucky to escape execution for treason.

Harriot conducted many optical experiments and some historians have claimed that he produced a six-powered telescope around the same time as Lippershey began to publicise his invention. Why Harriot did not exploit the commercial applications of this device is difficult to explain. It is possible that by this time (1608/9), unpopular with the new monarch, he was not in any position to do the most with his work. Hans Lippershey was from an entirely different mould, a practical designer and a man with a strong entrepreneurial streak. He was quick to realise the potential of his invention, and by 1609 he had begun to travel Europe hawking his device and trying to generate investment to develop it as a powerful military and scientific tool.

It is perhaps surprising that the telescope was not invented long before the start of the seventeenth century, and indeed its early development remains shrouded in mystery. Some uncorroborated stories tell of telescopes being used by Arabic scientists as early as the sixth century, but no examples or documents describing these devices have come down to us, so we can only assume they are fictional accounts.

Both Roberto Recorde, in 1551, and Leonard Digges around the same time, referred to 'prospective glasses' to view distant objects. William Borne, in 1585, and Giambattista della Porta a few years later claimed to have discovered a way to use lenses to see far off. It is also apparent that Leonardo da Vinci at least speculated on the uses of a telescope, and he documented his thoughts exactly a century before Lippershey in two different notebooks compiled between 1508 and 1510. 'It is possible to find means by which the eye shall not see remote objects as much diminished as in natural perspective,' he wrote in one account.[2] Elsewhere he was a little more specific. 'The further you place eyeglasses from the eye, the larger the objects appear in them . . . And if the eye sees two equal objects in comparison, one outside of the glass and the other within the field, the one in the glass will seem large and the other small.'[3]

Yet, the crucial thing to note about these comments is that Leonardo was almost certainly writing hypothetically. He had probably conducted some simple experiments with relatively inferior-quality lenses and made some interesting observations, but there is no hard evidence to suppose that he constructed a working telescope any more than that he was able to build a tank, an aqualung or a helicopter as he had described them in his wonderful notebooks.

Leonardo probably never made a working telescope, because the poor quality of the lenses he had at his disposal discouraged him from pursuing the exercise. This is also why no one else before Lippershey met with any real success; poorly ground lenses provided only meagre magnification, and a great deal of optical distortion. Lippershey spent years and all his skills as a spectacle-maker to produce a set of lenses that offered a clear image and a worthwhile magnification.

Like everyone else Galileo had heard rumours of the new invention, but preoccupied, perhaps, and unsure of the value of such whispers, he took little notice of them. The Parisian 'toys' he knew were mere playthings and he had little to go on when it came to Harriot's findings or the apparent accomplishments of the mysterious Dutch spectacle-maker from Middelburg. But then, in late July, he learned that more than six months earlier, in December 1608, his friend Paolo Sarpi had received a detailed intelligence report on Lippershey in which the potential for military exploitation of the man's invention had been considered. Because he had been caught up in other more pressing matters of state, Sarpi had done nothing about this report and had even overlooked passing on the news to Galileo, the one man in his acquaintance who could have done most with the news.

On 26 July, immediately after hearing that Sarpi had received official news about the telescope, Galileo went to see him to find out why he had not been informed of the Dutch breakthrough. Sarpi was staggered by his own stupidity and full of apologies. He immediately showed Galileo the full report sent to him at the end of the previous year, along with a letter he had written in January 1609 and sent to an interested party in the intelligence service, a mutual acquaintance of Galileo and Sarpi, named Jacques Badovere. The letter read:

> I have had word of the new spectacles more than a month and believe the report sufficiently not to investigate further. (Socrates forbids us to speculate about experiences we have not seen ourselves.) When I was young, I thought about such a possibility. It occurred to me that a glass parabolically shaped should produce such an effect. I had a demonstration, but since these are abstract matters and do not take into account the fractiousness of the matter, I sensed some difficulty. To pursue the matter would have been very tiresome, so I did not experiment. I do not know whether that Flemish artisan [Lippershey] has hit upon my idea.[4]

In his book *The Starry Messenger*, published in March 1610, Galileo recalled the events leading to his work with the telescope and offered a different version of how Sarpi had been involved:

About ten months ago a report reached my ears that a certain Fleming [*sic*] had constructed a spyglass by means of which visible objects, though very distant from the eye of the observer, were distinctly seen as nearby. Of this truly remarkable effect several experiences were related, to which some persons gave credence while others denied them. A few days later the report was confirmed to me in a letter from a noble Frenchman at Paris, Jacques Badovere, which caused me to apply myself wholeheartedly to investigate means by which I might arrive at the invention of a similar instrument. This I did soon afterwards.[5]

A few days after his meeting with Paolo Sarpi, Galileo learned that Lippershey had arrived in Padua to demonstrate his invention to the city fathers. Wasting little time, by 1 August he had finished up his affairs in Venice, and made all haste to his home in Padua. Arriving there determined to find out all he could about the telescope and to begin work on bettering the device, he discovered to his dismay that Lippershey had just left – for Venice. Galileo dashed back to Venice and hammered on Sarpi's door until a servant answered and was dispatched to wake up his master. Sleepy and disgruntled, Sarpi listened as Galileo implored him to intervene on his behalf. Calling upon their long friendship, he made it clear that the politician owed him over the knowledge he had carelessly withheld.

So between them Galileo and Paolo Sarpi worked together to realign matters in the scientist's favour and to effectively sideline Hans Lippershey, the man who had invented the telescope. Sarpi bought Galileo time by blocking any introduction to the doge and the Council requested by Lippershey, and Galileo worked feverishly to make his own telescope, with which he could usurp any business opportunities his Dutch rival might have hoped for.

Working from mere scraps of information and a large helping of intuition, Galileo spent forty-eight hours without sleep experimenting at his work bench, combining various lenses, reshaping them and positioning concave and convex lenses in different positions along a makeshift wooden tube.

The techniques for doing this would have been familiar to Galileo, who had always prided himself on his practical skills. He knew the biggest hurdle to overcome was to improve the resolution or sharpness of focus of the telescope as well as its magnifying power. There was no point in having a device that magnified many times but produced a very fuzzy image. Galileo had to grind lenses by hand to produce a slight concavity, or curvature. This concavity caused incoming light to refract, or bend. Difficulties arose, though, because light is refracted by different amounts, depending on its wavelength. So red light is refracted to a different degree from blue light at the other end of the visible spectrum. As a result, an astronomer looking at a distant object with a poor telescope would see the object surrounded by what appears to be a halo of colour a little like a circular rainbow. This is known as 'chromatic aberration'.

Galileo's first telescope was composed of two lenses separable by a controlled distance to set focus. One lens, the 'objective lens', had a less severe curve, to collect light and bring it to various points of focus depending on the frequency of the light source; but he was only able to focus the image near the middle of the eyepiece field of view, and focus could only be set based on the dominant colour emitted or reflected by whatever he was observing.

He later described his endeavours by reporting:

> My reasoning was this. The device needs more than one glass. The shape would have to be convex, concave or bounded by parallel surfaces. But the last-named does not magnify visible objects in any way. Furthermore, the concave diminishes them, and the convex, although it enlarges them, shows them indistinct and confused. I was confined therefore to considering what would be done by a combination of concave and convex. You see how this gave me what I sought.[6]

After the first day, Galileo had produced something approximating the toys he had heard about. Later that night he perfected a model that was a match for Lippershey's best telescope. Then, by guesswork and a dash of inspiration, he reshaped the lenses, repositioned them in the tube and succeeded in making the jump from a device that could magnify eight or ten times to a telescope that was able to make an image appear sixty times larger.

Without delay he sent a message to Venice, later recounting hyperbolically in his book *The Assayer*: 'The first night after my return to Padua I solved it, and on the following day, I constructed the instrument and sent word of this to those of my friends at Venice with whom I had discussed the matter the previous day.'[7]

This message sent to friends in Venice was really an instruction for Sarpi to use any means possible to stop Lippershey seeing anyone who mattered in Venice before he, Galileo, had a chance for a meeting with the doge. This meeting was arranged as quickly as possible by Sarpi, but even so it took over two weeks to find a space in the leader's busy schedule. This gave Galileo more time to refine his device and to construct something better than a rough laboratory model. Sparing no expense, he had a craftsman produce for him a beautifully made leather tube and, eschewing the use of his more powerful lenses, which still gave an unclear and confusing magnified image, he selected a combination of his finest lenses, which offered a magnification factor of ten and produced a clear image in the viewfinder.

Both Galileo and Sarpi were quite aware of the military applications of the telescope and knew this was the most important aspect to emphasise in any effort to convince the government of its value. 'The power of my *cannocchiale* [telescope] to show distant objects as clearly as if they were near should give us an inestimable advantage in any military action on land or sea,' he reported in a letter to the Venetian government. 'At sea, we shall be able to spot their flags two hours before they can see us; and when we have established the number and type of the enemy craft, we shall be able to decide whether to pursue and engage him in battle, or take flight. Similarly, on land it should be possible from elevated positions to observe the enemy camps and their fortifications.'[8]

The appointment with Doge Leonardo Dona (who was a personal friend of Galileo's and a long-time admirer) was stage-managed down to the last detail by the scientist and his friend Paolo Sarpi. In what was more a theatrical performance than a scientific demonstration, Galileo put his device through its paces.

After showing the doge and his advisers the hand-crafted object, the party were taken under guard to the Tower of St Mark's just a few dozen yards from the Doge's Palace. Galileo set up the telescope on a stand and turned it towards Padua. Through the eyepiece the astonished doge could see, over fifty kilometres away, the Tower of St Giustina in the centre of the city. Turning the tube closer to home, they could see across the city, magnified so that they appeared to be no further than the base of the tower, figures that were mere specks to the naked eye. Then, casting their gaze out towards the distant Adriatic beyond the Lido, the doge and his courtiers witnessed ships that would not be visible to the naked eye for at least another two hours.

After returning to the palace the doge was preparing to start negotiating a price for Galileo's amazing device when, quite unexpectedly, he told the doge:

> I Galileo Galilei, the humble servant of Your Highness, who always looks assiduously with all my spirit to perform my duty and always looks to find some utility to benefit Your Highness . . . I now bring this new artifice. Judging that this instrument is worthy of being received by you, I give it to you as a present, putting to your judgement whether more of these instruments should be built or not. This is one of the fruits of science, science which for seventeen years I have conducted in Padua, hoping to be able to present to you even greater inventions, if God wills it and Your Highness wills it, and if you and God want me to spend the rest of my life at your service.

Of course this was a very clever move. The doge and his advisers had been as impressed by the telescope as Galileo and Sarpi had expected them to be, and Leonardo Dona was certainly not slow to realise that he could have in his possession a device of enormous military importance, an invention that would very soon become famous throughout the world. At the same time, the Venetian leader had no idea that Galileo had more or less stolen the idea of the telescope. By the time he was escorted from the council chamber Galileo had been offered a thousand crowns a year (almost doubling his annual salary of 520 crowns), a lifetime appointment to his professorship in Padua and an immediate cash reward of 480 crowns.

The Council of Ten announced the news with great pomp and considerable inaccuracy: 'Signor Galileo Galilei, having lectured in Padua for seventeen years to the satisfaction of all, having made known to the world diverse discoveries and inventions, but in particular having invented an instrument by which distant things are brought within easy vision, it is proper that this Council do munificently recognise the labours of those who serve the public benefit.'[9]

This was a greatly publicised statement, but behind it was some disappointment on the part of the government, because they had just learned that Galileo had not been the first to invent the telescope and other neighbouring states were already in possession of similar devices (even if they were not as good as the one Galileo had made).

Galileo, too, was disappointed. He was pleased with the pay rise, but he could not ignore the fact that what had seemed like generosity came with strings. First, it was to be a once-and-for-all raise, so that as long as he worked at the university he could never expect to earn a single crown more than a thousand per annum. This was undeniably a handsome salary, but that was not really the point; he felt stifled, penned in. To make matters worse, the pay rise was to be delayed for a year.

Galileo may also have been aggrieved by the fact that the doge had moderated his offer because of Lippershey and the fact that the invention was not unique to Venice. Galileo felt no sense of guilt about ostensibly having stolen Lippershey's design. He was, we should remember, an egotistical man, and he may well have told himself (not without some justification) that what he had done was take a half-baked model of a telescope – one barely usable – and transform it into a genuine scientific instrument. It is a striking fact that Galileo had no theoretical knowledge of optics at the time and never did. Through the application of practical know-how and natural ingenuity he succeeded in making a telescope better than any that had previously existed.

Furthermore, Lippershey was gaining attention around Europe and was even then recognised as the true inventor of the telescope. He continued with a successful career in parallel with Galileo's, and although Galileo took much of the credit for introducing the telescope into Italy, this did little to damage the Dutch innovator. Indeed, his intervention obscured the fact that Lippershey's original was actually a rather primitive thing and that he should have been capable of producing something better, something comparable to Galileo's telescopes.

For Galileo the most unfortunate aspect of the government's offer was that he would have to remain in his teaching position at the University of Padua. His dislike for teaching undergraduates had never faded and by 1609 he could barely contemplate the thought of beginning a new academic year, with no end in sight for his labours.

Galileo had made his point as clearly as he possibly could when he presented the telescope to the doge. 'This [the telescope] is one of the fruits of science,' he had intoned, 'science which for seventeen years I have conducted in Padua, hoping to be able to present to you even greater inventions, if God wills it and Your Highness wills it, and if you and God want me to spend the rest of my life at your service' – in other words: 'Can't you fools see what wonders I could produce if only you would free me from the shackles of my damn teaching responsibilities and leave me to work?'

It may seem that Galileo was being impetuous and high-minded, but it is important to realise that his mood was not simply the reaction of an overindulged man resenting the simple demands of his job. It was ironic that he happened to be a very good lecturer who inspired his pupils and filled them with a lust for science; but he derived no pleasure from teaching.

More importantly for Galileo, every minute he spent in the lecture theatre was a minute away from his own experiments, and this was especially irksome now that he had an incredible new device with which he could study the glorious heavens and the wonders of nature that had so far been obscured.

At the same time, however, Galileo knew that there was little he could do to escape Padua. He needed a patron who would support him in the style to which he had become accustomed, but who did not expect him to teach or to carry out any mundane or time-consuming duties at court. There was really only one place where this could be achieved: the court of the Grand Duke of Tuscany – the Medici rulers he had left a decade and a half earlier.

When it came to decisions about patronage, the Medicis had always been extremely choosy. One hundred and forty years earlier, when Florence had been home to more than a dozen artists whose names have since become iconic, including Leonardo, Michelangelo and Botticelli, the first citizen, Lorenzo de' Medici, a man of great taste and talent, had shown almost no interest in Leonardo da Vinci but had spoiled and honoured Michelangelo to the point of excess. In a similar way, the Medici, perhaps stung by Galileo's desertion in 1592, lavished money and resources on far lesser men but offered Galileo only crumbs from the table.

Galileo had remained in touch with the Medicis – it would have been extremely foolhardy of him to have done otherwise; but between his leaving Pisa in 1592 and his period of greatest disillusionment with the rulers of Venice in 1609–10, his relationship with the first family of Italy was, at best, lukewarm. In 1608 Galileo had demonstrated at the Florentine court a lodestone which he had borrowed from his friend

Sagredo. It was considered a marvel: a small magnetic stone that could lift almost three times its weight in iron filings. The Grand Duchess Christina, the wife of Ferdinand I, appears to have enjoyed the scientist's company more than her husband did and, starting in 1604, each summer for three years Galileo had been invited to teach the couple's son Cosimo. When the boy was married, in 1608, Christina insisted on inviting Galileo, and when Ferdinand died, in 1609, Galileo was drawn closer to the Medici, raising his hopes of preferment.

When this opportunity presented itself, Galileo did everything he could to curry favour with the Medici. He had dedicated books to the family and been extremely attentive towards Cosimo, with whom he appears to have shared a genuine affection; but beyond flattery and attentiveness he could do nothing to influence such powerful figures or move things forward faster than diplomacy, tact and personal whim would allow. Turning away from such thoughts and letting matters take their own course, he threw himself into his scientific interests and began to study the infinite universe that awaited him through the eyepiece of his telescope.

After observing distant ships and towers in neighbouring towns it was, of course, logical for a scientist to point a telescope at the Moon. For the first three months of 1609 Galileo spent almost every night studying the lunar surface, and almost by accident he found his first real proof that Aristotle had been entirely wrong about the nature of the heavens.

According to Aristotle, the Moon was a perfectly smooth and featureless sphere, unchanging and unblemished. Galileo quickly demonstrated that this was nonsense. The Moon, he showed, was pock-marked, and its surface was undulating in places, jagged and riven in others. Indeed, it was hard to find even a tiny region on the surface that could be described as in any way smooth, featureless or unblemished. This prompted Galileo to note: '[The surface of the Moon] is uneven, rough, full of cavities and prominences.'[10]

Elsewhere he reported: 'The surface of the Moon is as spotted as the tail of a peacock is speckled with azure eyes, and resembles those glass vases which, while still hot, have been plunged into cold water and have thus acquired a crackled and wavy surface.'[11] Most significantly of all, he discovered that the Moon had mountains, some of which he calculated to be as much as four miles high.

From his observations Galileo made detailed sketches of the

changing face of the Moon as it went through its phases and the pattern of the Sun's reflected light altered the lunar features as seen from Earth. At the same time, he kept carefully worded records of his observations, noting the times at which his drawings were made, the position of the Moon in the sky and the relative positions of other fixed points, the stars.

By the end of what had been one of the most eventful and inspiring years of his life Galileo had improved his telescope to the point where it could magnify up to thirty times and still produce a clear, sharp image. Over Christmas 1609 he worked on, ignoring the festivities and the holidays, and in January, before the new college term began, he made one of the discoveries that was to immortalise his name and link him for ever with the telescope and the new astronomy this remarkable instrument had sired.

Galileo first observed the moons of Jupiter on 7 January 1610. He had no idea they were moons at the time and simply noticed three small bright objects close to the giant planet Jupiter, which he described in his notes as 'stars'. During his vigils for the following eight nights he plotted the positions of these 'stars', noting how they changed in brightness and how on certain nights a fourth object similar to the other three appeared.

Gradually it became clear that the objects he was observing were bodies much smaller than Jupiter itself and that these objects orbited the planet just as our Moon orbits the Earth. 'I had now decided beyond all question that three stars were wandering around Jupiter, as do Venus and Mercury, around the sun,' he wrote.[12]

Galileo later elaborated on this, declaring in his book *The Starry Messenger* (published in March 1610): 'Above all, since they sometimes follow and sometimes precede Jupiter by the same intervals, and they remain within very limited distances either to east or west of Jupiter, no one can doubt that they complete their revolutions about Jupiter and at the same time effect altogether a twelve-year period about the centre of the universe.'[13] In other words, the moons orbit the planet Jupiter and the whole system orbits the centre of the universe (be it the Earth or the Sun) once every twelve years.

For Galileo this was the clearest evidence yet that the Copernican theory was a true description of the mechanics of the universe. Within this Jovian system, he realised, he was observing a model of planetary dynamics that was similar to that described by Copernicus in which the planets orbited the Sun. Furthermore, a common argument of those who opposed Copernicus was that it would be impossible for the Earth to orbit the Sun without losing the Moon (presumably because it would shoot off into space). Yet, as Galileo could see, Jupiter was clearly capable of maintaining a grip on its satellites even though it was orbiting a central body (be it the Sun of Copernicus or the Earth of Aristotle's geocentric model).

He reiterated his point in a later chapter of *The Starry Messenger*, in which he wrote:

> Here we have a powerful and elegant argument to quiet the doubts of those who, while accepting without difficulty that the planets revolve around the sun in the Copernican system, are so disturbed to have the Moon alone revolve around the Earth while accompanying it in an annual revolution about the Sun, that they believe that this structure of the universe should be rejected as impossible. But now we have not just one planet revolving around another; our eyes show us four stars [moons] that wander around Jupiter as does the Moon around the Earth, and that all together they trace out a grand revolution about the Sun in the space of twelve years.[14]

By the end of January 1610 he had collected enough material to produce a book describing his discoveries. In great haste he put the finishing touches to his book in early February, rushed it to Tommaso Baglioni, a publisher in Venice, where the text was translated into Latin and copies were printed ready for distribution. By the middle of March Galileo's first truly important book, *The Starry Messenger* (*Sidereus Nuncius*) was published and the print run of 550 copies sent out to his associates, influential figures in the universities of Italy, and to bookshops in every major city.

On the first page of his book Galileo made his mission clear:

> I should disclose and publish to the world the occasion of discovering and observing four Planets, never seen from the beginning of the world up to our own times, their positions, and the observations made during the last two months about their movements and their changes of magnitude; and I summon all astronomers to apply themselves to examine and determine their periodic times, which it has not been permitted me to achieve up to this day . . . On the 7th day of January in the present year, 1610, in the first hour of the following night, when I was viewing the constellations of the heavens through a telescope, the

planet Jupiter presented itself to my view, and as I had prepared for myself a very excellent instrument, I noticed a circumstance which I had never been able to notice before, namely that three little stars, small but very bright, were near the planet; and although I believed them to belong to a number of the fixed stars, yet they made me somewhat wonder, because they seemed to be arranged exactly in a straight line, parallel to the ecliptic, and to be brighter than the rest of the stars, equal to them in magnitude . . . When on January 8th, led by some fatality, I turned again to look at the same part of the heavens, I found a very different state of things, for there were three little stars all west of Jupiter, and nearer together than on the previous night.[15]

He was in a state of feverish excitement and he had no doubts about the unique position in which he now found himself. He was perhaps fortunate to have stumbled upon the instrument that could open up an entire universe for him, but he was also a man prepared. As his countryman the great Machiavelli had stated in his masterpiece *The Prince* almost a century earlier:

[Fortune may be compared to] one of those raging rivers, which when in flood overflows the plains, sweeping away trees and buildings, bearing away the soil from place to place. Everything flies before it, all yield to its violence, without being able in any way to withstand it; and yet, though its nature be such, it does not follow therefore that men, when the weather becomes fair, shall not make provision, both with defences and barriers, in such a manner that, rising again, the waters may pass away by canal, and their force be neither so unrestrained nor so dangerous. So it happens with fortune . . .[16]

Galileo was prepared and he was to make the most of his good fortune. 'I have many and most admirable devices; but they could only be put to work by princes because it is they who are able to carry on wars, build and defend fortresses, and for their regal sport make most splendid expenditures.'[17]

His extreme mood had two very different but ultimately linked causes. First he was filled with the desire to make great scientific leaps forward, to learn to unthread the tapestry of the universe and to understand as no man had understood before. He knew he could now combine his mathematical knowledge with the enormous power the telescope provided him. He also knew there were few others in Europe

who could work in the same way: Kepler was a colleague who understood and sympathised; Lippershey was a purely practical man with no
interest in science; Sarpi was absorbed by other things and had slowed
down drastically since coming so close to death at the hands of the
pope's henchmen. Galileo was really the only one with all the requirements to publicise the new astronomy and to use it to further human
understanding of the universe.

The barrier to all this was, of course, the Roman Church; but for
now any clash with the Church could wait, for there was another more
immediate concern: Galileo realised that he might use his discoveries to
push the Medici into finally accepting him.

Writing to Cosimo de' Medici's secretary, Belasario Vinta, on 30
January, Galileo began to lay the groundwork by making it clear what
he had achieved: 'I feel an infinite amazement,' he gushed; 'that is, I
render infinite thanks to God, that he has been pleased to make me
alone the first observer of amazing things which have been obscured
since the beginning of time.'[18]

Next, Galileo dedicated *The Starry Messenger* to Cosimo. Ladling it
on thick, he began: 'Your Highness . . . scarcely have the immortal
graces of your soul begun to shine forth on Earth than bright stars offer
themselves in the heavens which, like tongues will speak of and
celebrate your most excellent virtues for all time . . .'

Not content with these moves, he pushed things almost over the
top by asking Cosimo for his permission to name the satellites of Jupiter after the duke and his brothers (Cosimo, Francesco, Carlo and
Lorenzo).

It worked. Suddenly Cosimo and his advisers found renewed interest
in the scientist. This reaction was helped by the fact that Galileo's new
book *The Starry Messenger* had been very well received across Europe. It
had become an instant success in Italy, and copies were being sold as far
away as England, Spain and the Netherlands.

On the day that *The Starry Messenger* was published – 13 March 1610
– Sir Henry Wotton, the British ambassador to Venice, wrote to his
home office about the 'strangest piece of news that hath ever yet
received from any part of the world . . .' He then went on to describe
Galileo's use of the telescope and his discovery of 'four new planets' (the
moons of Jupiter), and to explain that 'the Moon is not spherical, but
endued with many prominences', and 'illuminated with the solar light
by reflection from the body of the Earth'. He then predicted quite
accurately that these discoveries would overturn all astronomy and

astrology, saying that the place was abuzz with talk of Galileo and his book. 'Here in Italy, all corners are full of talk about these discoveries,' he enthused and concluded with the remark that Galileo 'runneth a fortune to be either exceedingly famous or exceedingly ridiculous'.[19]

Meanwhile, a no less enthusiastic response came from Kepler, who wrote to Galileo declaring: 'I may perhaps seem rash in accepting your claims so readily with no support of my own experience . . . but why should I not believe a most learned mathematician, whose very style attests the soundness of his judgement?'[20]

The negotiations with Cosimo's people were protracted but the outcome was never in doubt. Galileo was the hottest intellectual in Europe and any worthy patron would have perceived the man as a great asset to them – any, that is, except the Venetian leadership, who appeared completely out of step with the reaction to Galileo's sudden fame. Galileo believed his masters in Venice had simply taken him for granted and were complacent enough to believe that he would never leave to take up a better position.

If they indeed considered things this way they were quite mistaken, for by 1610 Galileo had become completely disillusioned with his position in Padua. He did not even consider the idea of playing one party off against the other to acquire a better deal for himself. Instead, through the spring and summer of 1610, he negotiated in private the fine details of the package offered by the Medici leadership in Florence.

Of paramount importance to Galileo was the condition that he should never have to teach again. He made this very clear to the grand duke's negotiator, Belasario Vinta: 'I wish to gain my bread by my writings, which I would always dedicate to my Serene Master.'[21] He was also happy to accept a salary to match that given by the doge – a thousand crowns per annum. Galileo's final quibble was over his official title. Always one to appreciate the importance of titles and the way the world perceived him, rather than accepting the title of Chief Mathematician Galileo asked that he be known as Chief Mathematician and Philosopher to the Grand Duke of Tuscany.

The distinction was subtle but very important to Galileo. There was much in this title to add kudos to his fame as the author of *The Starry Messenger*. It meant that his ideas officially extended beyond mathematics (still not considered an important subject in the early seventeenth century). It meant that he could challenge the propositions of other well-known philosophers on an equal footing.

By early July the fine print was agreed and Galileo's new position announced to the world. To the disgust of the Venetians, who had not been privy to the scientist's behind-the-scenes machinations, Galileo declared his intention to accept the offer of the grand duke and that he would serve his notice as Professor of Mathematics at the University of Padua. By mid-September he was ensconced in Florence.

9

Papal Secrets, Holy Intrigues

Galileo arrived in Florence just as the weather changed, and almost immediately he began to suffer pains from chronic rheumatism, a complaint that would plague him for the rest of his life. Indeed, his first six months in his new job were a rather fraught time. In too much of a hurry to leave Padua and to begin his new life as Chief Mathematician and Philosopher to the Grand Duke of Tuscany, he had made inadequate preparations for the move, and as a result his life was temporarily thrown into chaos.

He was better off materially and, most importantly, he was now free to dedicate his time solely to research; but at the same time he had given up the protection from Church censorship Venice could afford him. Tuscany was in thrall to Rome and ruled by an extremely religious family. His close friend Sagredo, who was by this time living in the Middle East, wrote a touching letter to warn him of this. 'Where will you find more freedom than in Venice?' he asked:

> Now you are in your noble native land, but gone from a place where you had many good things. Your prince is full of promise but here you had command over those who govern. Here you had only to serve yourself, as if you were the king of the universe . . . I do not condemn the youth of your prince. But who knows what the accidents of life can do? Who can guess at the schemes of envious people? Such people may sow in the prince's mind false and slanderous ideas that ruin a gallant man.[1]

Leaving Padua, Galileo had also said farewell to his mistress of ten years, Marina Gamba. The relationship had never been formalised by marriage, but after it came to an end Galileo took responsibility for the three children that had come from the liaison. The eldest, Virginia, who had just turned ten, had been in Florence for several months, staying there through the long summer with her grandmother, the 73-year-old Giulia. Taking the road to Florence, Galileo was accompanied by his second daughter, the 9-year-old Livia. His son, Vincenzo, just turned 4, would join his father later, when he was old enough to be away from his mother.

Within six months of their separation, Marina married a small-business owner, Giovanni Bartoluzzi. Galileo remained in touch with his former mistress; he helped out with the cost of her wedding and continued to send her money for many years after they separated. He also maintained a healthy relationship with Bartoluzzi, helping him to make business contacts with his wealthy Paduan friends. In return, Bartoluzzi found reasonably priced, high-quality lenses for Galileo's telescopes.

Galileo's first two or three months in Florence were spent attending to domestic responsibilities. He shared a house with his mother and daughters, which was rented to them by his brother-in-law Benedetto Landucci, who was clearly better disposed towards the scientist now that he was famous and wealthy and had paid his debts. The house had 'a high terraced roof from which the whole sky [was] visible', which was chosen because it offered a perfect view for making astronomical observations, when time allowed.[2]

When he was well enough, Galileo familiarised himself with the machinations of court protocol, with which he would have had some knowledge from the summers he had spent teaching Cosimo de' Medici a few years earlier. Things were different now, though: the boy had grown into a man and was the ruler of a wealthy and upwardly mobile state. Galileo was no longer a frustrated professor at a provincial university but had risen to become perhaps the most important scientist in Europe.

Soon after his move to Florence, in 1610, Galileo placed his two daughters, Virginia and Livia, into a nearby convent, the Franciscan Convent of St Matthew. Unfortunately for the girls, this was home to an order called the Poor Clares, a particularly extreme Franciscan sect who, as their name implies, were devoted to the notion of poverty and the reduction of the self to a mere vassal of Christ. One nun, Sister Maria Domitilla, who served as a Poor Clare, later advised any girls contemplating joining the order to be shown how we dress in vile clothing, always go barefoot, get up in the middle of the night, sleep on hard boards, fast continually, and eat crass, poor and lenten food, and spend the major part of the day reciting the Divine Office and in long mental prayers, and how all of our recreation, pleasure and happiness is to serve, love and give pleasure to the beloved Lord, attempting to imitate his holy virtues, to mortify and vilify ourselves, to suffer contempt, hunger, thirst, heat, cold and other inconveniences for his love.[3]

Livia was badly affected by this new life. From surviving letters between Galileo and his family it is clear the girl suffered some form of nervous breakdown. She turned in upon herself and was barely capable of communicating with anyone. After this, she rarely had anything to do with her father. Virginia was more stoical and genuinely devout. She drew closer to Galileo with each passing year and cherished his frequent visits to the convent and the small kindnesses he offered her – food, blankets and warm clothes.

All this supports the impression that Galileo's decision to place his daughters under such a regime was uncaring, even cruel; but we must remember that Galileo lived four hundred years ago, in a very different age from our own. In the seventeenth century the idea of female emancipation was completely alien. Women did precisely what men told them to do, especially if the man doing the telling was their father. There would have been no question that Galileo's daughters would do his bidding and it would never have occurred to him to consider their happiness. Such things were simply not issues in his world.

A relief from the pressures of the new job and the intrusions of his family came in the shape of a young devotee named Filippo Salviati. Salviati was precisely the type of disciple Galileo cherished – an impressionable but brilliant noblemen who would pamper him and flatter his ego; a perfect example of all that was good about Renaissance Italian nobility. He was extremely handsome, very rich and he possessed a sharp mind. Trained in the arts, he was a fine dancer and athlete and had come late to the intellectual world, particularly mathematics and science. He had studied *The Starry Messenger* before meeting Galileo and was so fired up with enthusiasm that, in spite of his dislike for teaching novices, Galileo was happy to take on the young man as a private student.

The two men became immediately simpatico, but Galileo was also clearly taken with Salviati because of what he could offer him: useful social connections, avenues into commerce and the homes of the wealthy, through which he could make considerable amounts of money selling telescopes. Salviati also insisted that Galileo should stay with him at his sumptuous country home, *Le Selve* (The Woods), fifteen miles to the west of Florence in the village of Lastra a Signa. In Salviati Galileo had found a Florentine Sagredo, and in his home, a new Ark.

Galileo spent the major part of the winter of 1611 at Le Selve, eating and drinking well, sleeping in a vast four-poster bed and keeping warm by an open log fire in a study that had been put aside for his private use. When he was well enough and the skies clear, he returned to the work he had been forced to leave when departing Padua – the observation of the planets and stars; and still more wonders were revealed to him.

His two great discoveries up to this time had been his studies of the surface of the Moon showing the craters and mountains, and following this came his observations of the Jovian moons.* The first of these discoveries had provided ammunition for his anti-Aristotelian view of the universe by offering clear evidence that the Moon was not, as the Greeks had supposed it to be, a perfect, unblemished sphere. The second discovery was even more significant, illustrating as it did that a planet could possess one or more moons and still orbit the centre of the universe, a fact that added weight to the validity of the Copernican model. In the winter of 1611 Galileo first turned his telescope to the second-brightest object in the night sky, the planet Venus, which throughout the summer had been too close to the Sun to be observable.

What Galileo saw over a period of several weeks was that Venus had 'phases', just like our Moon, going through a full illuminated sphere, a half-sphere and a crescent. What this meant to him was that the planet must be orbiting the Sun. This is explained by the fact that when Venus is furthest from the Earth (in other words, when the Earth and Venus are on opposite sides of the Sun), Venus is fully illuminated by reflected light from the Sun. At other points in the orbits of the two planets (when they are both on the same side of the Sun) Venus, as seen from the Earth, appears partly in shadow. This alters the appearance of

* Galileo had actually made a third important astronomical discovery in Padua: he had observed the rings of Saturn. However, because his telescope was insufficiently powerful to give a clear image of the planet, and because of the angle of the rings at the time, it appeared to Galileo that Saturn was actually what he called a 'triple planet'. It was not until 1657 that Christiaan Huygens, using a far more powerful telescope, was able to demonstrate that Saturn was surrounded by an array of rings.

Venus so that it ranges from being a largely illuminated sphere to a mere sliver, depending on the relative positions of the Earth and Venus.

Back in the 1540s Copernicus had, using just the naked eye, noted a discrepancy between his theory and the observations he had made. If his theory was right, he had supposed, when Venus and the Earth were furthest apart, on opposing sides of the Sun, Venus should appear much smaller than it did. However, he had not realised that when Venus and the Earth were in these relative positions, Venus appeared lit up as a 'full-Venus', which made it appear larger than it would otherwise be.

There remained, though, an argument, albeit a flimsy one, that supporters of Aristotle claimed could explain the phases of Venus without recourse to the Copernican model. A generation before Galileo Tycho Brahe had proposed a model in which Venus (and perhaps the other observed planets of the solar system) orbited the Sun and in which this whole sub-system circled the Earth, fixed as it was at the centre of the universe.

Tycho had been a great astronomer, a man who was receptive to many of the new scientific ideas of much younger men such as Galileo. He had rejected some of the ancient, traditional misconceptions, but he was never able to cast off the shackles of Aristotle entirely; and, although he lived in a country with relatively lenient attitudes to religious freedom, he was a devout man for whom theological considerations mattered. Tycho's model had offered a neat way to explain observations while appeasing the theologians.

Yet even if we ignore this, Tycho's proposition could be dismissed using Galileo's descriptions. If the planets of the solar system could be made to orbit the Sun in the way that Tycho described, then, Galileo reasoned, surely the force that made this possible would also exert an influence upon the Earth and alter its position. Tycho's model must then be a logical absurdity. If Tycho's model could be effectively ignored, and the traditional geocentric model of the universe could not account for the irrefutable evidence provided by Galileo's observations, at the very least these observations added weight to Copernicus's heliocentric model.

By the beginning of 1611 Galileo's fame was spreading as *The Starry Messenger* went to successive reprints and more and more experimenters across the continent turned their telescopes to the skies. However, many of these astronomers were inexperienced and, more importantly, their instruments were hugely inferior to Galileo's. This meant that many of those who owned Galileo's book and searched in the region of the planet Jupiter saw no sign of the moons. Those who turned their telescopes towards our own Moon did see mountains and craters, but even these were indistinct. This made it easy for those who did not want to believe in the existence of the things Galileo described to pretend they did not exist. At the same time, there were more than a few philosophers across Europe who flatly refused to even look through the eyepiece of a telescope. Consequently, ignorance and the poor quality of observations gave critics of Galileo ammunition with which to attack the astronomer and his new astronomy.

Around this time, from Bologna came a written attack on Galileo's astronomical findings. A young astronomer named Martin Horky published *A Very Brief Pilgrimage Against the Starry Messenger*. But Horky was little more than a self-serving nobody who attacked Galileo on fallacious grounds. For obscure reasons he believed that by criticising Galileo so openly he would gain preferment, especially from Johannes Kepler, who had once been his teacher. The plan backfired because Kepler was a great supporter of Galileo. Learning of Horky's antics, Kepler immediately wrote to his friend to apologise, referring to his former student as 'this scum of a fellow'.[4]

But the attacks kept coming. Another third-rate astronomer, one Francesco Sizzi, wrote his own treatise, *Dianoia Astronomica, Optica, Physica* attacking *The Starry Messenger* on theological grounds. In his book he claimed that Jupiter could not possess moons because they were not mentioned in the Holy Bible. Sizzi's nonsense could have been easily dismissed (and it was, by Galileo) except for the fact that the author had cunningly dedicated his book to Giovanni de' Medici, the only member of the Medici family who hated Galileo (because of their clash two decades earlier over the plan to dredge the harbour at Livorno). Sizzi's dedication did nothing to elevate the ideas contained in the book and forward-thinking scientists took the material in the treatise with a pinch of salt, but simply because it was attached to the Medici it succeeded in reaching a wide audience, and by some it was taken far more seriously than it deserved. One particularly muddle-headed passage from Sizzi's book called upon alchemical ideas in an attempt to discredit Galileo's work:

Just as in the microcosm there are seven 'windows' in the head (two nostrils, two eyes, two ears, and a mouth), so in the macrocosm God has placed two beneficent stars (Jupiter, Venus), two maleficent stars

(Mars, Saturn), two luminaries (Sun and Moon) and one indifferent star (Mercury). The seven days of the week follow from these. Finally, since ancient times the alchemists had made each of the seven metals correspond to one of the planets; gold to the sun, silver to the moon, copper to Venus, quicksilver to Mercury, iron to Mars, tin to Jupiter, lead to Saturn.

From these and many other similar phenomena of nature such as the seven metals, etc., which it were tedious to enumerate, we gather that the number of planets is necessarily seven . . . Besides, the Jews and other ancient nations as well as modern Europeans, have adopted the division of the week into seven days, and have named them from the seven planets; now if we increase the number of planets, this whole system falls to the ground . . . Moreover, the satellites are invisible to the naked eye and therefore can have no influence on the earth, and therefore would be useless, and therefore do not exist.[5]

Galileo became aware of the problem of poor-quality telescopes soon after arriving in Florence, and at first the only way he could think of countering the bad publicity and helping his cause was to offer telescopes free to as many genuinely interested people as he could. At the same time he took pains to help anyone who wrote to him claiming they could not see the Jovian system or that the images they had of the Moon were, at best, fuzzy. Even so, it was clear that Galileo's opponents had the potential to destroy all he had achieved if he did not do something to further support his claims; and it was this – the need to make a bold statement to confirm what he had written in *The Starry Messenger* – that led Galileo to propose to his patron Cosimo that he should make a high-profile visit to Rome, where his opponents were most vocal and influential. Writing to Cosimo's secretary Belisario Vinta, Galileo made the reason for his visit abundantly clear. He needed to go 'in order to put an end, once and for all, to malignant rumours'.[6]

Cosimo was easily persuaded. It was immediately clear to him that he would benefit from Galileo's plans. Letters of introduction from Cosimo to the elite of Rome were written and arrangements were made for his accommodation in the finest palaces, principally at the ambassador's residence, the Palazzo Firenze, close to the Pantheon. He was also given a generous allowance for a new wardrobe so that he could look his best before the pope and the noblemen who would gather to hear him speak.

In a letter to Giovanni Niccolini, the grand duke's ambassador to Rome, written at the end of February, Cosimo made it obvious how much importance he placed on Galileo's planned visit to the city:

> Our beloved Mathematician and Philosopher, Galileo Galilei, is going to Rome, and we have decided that he should stay with you in your palace there. It is our wish that you should make him welcome and take care of his expenses and those of one servant. Make a note of these in order to be reimbursed. You will be glad to see him and you will appreciate his intelligence and pleasantness. He will tell you himself why he is making the trip, and you will help him in every way possible, as he requests and as you see fit, more particularly with the advice of Cardinal del Monte for whom we have given him a letter of recommendation. The business that he will undertake is close to our heart both for its usefulness to the world of learning and the glory of our house. May God keep you and bless you.[7]

Galileo was always a confident man and he relished nothing more than being pampered and admired. He also adored being the centre of attention, so that he probably felt no nerves, no sense of self-doubt, even when he spoke before the most illustrious audiences. Arriving in Rome on 29 March 1611, he found that his fame had preceded him. He told Belisario Vinta:

> I arrived in good health on Holy Tuesday, and I handed over the letter of the Grand Duke to the Ambassador, who welcomed me very courteously and with whom I'm staying. On the very same day, I called on Cardinal del Monte to whom I gave the other letter from the Grand Duke, and I told him briefly about the purpose of my trip. The Cardinal received me very courteously and listened attentively to what I had to say before expressing the firm hope that I would not leave without having been able to give a full and satisfactory account of the complete truth of what I have discovered, observed and written.[8]

Many of those with whom he dined and debated did not actually agree with his scientific claims, but everywhere he went he was received with grace and indulged. One figure who held very different views from Galileo was the German Jesuit mathematician Christopher Clavius, then 73 and in his final year of life. Clavius had met him once before – twenty-four years earlier, when as a very green young man Galileo had asked the mathematician for help in securing a position at the University of Bologna. The Galileo who now returned to the Collegio Romano where Clavius had studied and taught for so long had been transformed by the years that separated the visits.

When he first heard of Galileo's discovery of the Jovian moons, Clavius is reported to have said: 'The whole system of the heavens is broken down and must be mended.' But he could not let go of his precious Aristotle and postulated a way around Galileo's discovery. If there were mountains and craters on the Moon, he declared, then the entire orb must be surrounded by a crystalline layer that did indeed make it a perfect sphere, just as the Greeks would have it. Galileo responded to this outlandish suggestion by professing: 'The imagining is beautiful, only it is neither demonstrated nor demonstrable.'[9] Later, he would be more forthright. In response to a letter of support for Clavius's ideas from a vigorous opponent of Galileo's new astronomy, he snapped: 'If anyone is allowed to imagine whatever he pleases, then someone could say that the Moon is surrounded by a crystalline substance that is transparent and invisible. I will grant this provided that, with equal courtesy, I be allowed to say that the crystal has on its outer surface a large number of huge mountains, that are thirty times as high as the terrestrial ones, and invisible because they are diaphanous.'[10]

Clavius and his assistants had recently made astronomical observations using their own telescope, and they could not deny that Venus had phases or that there appeared to be moons orbiting Jupiter. This led the Jesuit to vacillate over the matter of Galileo's observations. A few months before his death he seemed to be supporting Galileo, writing:

> Consult the reliable little book by Galileo Galilei, printed at Venice in 1610 and called *Sidereus Nuncius*, which describes various observations of the stars first made by him. Far from the least important of the things seen with this instrument is that Venus receives its light from the Sun as does the Moon, so that sometimes it appears to be more like a crescent, sometimes less, according to its distance from the Sun. At Rome I have observed this, in the presence of others, more than once. Saturn has joined to it two smaller stars, one on the east, the other on the west. Finally Jupiter has four roving stars, which vary their places in a remarkable way both among themselves and with respect to Jupiter – as Galileo Galilei carefully and accurately describes. Since things are

thus, astronomers ought to consider how the celestial orbs may be arranged in order to save these phenomena."

However, forsaking Aristotle was a step too far for Clavius and he died trying to show that the Jovian system was merely an isolated affair and that Tycho's model (described earlier) could adequately explain the observed phases of Venus.

Galileo realised that the most vocal objections to his ideas would come from the Jesuits. If he could sway them to accept his interpretation of recent observations, then the battle against Aristotelianism would be largely won; but he also understood this would not be easy. Taking the fight to them had been one of the reasons for his determination to visit Rome in the first place, and it lay at the heart of what Galileo saw as his duty, his mission in life: to educate and to inform, to radically alter perceptions. Writing to Vinta shortly after his visit to Clavius, Galileo told him optimistically:

I found that these Fathers [the Jesuits] have finally recognised the genuiness of the Medicean planets, and continue the regular observations that they began two months ago. We compared them with my own and they agree entirely. They are also working hard to find their periods of revolution but they agree with the Mathematician of the Emperor [Johannes Kepler] that it will be very difficult and almost impossible. I hope, however, to discover and determine them, and I trust that God Almighty, who made me the grace of discovering so many new marvels from his hand, will grant me to find the exact period of their rotations. Perhaps by the time I return, I shall have achieved this and be in a position to determine the places and positions that these new planets will have at any time in the future or that they occupied in the past, provided I have the strength to continue my observations late into the night, as I have done until now.[12]

Rome was an Aristotelian stronghold and by going there Galileo was taking the bull by the horns. But this did not worry him; he actually enjoyed shoving his new-found knowledge into the faces of his opponents. He did it all very politely, of course, just as at this stage those who disagreed with almost everything he stood for offered their resistance in a very mannered way. But beneath this veneer lay an undercurrent of clashing ideologies that would soon burst into the open.

Such a clash of opinion was particularly apparent at two of the most important meetings Galileo was invited to attend during his stay in Rome. The first of these was with the pope, Paul V; the other was a gathering at the Jesuit College, presided over by Cardinal Bellarmine, in which Galileo was awarded the equivalent of an honorary degree.

Paul V was, in all ways, an unexceptional Renaissance pope. He was self-obsessed and greedy, but he was no better and no worse than others who had worn the tiara before him. We need not look too far for evidence of this. When he failed to get his way, Paul V had excommunicated the entire government of Venice and had then ordered the assassination of his opponent Sarpi. He had then lionised those who had tried and failed to murder the Venetian.

Another example of Paul V's unsavoury behaviour is the sad case of a little-known author named Piccinardi. The unfortunate man had written a biography of Paul V's predecessor, Clement VIII. He had not even published the work but had mentioned to a friend that in it he had made a less than complimentary comparison between Clement and the Roman emperor Tiberius, who had been infamous for his interest in small boys. Hearing of this third or fourth hand, the pope had the writer arrested and flung into a dungeon. One night Paul, drunk and bellicose, decided, on a whim, to have Piccinardi executed. The prisoner was dragged from his cell and taken to the bridge of San Angelo, where he was hanged and left to swing until his body stank, pecked to the bone by carrion. Curiously, the online edition of *New Advent: the Catholic Encyclopaedia* makes no mention of any of these acts, saying merely that Paul V 'watched vigilantly over the interests of the Church in every nation'.

Galileo was treated to Paul's charming side and the pope surprised him immediately by insisting that the scientist stand rather than kneel while he explained his work to His Holiness. He then gave his blessing to the telescope and Galileo's discoveries; but, pointedly, he said absolutely nothing concerning any specific interpretation of astronomical findings. That he would leave to his Jesuit scientists.

Galileo was clearly excited by this encounter. The day after the audience with Pope Paul he wrote to his friend Filippo Salviati in Florence:

> I do not have time to write personal letters to all my friends and patrons, and in writing to you I shall imagine that I am writing to all. I have been received and fêted by many illustrious cardinals, prelates and princes, who wanted to see the things I have observed and were much

pleased, as I was too, on my part, in viewing the marvels of their statuary, paintings, frescoed rooms, palaces, gardens and so on.

This morning I went to pay my respects to His Holiness, and I was introduced by His Excellency our illustrious ambassador, who told me I had been treated with exceptional favour because His Holiness would not let me say a word kneeling but immediately commanded me to stand up.[13]

Shortly after this papal audience Galileo was the guest of honour at the Collegio Romano, close to the centre of Rome, a short walk from both the Pantheon and the Palazzo Firenze, where he was a guest of the Florentine ambassador. A social bulletin described the event: 'On Friday evening of the past week in the Collegio Romano,' it began, 'in the presence of cardinals and of the Marquis of Monticelli, its promoter, a Latin oration was recited, with other compositions in praise of Signor Galileo Galilei, mathematician to the grand duke, magnifying and exalting to the heavens his new observation of new planets that were unknown to the ancient philosophers.'[14]

Galileo was not invited to speak before the College, but instead a Jesuit, Father Odo Maelcote, read a prepared speech in which, before the gathering of cardinals, nobility and local dignitaries, he described Galileo's discoveries. Delivered in Latin, Maelcote's speech actually contained nothing of value; instead he offered purple prose to describe the appearance of the Moon through the telescope, made no mention of mountains or craters and offered an image of Galileo's findings as ingenious, but without presuming to interpret.

These were fine words, but the speech was, of course, just a performance, for even as Bellarmine, who acted as host for this occasion, offered platitudes and admiration, he was already growing suspicious of Galileo's ideas. Cardinal Bellarmine took his role as protector of the Church very seriously and prided himself on his ability to detect any threat to doctrine before it could make any impact. Sensing any ripples in the intellectual firmament created by men like Galileo, whom he considered a brilliant maverick, Bellarmine became animated and defensive. An illustration of this comes in a letter he wrote a few years later, in 1615, to a prelate in Calabria, the head of the Carmelite Order, Paul Anthony Foscarini, in which he insisted:

The words, '. . . the Sun also rises and the Sun goes down and hastens to his place where he arose, etc.', were those of Solomon, who not only spoke by divine inspiration but was a man wise above all others and most learned in the human sciences and in the knowledge of all created things. His wisdom was from God, and it is not likely that he would affirm something that went against some truth that was already demonstrated, or likely to be. Now if you tell me that Solomon spoke only according to appearances, and that it seems to us that the Sun goes around when actually it is the Earth that moves, as it seems to one on a ship that the shore moves away from the ship, I shall answer that though it may appear to a voyager as if the shore were receding from the vessel on which he stands rather than the vessel from the shore, yet he knows this to be an illusion and is able to correct it because he sees clearly that it is the ship and not the shore that is in movement. But as to the Sun and the Earth, a wise man has no need to correct his judgement, for his experience tells him plainly that the Earth is standing still and that his eyes are not deceived when they report that the Sun, the Moon and the stars are in motion.[15]

For Bellarmine, any deviation from such ideological confines could not be tolerated.

Shortly before his congenial performance at the Collegio Romano, Bellarmine had written to his colleague Christopher Clavius, who had met with Galileo only days earlier to discuss his discoveries. The cardinal had wanted to know what Clavius thought of Galileo's findings and claims.

The mathematician could do nothing but repeat what he had told Galileo himself. He was unable to deny the existence of the Jovian moons, nor could he deny that the image of Venus changed over a period of time, much as the Moon does. These findings, though, did not, he emphasised, challenge traditional cosmology. He did not believe the Moon possessed mountains, and held that the surface must either be covered with a transparent crystalline layer or else what was observed was nothing more than variations in the density of the lunar surface, regions he described as being: 'more rarefied and more solidified'.[16]

Finally, Clavius could make no comment on Galileo's own interpretation of his findings, and, like all other readers of his work, he had nothing else to go on apart from what he gleaned from *The Starry Messenger*.

This was of little help to Bellarmine, and for the moment he could determine no more. Yet he found it hard to do nothing when there might be heresy to unmask. In May, while Galileo was still very much the toast of the town in Rome, the scientist's name came up during another of Bellarmine's investigations.

On 17 May the Sacred Congregation of the Holy Office, the Roman Inquisition, decided to investigate the Paduan philosopher Cesare Cremonini, who had been a staunch but friendly critic of Galileo for many years and perhaps the greatest living fan of Aristotle. The source of Church anxiety over Cremonini was a book the elderly philosopher had written called *Disputatio de Caelo* in which, according to the blinkered vision of the cardinals, he appeared to come perilously close to a Gnostic view of nature.

During the investigation (which did not lead very far, though it ensured that Cremonini would remain under suspicion for the rest of his life), the Inquisitors learned that the professor had been on cordial terms with Galileo, and they assumed the worst. The link was duly recorded and another black mark put against the name Galileo. This, though, was particularly ironic, because the religious and scientific views of the two men could not have been more different: Cremonini was one of those who had boasted loudly that he had not even looked into the eyepiece of a telescope, and never planned to.

Bellarmine was extremely circumspect about his less-than-friendly investigations into the activities and ideas of the man he was forced to publicly admire and elevate, but his duplicity was sometimes exposed. Three years after Galileo's first official visit to Rome the Florentine ambassador recalled in a letter to Cosimo:

He [Galileo] spent a few days with me in 1611. His teaching, and something else, was not to the taste of the Advisers and the Cardinals of the Holy Office. Among others, Bellarmine told me that, however great their respect for the Grand Duke, if Galileo had stayed here too long, they could not have avoided looking into the matter. I gave Galileo a hint or a warning since he was staying here, but I fear that it did not give him great pleasure.[17]

If he had not already sensed it himself from friends, Galileo was made aware of a growing animosity that began to spread beyond Rome. One of his closest friends in the city, the painter Ludovico Cardi da Cignoli, with whom Galileo had spent much of his free time in Rome, wrote to him towards the end of 1611 with the warning:

I have been told by a friend of mine, a priest who is very fond of you, that a certain crowd of ill-disposed men envious of your virtue and merits met at the house of the archbishop in Florence and put their heads together in a mad quest for any means by which they could damage you, either with regard to the motion of the Earth or otherwise. One of them wished to have a preacher state from the pulpit that you were asserting outlandish things. The priest, having perceived the animosity against you, replied as a good Christian and a righteous man ought to do. Now I write this to you so that your eyes will be open to such envy and malice on the part of these sort of evildoers.[18]

Galileo's opponents were of many complexions, each finding a particular bone to pick with what the telescope was revealing. One of the noisiest but also the most irrational series of attacks came from a philosopher named Ludovico delle Colombe, a man who loathed Galileo, not least because the scientist had publicly ridiculed him very soon after the publication of *The Starry Messenger*. Delle Colombe had claimed that Galileo's discoveries were either false (i.e. specks on the lens) or misinterpreted. Galileo did not even deign to offer scientific answers to Colombe, seeing them as beneath his dignity. Instead, he simply made fun of him, calling him 'the Pigeon', which he derived from the Italian meaning of *colombe* (dove). From then on, Galileo and his supporters referred to Colombe and his friends as the 'Pigeon League'.

Colombe was a fanatic in an age dominated by religious extremists, and he clung desperately to the righteous path of Scripture over any form of discovery or observation, declaring: 'He who would render false all the belief of mathematics, philosophy and theology, who dares to demonstrate against all received wisdom and communion, that is a person who would put an end to Holy Scripture.'[19]

In fact, Colombe was motivated as much by self-aggrandisement as by any misplaced piety. By attacking Galileo he believed he would curry favour with the orthodox Church and boost his own career. He failed in this and is now rightly regarded as something of a shallow and naïve opportunist.

Galileo's opponents protested loudest over their distaste for what his observations and theories offered by way of support for Copernicus. A Florentine friend of Galileo's living in Rome, Piero Dini, reported to another of Galileo's acquaintances, the Perugian Cosimo Sassetti: 'Every day Galileo converts some of the heretics who did not believe him, although there are still a few who, in order to escape knowing the truth about the stars around Jupiter, do not even want to look at them.'[20]

Such opposition was not by any means confined to Rome or to Church circles. According to Sassetti's reply to Dini, some intellectuals in Perugia were inflamed by Galileo's ideas. 'Loud voices were raised against Galileo,' he reported. 'I spoke to two of the main protesters, who would not be converted by Ptolemy himself were he converted.'[21]

But, at the same time, Galileo knew he had some supporters, and there were many who had independently turned away from support for Aristotelianism. In attendance at the gathering of the professors and administrators of the Collegio Romano in Galileo's honour had been a young nobleman, the second Marquis of Monticelli, Federico Cesi. Cesi was a great admirer of Galileo and he considered *The Starry Messenger* to be one of the most important scientific books ever written. After the meeting he made a point of introducing himself to the scientist and inviting him to dinner at his lavish palazzo close by.

Cesi was a man who would make a great impact on Galileo's life, for he was the founder of a secret society called the Lyncean Academy, a small group of liberal-minded and anti-Establishment figures which is today considered to be one of the earliest scientific societies as well as being a group which explored the outer fringes of accepted philosophy and rationality.

Cesi was another of the extraordinary young men Galileo seemed to collect throughout his life, and in many ways he was the most important of this select group. At the time the two men first met Cesi was only 26, but he had already achieved a great deal. Born into an extraordinarily rich family and possessing a high social rank (he was made a prince in 1613), he was pretty much free to do what he wanted. Rather than simply devoting himself to a hedonistic lifestyle, the young Federico studied philosophy and the new science, and he was particularly taken with the work of those who espoused anti-Aristotelian perspectives. By the time he met Galileo, in 1611, he is said to have owned the finest private library of scientific, philosophical and occult materials in Italy.

Indeed, Federico became so taken with the whole movement towards liberal thinking and the radical new ideas at the fringes of philosophy that in 1603, when he was just 18, he formed the Lyncean Academy, so named in honour of the lynx, considered to be the sharpest-eyed big cat. The manifesto of the group was: 'Not only to acquire knowledge of things and wisdom and live together justly and piously, but also peacefully to display them to men, orally and in writing without any harm.' These were noble intentions and Cesi meant them, but he was also drawn to areas of investigation that many considered dangerously heretical; and he associated with some figures who were not viewed kindly by the Church.

For the first few years of its existence, the Lyncean Academy consisted of just five men. Cesi himself was joined by Giambattista della Porta, an elder statesmen of the occult and philosophy who had written books on natural magic and alchemy and had even endured questioning by the Inquisition in Rome when rumours of his involvement in sorcery had reached the ears of the pope. Another member was Jean Eck, a Flemish doctor and convicted murderer, who was known to have strong links with black-magic circles and had fled his homeland just ahead of persecution for heresy. The fourth and fifth members were the mathematician Francesco Stelluti and the philosopher Anastasio De Fillis, both of whom were known for their radical opinions.

Each of these men was a radical. Eck was probably the most unorthodox and extreme in his views, but none of them could have been described as anything but subversive and counter-cultural. To add an element of intrigue to their activities they each operated under a pseudonym, which they used to communicate with one another anonymously. Cesi was known as *Il Celivago* (The Astral Traveller), while Eck went by the name *L'Illuminato* (The Enlightened One). When Cesi's father, who was a famous drunkard and proud of his anti-intellectualism, discovered his son's preoccupation and the company he kept, he tried to stop him and to forcibly disband the group. When he failed in this attempt he promptly disinherited his son.

It is possible Cesi was drawn to intellectualism precisely because his father had shunned such interests, and although he was restricted financially by his father's action, by the time he was disinherited, Cesi had acquired independent means. Then, when he was promoted to the title of prince he achieved even greater kudos and social recognition, especially amongst the young nobles of Italy.

A striking aspect of the group Cesi formed around him was the way in which they managed to rise above even the power of the Church. Cesi's father succeeded in having two of the group expelled from Rome for a while and it is said that the man's constant hounding eventually drove one of his son's friends insane, but in all the time the academy was headed by Cesi, until his premature death in 1630, the group remained untouchable, left by the Vatican to do pretty much what they pleased.

The Lynxes were left alone thanks to the fact that Cesi was simply of too high a rank to be open to persecution by the Church. This implies that there was a confused set of rules about who could be left alone to hold extreme views and who could not. The radical philosopher Giordano Bruno, who was, of course, an extremist, had no social standing; he was from a poor, anonymous family and he never achieved official status as a professor or an intellectual. Bruno was burned, his bones crushed to powder and copies of his works destroyed publicly. Galileo, a renowned figure in the world of science, but nevertheless a commoner, was later given a very rough time by the Inquisition. Yet, Cesi, a royal figure, was untouchable.

Perhaps the most extreme case of this Janus attitude is the example of Franccsco Barberini, the nephew of Maffeo Barberini, who was made a cardinal in 1623. Barberini was known to be a supporter of Copernicanism and Galileo's science, and he became a prominent member of the Lyncean Academy, renowned for its occult connections.

So, what did the sharp-eyed members of the academy do? Were they genuinely dangerous, anti-Establishment figures? or merely rich young men messing around with radical ideas?

They took themselves very seriously and they also had extremely liberal, even radical views on science, philosophy and religion. Employing their self-styled pseudonyms, the members met regularly at Cesi's palazzo on the Via Maschera d'Oro (Golden Mask) to discuss the latest scientific ideas of the day. The Lyncean Academy was a scientific organisation. It published original works and supported the ideas of its members; as well as this, some members did important scientific research and shared their findings with the rest of the academy. Aside from Galileo's famous works, the strongest areas for the group were botany, zoology and geology, and they used a microscope to make beautifully detailed illustrations of fungi roughly forty years before Robert Hooke's famous *Micrographia*. The Lynceans also conducted some of the earliest serious research in the science of palaeobotany and they were early practitioners of animal and plant dissection. Prince Cesi himself began working on what he called 'phytosophical' tables to classify nature – work that was only interrupted by his untimely death.

But members of the academy were also open to talk of alchemy, necromancy and sorcery, and they probably carried this talk over into experiment. This would have made them dangerous subversives, and they were only protected by a combination of careful secrecy and the power invested in Prince Cesi.

Recently, interest has focused on a legendary mystical group or secret society called the Illuminati. Many believe this group started in the early Renaissance and continues to this day – that it has been an extremely important anti-Christian secret society led by some of the great figures of history, including Leonardo, Isaac Newton and Galileo. Sadly there is little evidence to support the existence of such a group, and even those who make extreme claims for the Illuminati (ranging from the saving of Galileo from the pyre to the assassination of JFK) offer conflicting and often contradictory ideas about the nature of the organisation and what it has done.

The closest link between Galileo and any group that had any connection with the occult and anti-orthodox opinion is his close association with Cesi's Lyncean Academy, which started during his visit to Rome in 1611. As I have said, this group was dedicated to liberalising intellectual endeavour and it also had strong associations with the occult; but the Academy did not last long. It rose to become an important scientific group with dozens of members drawn from the highest echelons of the scientific world, but then faded into obscurity. The only link between the Lyncean Academy and the Illuminati is the rather spurious one that the occultist and magus Jean Eck immodestly adopted the name *L'Illuminato* as his Lyncean pseudonymn.

Galileo maintained very strong associations with Cesi and the other enthusiasts of the Lynxes. Immediately after dining with Federico Cesi in early April (soon after the gathering at the Collegio Romano), when he met the other members of the academy, Galileo was invited to become the sixth member of their group. He accepted the invitation without hesitation, and in the membership book he wrote proudly: 'I Galileo Galilei Lyncean son of Vincenzo, Florentine, age forty-eight years, in Rome. Written in my own hand on 25 April of the year of grace 1611.'[22]

For Galileo, membership of the academy was no game. He was genuinely honoured by the invitation and, for their part, the other members were thrilled and inspired by the great man's ready acceptance of them. From April 1611 Galileo and Cesi remained intimate friends until Cesi died nineteen years later. Furthermore, the academy financed the publication of two of Galileo's works *Letters on the Sunspots* (1613) and *The Assayer* (1623). These books, each in its own way, contributed to the clash between Galileo and the Church. Each was eventually seen as a heretical work, and each was placed on the *Index Librorum Prohibitorum*. Each was considered by the Church authorities to be the work of an anti-Christian.

Galileo's trip to Rome finally came to an end in August. Upon his return to Florence he was received as something of a hero, and by Cosimo as a servant who had, by showing his brilliance and erudition, cast his master in a very fine light. Cardinal Francesco del Monte, who was one of Galileo's closest associates in the Church and a friend of Cosimo de' Medici, prepared a statement for the scientist to hand the grand duke which read: 'Galileo has, during his stay in Rome, given great satisfaction, and I think he received as much, for he had the opportunity of showing his discoveries so well, that the learned and notable in this city all found them no less true and well founded than astonishing. Were we still living under the ancient republic of Rome, I am certain that a statue would have been erected in his honour on the Capitol.'[23]

But for all the celebration and the high regard of many intellectuals, controversy continued to stalk Galileo. No sooner had he returned to work in Florence than he found himself attacked from several places simultaneously. Academics in Bologna had formed an anti-Galileo group, who tried to derail anything the scientist wrote or talked about in public. Tellingly, they were organised by Giovanni Antonio Magini, who had felt only resentment towards Galileo since the latter had beaten him to the position of Professor of Mathematics at the University of Padua in 1592, a full two decades earlier.

Such attacks were made simply in an effort to undermine Galileo's reputation. They failed completely, but they stung nevertheless. Galileo tried to rise above it all, but in private he seethed. To his patron, Cosimo, in a note accompanying some of his latest writing, he lamented: 'There is no point in disputing someone who is so ignorant that it would require a huge volume to refute his stupidities, which number more than the lines of this essay.'[24]

To a degree we have to accept that Galileo was to blame for many of these attacks and criticisms. He cannot be blamed for wanting to bring his radical ideas to public attention, of course, for he was right and his opponents entirely wrong, but he had never been the most diplomatic of men, nor was he at all modest. He was loud, forceful, argument-ative and combative. He loved vigorous debate, and the cleverer his opponent, the more he enjoyed arguing.

But then some of his detractors were horrendously ignorant. In

November 1612 a Dominican named Niccolo Lorini, who knew no astronomy but objected to Galileo's theories on principle, launched an attack on the scientist at a meeting of clerics in Florence. News of this reached Galileo, who then asked Lorini for an explanation. The Dominican backed down and claimed that he had only criticised the astronomer at an informal gathering of churchmen. Replying to Galileo's letter, he said:

> The suspicion that I entered into a discussion of philosophical matters against anyone on All Souls' Day is completely false and without foundation . . . I did, however, not in order to argue but merely to avoid appearing a blockhead when the discussion was started by others, say a few words just to show I was alive. I said, as I still say, that this opinion of Ipernicus – or whatever his name is – would appear to be hostile to divine Scripture.[25]

We should also keep in mind that Galileo loved attention, relished stirring things up and revelled in his unorthodoxy. At times he probably also believed he was infallible and too important ever to get into serious trouble for his views. He was immensely popular with a large group of supporters; he was patronised by the influential and esteemed Cosimo de' Medici; he was an acclaimed academic, and, most importantly, he had offered staggering discoveries to the world.

Of course, Galileo was deluding himself: few were safe from the claws of the Church. To many powerful Catholics, intellects possessed little real value. Wealth and social status might protect some men, but Galileo was neither rich nor aristocratic. At this stage of his conflict with the Church (before he had heard the faintest murmur of resentment from Rome), Galileo was buoyed up by a misplaced sense of self-importance. He was also singularly focused on the scientific truth of what he had discovered, and this caused him to walk blindly into trouble.

A perfect example of how Galileo stumbled into dangerous territory over his views and did not see how he was opening himself up to trouble is the way he excited damaging reactions to another important astronomical discovery. As early as the summer of 1609, around the time when he first observed the Jovian system and the irregular surface of the Moon, Galileo first noticed odd blemishes on the face of the Sun (what he later called sunspots). While he was in Rome, he had mentioned these findings to a few close associates, including the members of the Lyncean Academy and his good friend, the painter Cignoli.

Upon his return to Florence in late August 1611, Galileo began an intimate study of sunspots. He worked closely with the enthusiastic Filippo Salviati, who had been carrying on with his own nightly observations using a powerful telescope while Galileo was away. The pair were also greatly assisted by an innovation of one of Galileo's former students in Padua, Benedetto Castelli, who had become a Benedictine monk but remained dedicated to Galileo and his views on astronomy. Castelli had, like his master, tried to make meaningful observations of the Sun by looking with the naked eye for just a few seconds through a telescope. This was extremely hazardous. To protect his sight, Castelli devised the technique of letting the image of the Sun fall on to a white card placed at an appropriate point close to the eyepiece of the telescope. This image could then be studied at leisure and without danger. Using this method, Castelli, Salviati and Galileo each observed inexplicable dark areas scattered randomly across the face of the Sun. Writing to Cesi in Rome, Galileo reported: 'I will not neglect celestial observations,' and added confidently, 'expect an exquisite addition to my findings.'[26]

Throughout the winter of 1611 and into the early spring Galileo worked on making observations of the Sun, watching the movements of the blemishes, noting how new ones appeared unexpectedly while others disappeared without warning. By March 1612 he was ready to publish a new book on the subject. But then he received a shock: a letter arrived in Florence from a trusted associate (and later a member of the Lynceans), Mark Welser, who was not a noted scientist but a banker and Sheriff of Augsberg in Germany. The letter contained the news that an astronomer working anonymously under the pseudonym Apelles was claiming to be the first to have seen sunspots. Furthermore, he was publicising his belief that these sunspots were due to stars moving in front of the Sun.

Galileo's explanation for what he had seen was very different. Writing to a friend, he summarised his thoughts:

I do not assert [on this account] that the spots are clouds of the same material as ours, or aqueous vapours raised from the Earth and attracted by the Sun. I merely say that we have no knowledge of anything that more closely resembles them. Let them be vapours or exhalations then, or clouds, or fumes sent out from the Sun's globe or attracted there from other places; I do not decide on this – and they may be any of a thousand other things not perceived by us.

He went on:

If I may give my opinion, I shall say that the solar spots are produced and dissolve upon the surface of the Sun and are contiguous to it, while the Sun, rotating upon its axis in about one lunar month, carries them along, perhaps bringing back some of those that are of longer duration than a month, but so changed in shape and pattern that it is not easy for us to recognise them.[27]

Just as he received the disturbing news from his rival, Galileo was again feeling physically ill and emotionally low. Two things were concerning him about this new discovery. First, that the mysterious astronomer named Apelles wanted to popularise what Galileo was sure was an incorrect explanation for the phenomenon. But secondly, the man was claiming priority for the discovery of sunspots. Galileo was reassured by the fact that his earliest observations, from the summer of 1609 in Venice, had been mentioned to friends and colleagues and that his data had been well documented from that time; but feeling the pressure of enforced rivalry from someone who clearly had a very different perspective on the discovery made him uncomfortable. This feeling was exaggerated when, in January 1612, Apelles became the first to publish on the subject with his *Three Letters on Solar Spots*.

Angry but undaunted, Galileo pressed on with his research and, as he prepared his own discourse, he took the cautious step of asking for Church approval of his explanation for the blemishes he had observed. Writing to Cardinal Conti, who was then Prefect of the Roman Inquisition, Galileo noted that his explanation was anti-Aristotelian, but needed the theologian's opinion on whether or not it was actually anti-doctrinal.

Conti, of course, had no idea, but he could not admit as much. Instead, he merely sat on the fence. Galileo's explanation for sunspots was not at odds with Scripture, he admitted, because no mention of such a phenomenon could be found in the Bible. He could only assume, then, that the blemishes, which could not simply be ignored, were in fact stars moving in front of the face of the Sun. Yet, such a response was as good as useless and provided only contradiction, for

GAILILEVS
GAILILEVS
MATHVS:

Galileo Galilei in his prime. This was painted in 1606 when he was a professor at Padua and already renowned as a great intellectual.

A bird's-eye view of Venice showing St Mark's Square with the Doge's Palace on its right. It dates from around the time Galileo was working in the nearby city of Padua.

(*inset*) Leonardo Dona (sometimes known as Leonardo Donato, 1536–1612), Doge of Venice from 1606 until his death. He knew Galileo well and was the Venetian ruler who bought the first telescopes produced by the scientist.

(*above left*) Pope Paul V (1550–1621). Paul V was a supporter of Galileo, but he worked with Robert Bellarmine to caution him about proselytising Copernicanism as anything more than a hypothesis.

(*above right*) Pope Urban VIII (1568–1644). Urban was an intellectual and initially a supporter and friend to Galileo, but he was greatly aggrieved by Galileo's *Dialogue* and he consequently led the persecution of the scientist.

(*left*) Christina, Grand Duchess of Tuscany (1565–1637). A great Medici dowager, Christina was a supporter of Galileo and did much to further his career. However, she was also a devout and orthodox Catholic who remained doubtful about many of Galileo's anti-Aristotelian ideas.

(*main picture*) Galileo before the Inquisition. The real reason for the trial of Galileo has been obscured by the Church for almost four centuries. The accusation that Galileo's writing was heretical because of his support for Copernicanism was nothing more than a smokescreen to conceal a discovery far more radical and potentially dangerous to the Church.

ED·CÆSIVS·LYN·P·I·M·CÆL·MA

LVS SARPIVS VENET VS
NCILII TRIDENTINI
EVISCERATOR

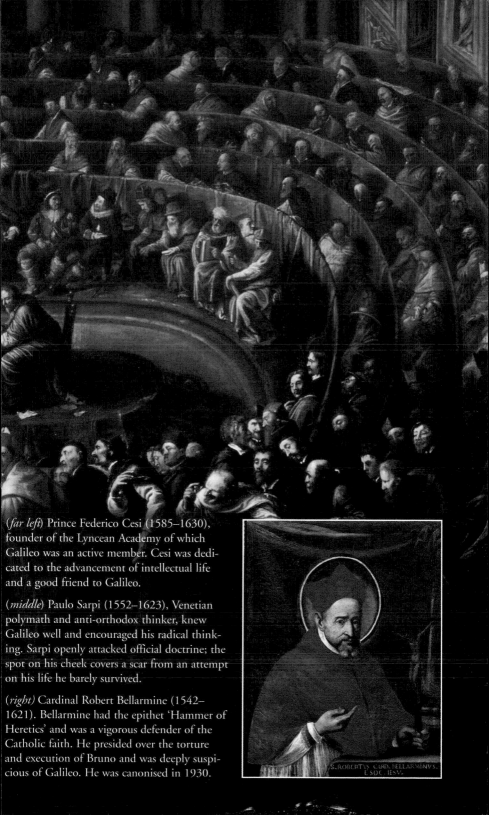

(*far left*) Prince Federico Cesi (1585–1630), founder of the Lyncean Academy of which Galileo was an active member. Cesi was dedicated to the advancement of intellectual life and a good friend to Galileo.

(*middle*) Paulo Sarpi (1552–1623), Venetian polymath and anti-orthodox thinker, knew Galileo well and encouraged his radical thinking. Sarpi openly attacked official doctrine; the spot on his cheek covers a scar from an attempt on his life he barely survived.

(*right*) Cardinal Robert Bellarmine (1542–1621). Bellarmine had the epithet 'Hammer of Heretics' and was a vigorous defender of the Catholic faith. He presided over the torture and execution of Bruno and was deeply suspicious of Galileo. He was canonised in 1930.

A blind and ailing Galileo at 'Il Gioiello' (Little Jewel), the villa in Arcerti in which he was placed under house arrest. With him is his amanuensis and disciple, Vincenzo Viviani.

A view of Venice from 'Il Gioiello', Arcerti, where Galileo died in 1642.

The monument to Galileo and his disciple and biographer Viviani in the church of Santa Croce, Florence. This was constructed in 1737, almost a century after the scientist's death. Any plans for a monument to Galileo during the first decades after his death were quashed by the Vatican.

Aristotle had also stated that the stars were fixed in space. How then could they move in front of the Sun?

While Galileo wasted his energies trying to get uncomprehending clergymen to offer a little clarity, Cesi, who had recently taken on the role of Galileo's publisher and literary benefactor, was trying to clear the way for publication of the astronomer's planned book on sunspots.

For more than a century, ecclesiastic approval for publication had been an essential requirement. In 1515, Pope Leo X had decreed that all books published in Italy had to be passed by the papal censor. If this was not done, the author, the printer and even the readers of illegal books could face severe fines, excommunication and imprisonment, their books burned in public.

Such a draconian move was one of the many consequences of the Council of Trent. The papal office had decided (quite correctly) that one of the most dangerous forces working against them was the ubiquitous written word and the fact that so many more people in Europe could read and understand a given work. By censoring, banning and burning, they believed they could maintain some sense of control. It was not enough to monitor and 'correct' books of a religious or a scientific nature because (again, quite rightly) it was assumed that all sorts of worrying concepts and radical ideas might emerge from books that appeared on the surface to be quite innocuous. Far better, then, simply to censor everything.

Cesi finally received approval to publish Galileo's book *History and Demonstrations about Sunspots and their Properties* in January 1613, and it left the printing press in March. Before its publication Galileo predicted that he would receive unprecedented criticism for his ideas; writing to Cesi, he stated: 'I expect the tempest over the mountains of the Moon will be a joke compared to the lashings I will receive over these clouds.'[28]

He was not wrong. Attackers came from all directions. There were those who, without checking their facts, objected to the treatise on theological grounds, even though Galileo's interpretation did not contradict Scripture (because, as Conti had pointed out, there was no mention of sunspots in the Bible); and there were those who could simply not let Aristotle go, yet were unable to offer explanations for the phenomenon without themselves breaking one or other of the ancient dogmas. There were also those who simply attacked Galileo and his latest publication because it was Galileo and his work; and there were those, especially amongst the clergy, who were scandalised by the fact that Galileo and his friends in the Lyncean Academy had deliberately published a book of philosophy written in the vernacular, thus compromising the exclusivity of intellectual property and allowing ordinary people to read his dangerous ideas.

Galileo fumed, declaring in a letter to Prince Cesi that spring: 'There are men with horse sense, but because they are unable to read things that are "Greek to them", they become convinced that the logic and philosophy are over their heads. Now I want them to see that just as nature has given them eyes with which to see her works, so she has given them brains to penetrate and to understand.'[29]

Clearly, Galileo was affected by the scorn of his many critics, and he continued to become irritated by what he considered mindless barbs. To some he responded directly, writing patronising or simply rude letters, while others became the subject of his scathing wit in private correspondence with friends, through which he could let off steam. The fact that he took the attacks badly is clear from the fact that eight years later, in his book *The Assayer*, he could write: 'How many men attacked my letters on sunspots, and under what disguises! The book should have opened the mind's eye for admirable speculation. Instead, it met with scorn and derision. Many people disbelieved it or failed to appreciate it. Others, not wanting to agree with my ideas, advanced ridiculous and impossible opinions against me.' Then, with customary immodesty he concluded: 'And some, overwhelmed and convinced by my arguments, attempted to rob me of that Glory which was mine, pretending not to have seen my writings and trying to represent themselves as the original discoverers of these impressive marvels.'[30]

One small personal compensation for facing these attacks came when his rival and earliest critic over the nature of sunspots, the elusive Apelles, revealed his true identity as that of Father Christopher Scheiner, a Jesuit priest and a professor of mathematics from the tiny town of Ingolstadt in Bavaria. Early in his career, Scheiner had made some important contributions to the design of scientific instruments and had invented a useful device called a pantograph, used for copying and enlarging drawings. But over the issue of sunspots he had let his obsession with Aristotle cloud his scientific detachment.

Galileo learned that part of the reason for Scheiner's decision to remain anonymous had been the local head of the Jesuit order, Scheiner's superior, who had warned him not to get involved in the subject. In a letter to Scheiner the Jesuit had declared: 'I have read everything written by Aristotle and, I can assure you, my son, that I have found nothing similar to what you describe. Go and calm yourself. Your sunspots are the defects of your glasses and your eyes.'³¹

For a brief moment this news lightened Galileo's mood, but it came just before he inadvertently walked into a trap that would be seen later as a major turning point in his career. In December 1613 Galileo found himself exposed. He had many supporters, but he was also, as we have seen, the subject of attacks from hostile opponents. Most importantly, he was now living in Tuscany, a state under the control of the conformist and conservative Medici, far from the sanctuary of liberal Venice. In the course of the next few years Galileo would come to regret his decision to abandon the Most Serene Republic and learn that, when it came to making a stand for what he truly believed, he could trust almost no one.

10

The Fight Begins

It all began with an innocent conversation over lunch on 12 December 1613. To be sure, it was no ordinary lunch at the Verga d'Oro, the Medicis' Pisan palace. The advisers to the duke had invited the professors from the university and amongst these was Galileo's former student and fellow anti-Aristotelian Father Benedetto Castelli. Also in attendance were their royal personages the Grand Duke Cosimo II, his wife, Archduchess Maria Maddelena, and Cosimo's mother, the Grand Duchess Christina.

Castelli had done much to help his former master in his work on sunspots and he had had the favour reciprocated when Galileo had helped him secure the Chair of Mathematics at the University of Pisa (the position Galileo had once held there). Castelli had taken up his new post in the autumn of 1613.

It was an enormous step up the academic ladder for Castelli, but the University of Pisa had changed little since Galileo's unhappy years there at the end of the previous century. Conservative and staid, it was no place for innovative thought and Castelli was known for his strong views. Indeed, it shows how influential Galileo was in Tuscany that the university had taken on the priest at all. It is even possible some arm-twisting had been required, because within weeks of Castelli's appointment he had been called to the office of the overseer of the university, Arturo d'Elci, and told in no uncertain terms that if he wished to keep his job he was not to teach a single word of anti-Aristotelian ideology.

Castelli complied and taught only what was prescribed, but at the same time he continued with his private researches, published, and kept up regular correspondence with Galileo. Such circumspection was imperative for an ambitious junior professor and Castelli knew he could leave most of the cause-fighting to his guide, Galileo.

The lunch at the Verga d'Oro was simply a diversion for the Medici, but both Cosimo and his mother liked to think of themselves as intellectuals. They enjoyed lively debate about the latest ideas in philosophy and were keen to demonstrate their erudition before the academics invited to their table. Because of this, Castelli was drawn into a discussion he might well have wished he could have avoided: a debate on the nature of Galileo's findings and what they meant for Aristotle.

The details come to us from a lengthy letter Castelli wrote to Galileo two days after the lunch:

> Thursday morning I was at lunch with our patrons and when asked by the Grand Duke about the university, I gave him a detailed account of everything, with which he showed himself much pleased. He asked me if I had a telescope. I said yes, and I began to tell about observation of the Medicean planets [Jupiter's moons] I had made just the night before. Madama Christina wanted to know their position, whereupon the talk turned to the necessity of their being real objects and not illusions of the telescope.

He then went on to recount how after lunch he was leaving the venue when he was met by a servant of Cosimo's, who told him that the Grand Duchess Christina wished to have a word with him. 'But before I tell you what followed,' Castelli reported, 'you must first know that while we were at table Doctor Boscaglia had had Madama's ear for a while, and while conceding as real all the things you have discovered in the sky, he said that only the motion of the Earth was somehow incredible, and could not take place especially because Holy Scripture was obviously contrary to this view.'[1]

The Grand Duchess was a formidable woman. Not only was she rich and powerful, she also had a great deal of control over the running of her son's dominion. She was, besides, a famously devout and traditional Catholic. But there was more to this woman than simple piety and power: she was also intellectually curious and had a genuine desire to understand God's creations. She was not content to be milk-fed.

Not surprisingly, by the time Christina had finished questioning her academics, she remained unconvinced. As Castelli boasted to Galileo:

> The Grand Duchess began to argue. After making suitable disclaimers, I commenced to play the theologian with such assurance and dignity that it would have done good to hear me. Don Antonio [another guest]

assisted me, giving me such heart that instead of being dismayed by the majesty of Their Highnesses I carried things off like a paladin. I quite won over the Grand Duke and his ArchDuchess [his wife], while Don Antonio came to my assistance with a very apt quotation from Scripture. Only Madama Christina remained against me, but from her manner I judged that she did this only to hear my replies. Professor Boscaglia never said a word.[2]

Castelli probably thought that his letter would simply impress and add colour to their relationship, but it actually alarmed Galileo greatly. He was very aware of Christina's character and he owed her a great deal, for it was she who had been most influential in encouraging the Medici to employ him, and she had always shown him respect and favour. The last thing he wanted, especially as his enemies began to circle, was for the dowager to be affronted by his discoveries.

Galileo decided he should act quickly to head off any problems that might arise from this incident. Preferring the pen to the spoken word, he began a letter to Castelli that would state clearly his position and that he knew would be circulated widely through the man's academic contacts, so serving to counter any negative rumours from the stately lunch that might already be leaking into the community of Tuscan intellectuals. This letter was later reworked (and published in 1615) as 'Letter to the Grand Duchess Christina of Tuscany' (see Appendix II).

As to the first general question of the Madama Christina [he wrote], it seems to me that it was most prudently propounded to you by her, and conceded and established by you, that Holy Scripture cannot err and the decrees therein contained are absolutely true and inviolable. I should only have added that, though Scripture cannot err, its expounders and interpreters are liable to err in many ways . . . when they would base themselves always on the literal meaning of the words. For in this wise not only many contradictions would be apparent, but even grave heresies and blasphemies, since then it would be necessary to give God hands and feet and eyes, and human and bodily emotions such as anger, regret, hatred and sometimes forgetfulness of things past, and ignorance of the future.

'Holy Scripture and Nature', he went on stridently, 'are both emanations from the divine word: the former dictated by the Holy Spirit, the latter the observant executrix of God's commands.'[3]

For anyone viewing the matter dispassionately, Galileo's statements were clear and refined, logical and coherent. But, given the climate of religious paranoia and also bearing in mind that Galileo had many enemies, this letter, which was indeed circulated widely, led him further into dangerous territory. Galileo may not have realised it, but by making these statements he was again intruding into the sacred domain of the theologians. He had already suffered the hostile reaction of orthodox clerics to his discoveries using the telescope. Such men loathed the idea that anyone, most especially a 'mere' mathematician and philosopher, should ever question their opinions or, worse still, the very foundations of their faith system.

It took a year for the thunderbolt of reaction to strike, and as he continued with his researches and parried the attacks of his detractors, Galileo may have been forgiven for thinking that his letter had kept the trapdoor closed, quelling opposition with reasoned argument before a row could break out.

He was also preoccupied with personal tragedy: in January 1614 his dear friend and assistant Filippo Salviati was killed in Spain. Salviati was possibly the most talented pupil Galileo ever had, possessing a powerful imagination and adventurous intellect. Galileo later said of him: 'He had a sublime intellect that knew no more exquisite pleasure than elevated speculations.'[4]

Salviati was also hot-headed, however, and in the autumn of 1613 he had become embroiled in a violent dispute with one of the Medici (Don Bernardetto de' Medici). Forced to back down, his pride had driven him away from Florence and he had embarked on a journey around Europe. Late in 1613, he had visited Sagredo in Venice and during the closing weeks of the year had debated with Galileo's supporters and opponents in Genoa before moving on to Spain. There he had been drawn into a bar brawl and been murdered.

Galileo was devastated, not least because of the terrible waste: Salviati had been only thirty-one and at the height of his powers when he had been cut down, over nothing.

By December 1614 Galileo had moved on from his theological musings and was engaged in a set of mechanics experiments, but others had not forgotten, nor had they forgiven. On the morning of the twenty-first he heard news that immediately made him realise that the past was catching up with him and his incendiary 'Letter to the Grand Duchess Christina of Tuscany' was about to light up the sky.

Some hundred and twenty years before these events, during the

1490s, in the time of Leonardo and Machiavelli, the Florentine government had been led briefly by a crazed evangelical Dominican monk called Girolamo Savonarola. He had not lasted long, executed by the very people he had temporarily quashed, but his influence had continued. The river of his madness had dwindled to a trickle in a group of overly pious clerics who had formed in Florence a tight-knit cabal set against any progressive thought or what they considered 'anti-orthodox speculation'.

On the fourth Sunday of Advent, which in 1614 fell on 21 December, a young Dominican named Tommaso Caccini, who lived and breathed the fire of Savonarola's teachings and had changed his name from Cosimo to Tommaso because he believed he was a new Thomas Aquinas, decided to openly attack from the pulpit a figure whom he considered a genuine antichrist: Galileo Galilei.

In truth, Caccini was another third-rater seeking preferment. He fancied himself as a Savonarola or an Aquinas, but he was nothing of the kind and was far too interested in personal advancement, placing his own betterment above the doctrines he preached. But he was certainly keen. Noticed as a young radical, he was encouraged by his superiors and began to deliver fire-and-brimstone sermons at one of the most important churches in Tuscany, Santa Maria Novella in Florence. On 21 December 1614, having been inspired to the task by his associates, who despised Galileo – most notably by the 'Pigeon League' of Colombe and their friends – he took to the pulpit with only one aim: to destroy the reputation of the scientist Galileo Galilei.

Caccini had two pieces of ammunition: he had a copy of the letter Galileo had sent to Castelli a year earlier, and he had an intimate (if warped) familiarity with the Bible. He also knew his audience and how to get the reaction he wanted. He wished to stir up what he considered righteous indignation in his audience, to incite resentment over the idea that a mathematician had the nerve to interfere in matters that were not for him to meddle with. He began the sermon by quoting Joshua 10:12–14:

> Then Joshua said . . . in the sight of Israel, Sun, stand thou still upon Gibeon; And thou, Moon, in the valley of Ajalon.
>
> And the sun stood still, and the moon stayed, until the people had avenged themselves upon their enemies . . . So the sun stood still in the midst of heaven, and hastened not to go down about a whole day.

And there was no day like that before it or after it, that the Lord hearkened unto the voice of man.

Filled as this is with references to the Sun, the Earth and the immutability of the universe, Caccini claimed that God's words were proof against any notions of anti-Aristotelian troublemakers. Deep in his soul Caccini probably knew that whatever one believed, these lines of Joshua had precious little to do with the questions raised by men like Galileo, but he was intelligent enough to know how to manipulate his audience. From Joshua, Caccini moved on to the New Testament and recited in Latin lines from the Acts of the Apostles including: 'Men of Galilee, why do you stand here looking at the sky?' He then attacked Galileo directly and quoted him as having taught that the universe could not be understood until we have learnt the language and become familiar with the characters in which its story is written. The very fact that Galileo believed the cosmic model could be described in mathematical language, and that without knowing this language it was impossible to comprehend the universe, struck the priest as pure blasphemy: 'Geometry is of the devil and mathematicians should be banished as the authors of all heresies,' Caccini stormed.[5]

You have to admire the man's chutzpah, his sense of drama and spectacle. It was a performance that would make any televangelist proud and it had precisely the desired effect. Galileo had been attacked from the pulpit before but never with such aggression or vitriol.

Caccini's onslaught proved devastating and it damaged both men. On the one hand, it led to Galileo's first direct clashes with the ecclesiastical authorities, who were becoming increasingly aware of just how damaging Copernican ideas could be for orthodoxy (though these ideas had not yet been deemed officially heretical). On the other, Caccini was lambasted by those who held the middle ground. The Archbishop of Bologna officially reprimanded him, clergymen from across Italy wrote to Galileo with words of support against the scurrilous attack and, most tellingly, perhaps, Caccini's own brother Matteo, who was then a junior assistant to Cardinal Barberini in Rome, wrote a letter to the priest in which he declared:

It may come to pass that you'll regret ever having learned to read. You could have done nothing more annoying to the high authorities here, up to the very highest . . . truly it is a great impertinence . . . Take it from me, reputation rules the world, and just as we were trying to open up a career for you through high protections. Try to think where you would like to go, because you are disliked there, and here even more . . . You have behaved like a dreadful fool.[6]

Galileo considered it beneath him to retaliate publicly, and the grand duke would not have wanted his servant to do such a thing; but in private he was incandescent, describing Caccini as a man 'of very great ignorance, no less a mind full of venom and devoid of charity'.[7]

Meanwhile, Prince Federico Cesi, who considered such men as Caccini to be little more than vermin, called the priest and his friends 'enemies of knowledge, perfidious madmen who will never keep quiet'.[8] But Caccini's was not the last of the attacks on Galileo and the priest's words resonated far beyond the houses and churches of the city in which they were proclaimed. Indeed, they reached as far as Rome and the ever-alert ears of the Holy Office.

It is possible that the Inquisition might simply have noted the incident in the file they had opened on Galileo and, for the moment at least, no more would have been said; but Caccini was not content with leaving the matter there: he was on a mission, and he had been stung by unexpected venom from those whom he had considered allies. He made a personal request for an interview with the Holy Office so that he could have his chance to lay before them the case against Galileo and the 'new science'.

It appears the Inquisition were not entirely convinced it was worth talking to Caccini, but eventually a request to add the matter to the agenda of a regular meeting of the Tribunal of the Inquisition was put before the pope and approved. On 20 March 1615, Caccini met with the Roman Inquisition.

In truth, his claims were pretty uninspiring. Caccini merely reiterated his belief that Galileo's theories and his support for Copernicus were in conflict with Scripture and Aristotle. He reminded the tribunal that the scientist was a good friend of the arch-heretic Paolo Sarpi, who was still freely scheming against His Holiness; and for good measure he added that Galileo was a member of the Academy of Lynxes, a close friend of Cesi and his associates, many of whom were known to have links with occultists and black magicians. He then went on to offer the evidence of two witnesses in Florence who had overheard Galileo making unorthodox comments about the Scriptures.

Rather reluctantly, it seems, the tribunal contacted the Florentine Inquisitor, who was instructed to interview the two witnesses and file a report to Rome. This was eventually done (some eight months later, in November that year) and the unremarkable testimonies of the two witnesses were added to Galileo's Vatican file.

The witnesses were Ferdinando Ximenes, a young Dominican priest, and a Florentine nobleman named Gianozzo Attavanti. Ximenes told the Inquisitor that he had overheard Galileo comment that he believed in a sensuous God, a being who laughed and cried; while the best Attavanti could offer was that he had overheard the scientist delivering a discourse to a gathering in which he supported the Copernican model and claimed it to be the true mechanism via which the universe operated. But all concerned knew that, unsavoury as Copernicanism may have been to the devout in 1615, it was not actually heretical. Attavanti then went on to mention Galileo's *Letters on the Sunspots*, and the tribunal sought out a copy for further investigation.

During these interviews both witnesses made it clear that in their opinion Galileo was nothing other than a good Catholic and they stressed the point that if he had been anything other than this, then he would not have remained in the employ of the grand duke, nor would he have been patronised by the Medici in the first place. Cosimo and his family would have had no wish to be associated with any form of scandal or inappropriate behaviour on the part of their servants, for any criticism of Galileo would be a criticism of them.

Through contacts in Rome, Galileo learned what had happened at the tribunal as well as in the interviews conducted by the Florentine Inquisitor. It did nothing to dampen his feelings towards Caccini, but most importantly it acted as a clear sign the furore over the priest's sermon had not simply dissipated, as he might have hoped it would. Indeed, this news made it clear his now very public views might lead him into real danger.

Galileo's friends rallied in support. Two such close allies worked in Rome: Monsignor Piero Dini, a supreme diplomat who had connections at the highest level in the Vatican, and Giovanni Ciampoli, one of Galileo's most dedicated disciples and a trusted friend; both did their best to counter the claims of Caccini and the Pigeon League within influential circles in Rome.

Galileo was now alert to danger and he began to suspect that the copy of his letter to Castelli on sunspots which had been passed on to the Inquisition in Rome for their investigation was in fact inaccurate and had been tampered with. To protect himself, through Dini he passed on to Cardinal Bellarmine a slightly amended copy of the original letter and asked for his opinion on the contents.

According to Dini, the Cardinal's response was unequivocal:

Cardinal Bellarmine, who as you know from experience has always admired your worth, told me only yesterday evening that with respect to those opinions he would like greater caution in not going beyond the arguments of Ptolemy, and, finally, in not exceeding the limitations of physics and mathematics. For theologians claim that the explanation of Scripture is their field, and if new things are brought in, even by an admirable mind, not everyone is dispassionate enough to take them as they are said.[9]

Such a response simply irritated Galileo. At the same time, he was justifiably nervous about other people representing his opinions. The inflammatory nature of the 'new science' was clear for all to see, and if he was to defend himself against his increasingly volatile and vocal opponents and the blinkered attitudes of men like Bellarmine he would have to act for himself. There was nothing for it but another trip to Rome.

It has been suggested by some historians that Galileo was actually a rather unsophisticated man thrown into a maelstrom in Rome, that he was easily duped and manipulated.[10] But I find this image very difficult to square with his background and his pronouncements in letters and in official documents. Instead, I see Galileo as very much a man of the world, a player. For almost two decades he had lived in Padua close to one of the great centres of world culture and he had mixed in exalted circles for even longer. His family had once been part of the Florentine elite and he was accepted and honoured by some of the most powerful people alive at the time, from Medici dowagers to future popes.

To claim that Galileo was overwhelmed by stronger personalities who moved in a more rarefied world is fanciful, but that is not to say Rome was in any way an easy place in which to operate – quite the contrary: Rome in 1615 was filled with scheming chancers, oily bureaucrats and self-interested nobility. In some ways, it was a dangerous, frightening place for anyone with unorthodox views, and only the foolish would have entered the whirlwind of ecclesiastic affairs in Rome without keeping a wary eye over their shoulder ready for the approaching dagger.

The charming Caccini had been determined to destroy Galileo and the scientist went to Rome with very clear intentions: he wanted to clarify the position of the Church over the matter of Copernicus and he wanted to expunge any hint of a shadow over his name, to repair the damage caused by the Pigeon League. Writing to Piero Dini in early May 1615, Galileo made his feelings clear:

> As far as I am concerned, any discussion of Sacred Scripture might have lain dormant for ever; no astronomer or scientist who remained within proper bounds has ever got into such things. Yet while I follow the teachings of a book [Copernicus's *On the Revolutions of the Heavenly Spheres*] accepted by the Church, there come out against me philosophers quite ignorant of such matters who tell me that they contain propositions contrary to the faith. So far as possible, I should like to show them that they are mistaken, but my mouth is shut and I am ordered not to go into the Scriptures. This amounts to saying that Copernicus's book, accepted by the Church, contains heresies and may be preached against by anyone who pleases, while it is forbidden for anyone to get into the controversy and show that it is not contrary to Scripture.[11]

In response, his friend suggested that he come to Rome, 'because you would be welcomed by everybody because I am told that many Jesuits secretly share your position although they remain silent'.[12]

By this time Galileo had already given the trip serious consideration and he wasted no time in organising it through his master, Cosimo. Once again the grand duke cleared the way for him. On 28 November his minister Vinta wrote to the new Tuscan ambassador Piero Guicciardini (who had replaced Giovanni Niccolini): 'Galileo Galilei requests leave to go to Rome to defend himself against the accusations of his rivals. He needs peace and quiet on account of his poor health.' In conclusion Guicciardini was told he must 'offer full board to Galileo, as well as one servant and a valet. You will also provide him with a small mule.'[13]

In 1611 Galileo had gone to Rome to demonstrate the wonders of the telescope and to promote his book *The Starry Messenger* as well as to see off his detractors. On the eve of this new trip he was preparing himself for a visit he knew would be far more confrontational. There were three areas in which the Church viewed him with deepening suspicion. First, in the face of rising criticism he had published a version of his letter to Castelli, *Letter to the Grand Duchess Christina of Tuscany*, in which he had had the temerity to argue with theologians and to place science above the interpretation of Scripture. Secondly, he had continued to write in Italian so as to reach as many ordinary people as possible; and thirdly, he had insisted upon supporting Copernicanism and espousing an anti-Aristotelian stance.

If he had been privy to the grand duke's correspondence, Galileo would have been made aware of the difficulties that faced him in Rome. In response to Vinta's instructions to accommodate Cosimo's Chief Mathematician and Philosopher, Guicciardini had been grudging and anxious: 'If Galileo stays here any length of time, he is certain to come out with some defence of his opinions. I do not know whether he has changed his opinions nor whether his temper has improved. But I know for certain that some Dominicans who are very influential with the Holy Office bear him no good will. This is not the place to come to dispute about the Moon, nor is it the time to defend novelties.'[14]

A clash of some sort was inevitable. For his part, Galileo was in a stubborn mood, his anger suppressed but ready to burst forth. He was aware of the volatility of the Church leaders, but he was also an evangelist when it came to intellectual freedom, and it was clear to him that science was being threatened with suffocation. 'I believe,' he would declare a few years later, 'that [philosophical] knowledge equals the Divine [theology] in objective certainty, for it is able to comprehend necessity, above which it is not possible to have greater certainty.'[15]

Bellarmine's opinions on the matter of Copernicus versus Aristotle were quite clear, and they carried enormous weight. His view was uncomplicated. He had considered modern astronomy at some length, but he could not take it seriously without proof. His faith was completely orthodox; there was no room in his mind for any form of contradictory thought system. If, by some chance science could offer irrefutable evidence that the Earth was not the centre of creation, then, he claimed, theologians might have to reconsider the interpretation of the Bible in an effort to understand where they had gone astray. But the problem for Bellarmine was simple: he considered the Catholic Church to be a divine institution, created by God's servants, and guided by the infallibility of the pope. If the Holy See was infallible, how could the Church's interpretation of divine Scripture be wrong?

The Church needed to stamp out any flame of innovation, and as Galileo returned to Rome to defend science, Bellarmine's line was this: Copernicanism could be discussed and written about; Galileo could proclaim what he liked, as long as he made it clear that his description was nothing more than a hypothesis. He might as well have said that anyone who taught that the Copernican model described the real world must be silenced and their writings banned.

Galileo's objection to this was understandable. We must remember that he was a new kind of philosopher, a 'proto-scientist', and he was forging a revolutionary way to perceive the universe. To him, the idea that a philosopher might accept being told he could think only in terms of hypotheses was quite unacceptable. He understood that what we would call 'scientific advancement' could not operate under these restrictions. He knew the power of the 'new science' he was initiating and that it took reasoning beyond hypothesis to theory, to proof, and to understanding. Without those steps beyond hypothesis there was no meaning to what Galileo was trying to achieve. Bellarmine was quite aware of this too, but he thought in very different way, and it was his aim to stifle science if it threatened religion. To him, Faith was everything; Truth was provided by God as 'insight', a product of Faith; in his universe there was really no need for Galileo's innovations.

It is likely Bellarmine did not relish the thought of Galileo returning to Rome. He had made his views clear to the devout, so there was nothing more to be said on the matter, and he would rather have been left to his duties than be drawn into theological debate. But although Galileo had begun to irritate Bellarmine and to ruffle the feathers of the clergy, he had not yet stepped over the line into anything approaching heresy. For the moment, the best Bellarmine could do was freeze out the man in an effort to send him back home as soon as possible.

Within a few weeks of arriving in Rome Galileo was beginning to get the message. Associates and acquaintances were suddenly not so keen to see him or for him to address philosophical meetings. Bellarmine had engineered this, but Galileo was also responsible for creating a frosty atmosphere. Never shy, and believing that the best way to get his ideas across was to shout them from the highest roof, he had quickly started to annoy people by using any opportunity to loudly proclaim his views.

During the first week or two of his stay in Rome new associates had been enthralled by Galileo's presence. Writing to his superior Cardinal Alessandro d'Este, a Roman priest, Monsignor Querengo, who had attended a social gathering, declared:

You would be delighted to hear Galileo argue, as he often does in the midst of some fifteen or twenty persons who attack him vigorously, now in one house, now in another. But he is so well buttressed that he laughs them off; and although the novelty of his opinion leaves people unpersuaded, yet he shows that most of the arguments, with which his opponents try to overthrow him, are spurious. Monday in particular, in the house of Federico Ghisilieri, he performed marvellous feats. What I liked most was that, before answering objections, he improved on them and added even better ones, so that, when he demolished them, his opponents looked all the more ridiculous.[16]

Others though had been less impressed from the off. The Florentine ambassador, Piero Guicciardini, who had never taken to Galileo, wrote a swingeing report to Cosimo:

He is passionately involved in this fight of his and he does not see or sense what it involves, with the result that he will be tripped up and will get himself into trouble, together with anyone who supports his views. For he is vehement and stubborn and very worked up in this matter and it is impossible, when he is around, to escape from his hands. And this business is not a joke, but may become of great consequence, and the man is here under our protection and responsibility.[17]

As doors began to close, Galileo lamented to a friend Curzio Picchena:

My business is far more difficult and takes much longer, owing to outward circumstances, than the nature of it would require, because I cannot speak openly with those persons with whom I have to negotiate, partly to avoid causing a prejudice to any of my friends, partly because they cannot communicate anything to me without running the risk of grave censure. And so I'm compelled, with much pain and caution, to seek out third persons who, without even knowing my purpose, may serve as mediators with the principals, so that I can set forth, incidentally as it were, and at their request, the particulars of my case. I have also to set down some points in writing, and to arrange that they should come privately into the hands of those I want to read them, for I find in many quarters that people are more ready to yield to dead writing than to live speech, for the former allows them to agree or dissent without blushing and, finally, to yield to the arguments since in such discussions we have no witnesses but ourselves. This is not done so easily when we have to change our mind in public.[18]

Some positive news came in February when, after another meeting of the Tribunal of the Inquisition, it was decided that Galileo was innocent of any charges brought by the imbecile Caccini. A few days later Caccini paid Galileo a visit at the embassy, ostensibly to apologise, but perhaps also to spy.

Galileo was secretly amused by the encounter and gave Caccini no leeway, neither accepting his apology nor forgiving his opponent. To Picchena he wrote: 'In the first half hour in which we were alone, he tried, very humbly, to excuse what he had done, saying he was ready to give me satisfaction. Then he tried to make me believe that he was not the engine behind his accusation. At last he tried to dissuade me from what I know for sure.'[19] Caccini's approach to Galileo was little more than flummery. He was never reconciled with the scientist and continued to do his best to cause trouble for decades to come.

The tribunal had cleared Galileo against any of Caccini's vague accusations, but the attacks of the priest had not been ignored entirely, and the more Bellarmine was exposed to Galileo's ideas the more suspicious he became. As a precaution, he created a committee to investigate the nature of Galileo's scientific claims. Initially this was little more than a fact-finding exercise, but it soon became much more.

Bellarmine's committee of eleven 'qualifiers', or experts, was gathered from several different groups within the Faith, including Dominicans and Jesuits, academic theologians and high-ranking members of the Holy Office. Their remit was to make a judgement on the heretical nature of the heliocentric model of the universe, but they were all trained in theology and none of them understood a word of science, philosophy or mathematics.

As one would expect from such poorly educated men, they came down heavily on Copernicanism. This was particularly ironic, since Copernicus's book explaining the heliocentric model in detail, *On the Revolutions of the Heavenly Spheres*, had been published seventy-three years earlier and had already been widely read. But since the book had first appeared, intellectuals had started to publish others in the vernacular in which they offered support for the heliocentric model and put it in a form that was understandable to more than just an elite few. Galileo was the prime mover in this new scene, but he was not the only Copernican. Giordano Bruno had spearheaded the charge two decades earlier and in 1600 had paid the ultimate price in the Campo di Fiori. More recently, a Catholic priest, Paul Anthony Foscarini, had written a treatise, *Opinion of the Pythagoreans and Copernicus Regarding the*

Motion of the Earth, in which he had made a genuinely pious attempt to reconcile the differences between Copernican science and Catholic doctrine.

Foscarini was lucky to escape Bruno's terrible fate, for the Holy Office considered his attempt to clarify things as totally misguided. Bellarmine took great exception to the book and reprimanded the priest personally. His reason? The same as ever: it was permissible to talk about Copernicanism as a hypothetical idea, an abstract construct, a mere mental exercise. It was anti-doctrinal to honour it with the status of a real model that could be mentioned on the same page as divine Scripture.

On 19 February the committee created by Bellarmine to bring ecclesiastical judgement to the matter of Copernicus reached two sweeping and very predictable conclusions. First: '[That] the Sun is the centre of the world and completely immovable of local motion is foolish and absurd in philosophy, and formally heretical, inasmuch as it expressly contradicts the doctrine of the Holy Scripture in many passages, both in their literal meaning and according to the interpretation of the Fathers and Doctors.' Second: 'The assertion that the Earth moves receives the same censure in philosophy and, as regards theological truth, is at least erroneous in Faith.'[20] These were damaging conclusions for Galileo; he was, after all, the best-known supporter of Copernicanism and defamer of Aristotle.

The pope and Bellarmine met to decide upon affirmative action. They wanted to draw a line under the entire business of Copernicus, the fashion for anti-Aristotelianism and the dispute over the nature of the universe, heliocentric or geocentric. Most specifically, they wanted to stop Galileo's insistence on popularising anti-doctrinal ideas. Between them it was decided they could follow one of three possible courses.

First, Bellarmine would admonish Galileo to abandon Copernicanism and agree to discuss it only hypothetically. Galileo would be expected to acquiesce. If he did, the matter would be dropped.

If Galileo did not submit to this, then a second course of action would be followed: Bellarmine would issue an injunction, signed by a notary and proper witnesses, commanding Galileo to abjure Copernicanism and not even to discuss it hypothetically. If this failed, then the cardinal would have no choice but to order the immediate imprisonment of the scientist.

This discussion was formalised in a document signed by Pope Paul

V, in which it is noted: 'His Holiness ordered the Most Illustrious Cardinal Bellarmine to call Galileo before himself and warn him to abandon these opinions; and if he should refuse to obey, the Father Commissary, in the presence of a notary and witnesses, is to issue him an injunction to abstain completely from teaching or defending this doctrine and opinion or from discussing it; and further, if he should not acquiesce, he is to be imprisoned.'[21]

On 26 February Galileo was invited to Bellarmine's house and the cardinal asked Galileo for his decision. Would he agree to acquiesce in official doctrine in the matter of the Copernican model?

It is from this point on that the exact events have become clouded by opinion and conjecture. We know that Bellarmine and Galileo were not alone at this meeting, that they had been joined by the Dominican Commissary of the Inquisition Michelangelo Seghizzi, members of his staff and two further unnamed witnesses; but beyond that it is quite unclear who said what and who guided proceedings.

What is certain is that Galileo readily agreed to Bellarmine's demands and promised that he would not teach or write about Copernicanism as anything more than a hypothesis. It seems that Bellarmine was content to take his word for it, but then the Commissary Seghizzi stepped in to add further force to the warning by insisting that Galileo should not 'hold, teach, or defend Copernicanism in any way whatsoever'.[22] Seghizzi then called for Galileo to sign an official document reiterating this command.

This is odd, because Bellarmine and the pope had agreed in a private session that this course of action would only be necessary if Galileo had refused the original order. Furthermore, the document proffered by Seghizzi was never signed and the official record of the meeting at Bellarmine's house describing Seghizzi's intervention also remained unsigned by either Bellarmine or Galileo.

To make things even more confusing, when Seghizzi's document was brought from the files some seventeen years later at the time when Galileo was put on trial before the Inquisition, it was found to have been filed in the wrong place. Furthermore, it had been written on the reverse side of another, earlier document. Both of these were uncharacteristic flaws for the Inquisition, who were famed for being fanatically thorough in their record-keeping.

What actually happened that day in Bellarmine's house remains a subject for debate. Some historians have suggested that the document mentioned here was actually a fake, that it was added to the Inquisition files some time after the event and was planted there by Galileo's enemies.

Today the consensus of opinion supports the view that the document is in fact genuine and that it was indeed written at the time of the encounter. If this is true, we might reasonably assume that Cardinal Bellarmine did not sign the document for two reasons. First, he did not agree with the action of Seghizzi, because his stance on the matter of Copernicus was that it could be discussed openly but only as a hypothesis. Forcing Galileo not to mention the subject at all was, he believed, unreasonable and unnecessary. The second motivation for Bellarmine not to sign might be that he was simply very put out by Seghizzi's interference.

Although Seghizzi was a powerful member of the inner circle at the Vatican, Bellarmine was, strictly speaking, his superior and he was certainly closer to the pontiff. Moreover, Bellarmine had decided upon the action to take that day after having discussed it with the pope. So he had a clear mandate, which did not involve Seghizzi.

We should also recall that Seghizzi was a Dominican. Two months earlier, the Florentine ambassador Piero Guicciardini had made the point that he knew *for certain that some Dominicans who [were] very influential with the Holy Office [bore] him [Galileo] no good will*. One of the things any good diplomat relies on, especially in a viper's nest like Rome circa 1616, is efficient intelligence. Piero Guicciardini may have known a great deal more about the scientist's enemies than Galileo did himself.

The details of the meeting on 26 February at the home of Cardinal Robert Bellarmine were to play a pivotal role in Galileo's later life, but for the moment they were of little real consequence. He had been given no choice but to acquiesce over his scientific views and it had left him brimming over with rage.

His fury stemmed from what he viewed as interference by the Church, who wanted to censor science. He had only agreed verbally never to write about, teach or hold forth in any way on Copernicanism without making it clear he was discussing the matter hypothetically, but even so he loathed and resented this restriction. Galileo felt suffocated by the demands of those he considered lesser men. 'Of all the hatreds,' he declared, 'none is greater than that of ignorance against knowledge.'[23]

The leaders of the Church had finally come off the fence and had brought down with them the heavy hand of papal censorship. Soon it became clear that this was merely the beginning – that the pope and his henchmen were tired of letting anti-doctrinal science go uncensored.

Eight days after Galileo was officially muzzled, *De Revolutionibus Orbium Coelestium* was taken out of circulation until it was amended to comply with official Church doctrine. The statement from the Vatican's Congregation of the Index, the body responsible for this censorship reads:

> It has come to the knowledge of the Congregation that the Pythagorean doctrine of the motion of the Earth and the immobility of the Sun, which is false and altogether opposed to Holy Scripture is also taught by Nicolaus Copernicus in his *De Revolutionibus Orbium Coelestium*, and Diego de Zuniga in his *Commentary on Job*, and is now being spread abroad and accepted by many. This can be seen from a certain letter of a Carmelite Father entitled *Letter of Father Paolo Foscarini, Carmelite, on the Opinion of the Pythagorean and of Copernicus Regarding the Motion of the Earth, and the Stability of the Sun, and on the New Pythagorean System of the World*, printed in Naples by Lazzaro Scorrigo, 1615. In this letter the said Father tries to show that the aforesaid doctrine of the immobility of the Sun in the centre of the world and of the Earth's motion is true and not opposed to Holy Scripture. Therefore in order that this opinion may not insinuate itself any further to the prejudice of Catholic truth, it has been decided that the said Nicolaus Copernicus's *De Revolutionibus Orbium Coelestium*, and Diego de Zuniga, *Commentary on Job*, be suspended until corrected. The book of the Carmelite Father, Paolo Antonio Foscarini, is altogether prohibited and condemned, and all works in which the same is taught are likewise prohibited, and the present Decree prohibits, condemns, and suspends them all respectively.*

This may have been a very straightforward and aggressive move on the part of the Holy See, but just as these strictures were being imposed, Galileo was receiving mixed signals. He had tarried in Rome, determined to salvage something from the wreckage created by his opponents; but by staying there he had begun to annoy the Church authorities.

---

* It is interesting to note that a month after this declaration, the printer of Foscarini's book, Lazzaro Scorrigio, was arrested, and in June 1616 Father Foscarini himself died suddenly aged just 36.

Bellarmine had perhaps considered the arguments between the scientist and the Church as being over on 26 February, and that the proclamation of the Congregation of the Index the following week had settled the matter. Doubtless the pope concurred. But instead of shunning Galileo, both Bellarmine and Paul now became more open towards him. He was invited to an audience with the pope, and the two men walked through the gardens of the papal office. Writing to his friend Curzio Picchena, Galileo boasted that he had come straight out and told His Holiness of his grievances against his persecutors and that the pope had told him

> he was well aware of my uprightness and sincerity and, when I showed signs of being still somewhat anxious about the future because of the fear of being pursued with implacable hate by my enemies, he cheered me up and said that I could put all care away because I was held in such esteem by himself and the whole Congregation, that they would not lightly lend their ears to calumnious reports, and that I could feel safe as long as he was alive. Before I left, he assured me several times that he bore me the greatest goodwill and was ready to show his affection and favour towards me at all times.[24]

Bellarmine, too, was being more accommodating. Galileo had heard through the grapevine that rumours were circulating that the previous December he had been summoned to Rome and had not travelled there of his own volition. These rumours had been started by his enemies, who were still determined to ruin his image and erode his standing; and such was the volatile atmosphere in the Vatican over Galileo and the new science that such rumours might well have succeeded in damaging the man's reputation. This had only been prevented because Galileo was shrewd enough to have informed Bellarmine of these reports as soon as he had heard them.

Cardinal Bellarmine had ears and eyes everywhere in Rome and so he had almost certainly heard the rumours for himself. He took the extraordinary step of writing an official exoneration, the contents of which were distributed widely. Bellarmine's statement announced:

> We, Robert Cardinal Bellarmine, having heard that it is calumniously reported that Signor Galileo Galilei has in our hand abjured and has also been punished with salutary penance, and being requested to state

the truth as to this, declare that said Galileo has not abjured, either in our hand, or the hand of any other person here in Rome, or anywhere else, so far as we know, any opinion or doctrine held by him. Neither has any salutary penance been imposed on him; but that only the declaration made by the Holy Father and published by the Sacred Congregation of the Index was notified to him, which says that the doctrine attributed to Copernicus, that the Earth moves around the Sun and the Sun is stationary in the centre of the world and does not move from east to west, is contrary to Holy Scriptures, and therefore cannot be defended or held. In witness whereof we have written and subscribed the present document with our own hand this twenty-sixth day of March 1616.[25]

It was as though the upper echelons of the Holy Office were playing a game of good priest, bad priest, and it did nothing to ease Galileo's confusion. Six months after arriving in Rome he was still not content to leave and still believed he had work to do there. But in this he was quite misguided. There was nothing more for him to do in the city and his continued presence was merely causing irritation. In late May, Ambassador Guicciardini wrote to Cosimo with this news: 'Galileo seems disposed to emulate the monks in obstinacy and to contend with personages who cannot be attacked without ruining oneself. You should soon hear at Florence that he has madly tumbled into some abyss or other.'[26]

Cosimo valued both Guicciardini and Galileo, but he also thought that his Chief Mathematician and Philosopher had been given all the time he needed to sort out his private conflicts. With well-practised diplomacy he suggested that Galileo should return to Florence, where his expertise and company were sorely missed.

Galileo got the message and started on the road home. He believed quite rightly that his life had been diminished because of his clash with the Church; but, perhaps more importantly, he was growing convinced that the interference of the cardinals was going to slow the advance of the 'new science', if not damage it severely. At the same time, he could take some small comfort from the fact that both Bellarmine and Pope Paul V appeared to respect him enough to leave him to his researches. Copernicus had been officially censored; he, Galileo, had agreed to treat Copernicanism purely as a hypothesis and nothing more, but nothing had been put in writing to that effect; there was no official, signed order to obey. Bellarmine's stern words, he concluded, were simply cautionary. He would have to tread carefully – that much was certain; but he could not and would not allow any misguided doctrine to sway him from his path.

II

The Calm before the Storm

It has often been claimed that Galileo was tried twice. But the implication of this is that the scientist's appearance before Bellarmine at the cardinal's house was a trial. It was, though, no such thing. The real trial of Galileo took place during 1633 and it was of a very different order from the wrist-slapping of 26 February 1616.

Between these two milestones Galileo's life changed in many profound ways. Some of the leading characters in his life, both supporters and detractors, disappeared from the stage, and the man at the heart of our story, Galileo himself, suffered both agonies and times of euphoria and triumph. It was also the period when he produced his greatest works of science and laid some of the foundations for what Newton and others were to develop in later centuries. As well as this, the sixteen years between papal censure and inquisitional thunderbolt saw Galileo stray further and further from orthodoxy. This was a time during which he wilfully challenged the Church and offered up theories and ideas that would strike at the very core of Catholic dogma, setting the scene for the great showdown that was to strip him of his freedom.

Leaving Rome on 4 June 1616, Galileo must have been in a confused state of mind. As the carriage bearing him north swayed with the road, his thoughts must have been tossed around like so much driftwood. How was he to proceed? He valued his life and had no wish to follow in Giordano Bruno's shoes, but at the same time he also treasured the freedom of science.

His confusion is evident in the fact that for the next two years he did little more than tread water. In 1616 he moved residence, renting a large country home called Bellosguardo nestled high up in the hills to the west of Florence. It offered him peace and seclusion and it was also close to the convent where his daughters now lived. At Bellosguardo he conducted experiments, devised gadgets to aid marine navigation and worked on the mechanics of the Jovian system. This last was one of the few areas of astronomical research considered innocuous by the Church.

Galileo might have continued with these efforts for some years, but in October and November 1618 three comets appeared in the sky in quick succession. This series of events drew him back into the fray. As always, the appearance of comets provoked wide-ranging and intense speculation, and because Galileo was the most famous astronomer in the world, his opinion on their nature was highly sought after.

At first, he remained reticent. In fact, he was ill again and unwilling to be drawn into a debate on what he knew might, in the light of recent events in Rome, provoke trouble. Disappointing his friends and opponents alike, he stayed quiet. But then, early in 1619, he was drawn out of his silence by a publication entitled *On the Three Comets of the Year MDCXVIII. An Astronomical Disputation Presented Publicly in the Collegio Romano of the Society of Jesus by one of the Fathers of that Same Society.* Despite the sheepish title, the author became known very quickly: the discourse had been written by a powerful and highly regarded figure in the worlds of both astronomy and religion, Orazio Grassi, a devout Jesuit and Professor of Mathematics at the Collegio Romano – the man who had succeeded Christopher Clavius.

Grassi proposed that the comets originated somewhere between the Earth and the Moon. This was a safe, Aristotelian explanation because it meant that they did not come from the region of the 'perfect heavenly sphere' in which, according to received wisdom, lay the immovable and perfect stars. Galileo had long held the view that comets were an Earthly phenomenon, a purely atmospheric effect.

Over this matter Galileo and Grassi were both wrong. Grassi's ideas were closer to the truth, but he was chiefly concerned with using his observations to disprove Copernicus. His reasoning was based on the fact that the comet moved so quickly it must have a very large orbit. Grassi's calculations also showed that the orbit of the comet would be an extremely elongated ellipse rather than a perfect circle. Supporters of Copernicus supposed that the paths of all planets were circular (until Kepler showed this to be untrue). Galileo learned of Grassi's efforts from a friend in Rome, Giovanni Battista Rinuccini, who wrote to him with the news: 'The Jesuits . . . discuss the comet in a public lecture now in press, and they firmly believe that it is in the heavens. Some outside the Jesuit Order say that this is the greatest argument against Copernicus's system and that it knocks it down altogether.'[1]

The true nature of comets has only gradually been revealed over the centuries since the time of Galileo and Grassi. Today astronomers believe most comets originate in a region far beyond the edge of the solar system called the Oort Cloud. However, the new battle into which Galileo was drawn was not much to do with pure scientific rivalry. Galileo hated the Jesuits and blamed them for the muzzling of science and what he considered the unreasonable behaviour of the Church towards original thought. Christopher Clavius he had viewed as a man completely out of step with modern thinking and long past his prime. Grassi, though, was dangerous. He was very clever, politically astute, determined and pious.

The publication of Grassi's book drew Galileo from introspection and led to an exchange that was often childish and garnered with insult; each man hid behind a diaphanous pseudonym. 'With poorly coloured and badly designed pictures, they have aspired to be artists,' Galileo wrote of Grassi and his associates, 'though they could not compose in skill even the most mediocre pictures.'[2] Elsewhere he described Grassi's idea as 'like that of a lacerated and bruised snake, which has no vitality left except at the tip of its tail, but which nevertheless continues to wriggle, pretending that it is still healthy and vigorous'.[3]

Grassi parried with the biting comment: 'Even with the telescope the lynx-eyed *astrologer* cannot look into the inner thoughts of the mind.'[4]

On each side the associates of the two men lined up in a face-off. The Jesuits backed their academic figurehead, and the Lyncean Academy acted as Galileo's defenders. But in the end, the dispute over the nature of comets fizzled out. Neither Galileo nor Grassi could prove their arguments and it would be centuries before astronomers understood the origin and structure of this celestial phenomenon. However, the bitterness behind the dispute lingered; and for Galileo it was a particularly bruising clash. He had many supporters but no real political influence, whereas Grassi was a man with important connections. Driven by envy and resentment, he could and would do much to harm his rival.

As Galileo and Grassi fought over theories, the Thirty Years War began, and it soon became a backdrop to the deterioration in Galileo's relationship with the Church. It was a war in which Italy was not directly involved, but at its core it was a dispute between Catholic and

Protestant states and, although Vatican forces took no part in the fighting, the war influenced papal policy enormously. In Rome it became a constant distraction and was perceived as a broadening of the schism created by Luther.

At Bellosguardo, Galileo was a long way from any real battlefield, but he was actually in the thick of ideological disputes. He never lost sight of the fact that he was first and foremost a natural philosopher, and as the war escalated he continued to experiment and to write. He was at the height of his powers and, in spite of the muzzle, he had much to say and do.

As one might expect, papal censure had the effect of dampening Galileo's interest in astronomy; but at the same time it allowed his attention to be drawn to other areas of science. In particular, from 1616 onwards he became very interested in atomic theory and the properties of matter (disciplines that had not yet been subjected to papal scrutiny). The book that grew out of this interest, arguably one of his greatest achievements, *The Assayer* (*Il Saggiatore*), dedicated to the new pope Urban VIII, offered the clearest and most carefully reasoned arguments about the microcosm since Lucretius's *De Rerum Natura*, written some sixteen hundred years earlier. But, by turning from a consideration of the cosmos to avoid trouble with Rome and writing *The Assayer*, Galileo actually produced what was to become his most controversial piece of work.

I will consider the contents of *The Assayer* in more detail in the next chapter, because, although it was published in 1623, when it was heralded as a remarkable and innovative piece of natural philosophy, its true importance was only realised a decade later when it became the centrepiece of Galileo's disastrous clash with Urban VIII and his intransigent cardinals.

With this book Galileo was principally concerned with the very basics of physics and it offered a cogent and forceful alternative to Aristotle's notion of the fundamental structure of matter. In it he espoused experiment and mathematical verification over pure thought more intensely than in anything he had written up to this time and he delved deep into the fundamental principles of nature. In one gloriously combative passage, Galileo declared:

> I cannot but be astonished that Sarsi [Grassi's pseudonym in the exchange with Galileo] should persist in trying to prove by means of witnesses something that I may see for myself at any time by means of

experiment. Witnesses are examined in doubtful matters which are past and transient, not in those which are actual and present. A judge must seek by means of witnesses to determine whether Pietro injured Giovanni last night, but not whether Giovanni was injured, since the judge can see for himself. But even in conclusions which can be known only by reasoning, I say that the testimony of many has little more value than that of a few, since the number of people who reason well in complicated matters is much smaller than that of those who reason badly. If reasoning were like hauling I should agree that several reasoners would be worth more than one, just as several horses can haul more sacks of grain than one can. But reasoning is like racing and not like hauling, and a single barbary steed can outrun a hundred dray horses.[5]

The incubation of this most remarkable work was not easy and it coincided with many personal traumas. During the two years between conception and publication of *The Assayer*, six people Galileo knew well died. The mother of his three children, Marina Gamba, died in February 1619. The following year, on 28 February, Galileo's patron, the grand duke, only thirty years old, succumbed to an illness that had been with him for the past six years. His kingdom was left in the hands of his wife the archduchess and his mother the grand duchess until his ten-year-old son, Ferdinand II, could succeed to the title eight years later.

The loss of the grand duke was painful for Galileo. It did not affect his relationship with the Medici family (because he had strong links with Christina and other prominent Medici), but Cosimo had been a friend as well as a patient and trusting patron. Galileo mourned the young leader, but it would not be until a decade after Cosimo's death that Galileo would feel the duke's absence most profoundly.

But for Galileo, the most painful loss this dark season was the passing of his old friend, the eccentric Gianfrancesco Sagredo, who died from influenza less than a week after Cosimo. Sagredo and Galileo had been inseparable during the scientist's first few years in Padua. In 1609 the former had taken an important official post in the Middle East and had lived in Syria for some years before returning to Padua just as Galileo was leaving. During the years since then, their relationship had remained as warm as ever; they met rarely but had often exchanged affectionate letters and gifts. Sagredo was a man whose beliefs and ideas had chimed well with Galileo's own, and they had shared many characteristics – including an irreverent sense of humour and a healthy lack of respect for orthodoxy.

Naturally, Sagredo sided with Galileo in his dispute with the Jesuits, and from the relative safety of the Most Serene Republic he expressed a distaste for the bullying of the clergy. He had never given up trying to persuade Galileo to return to Venice and he considered it the scientist's natural home. Soon after Galileo had returned to Florence after his brush with the Church in 1616 Sagredo sent him the gift of an Indian bird with a note that read:

It does not sing and has another virtue of living simply on millet and water, without a care. When it finds itself, as often happens, without any food, it makes considerable noise day or night, with considerable insolence. If you will take it, I would be free of requests of many who keep asking for it. Frankly I would not be too upset if I see him dead due to lack of care. Indeed, I will be obliged to you if you free me of this bird, in the same way I pray God to free you from these awful beasts who torment you. I also pray that by your acceptance, I should be assured that their diabolic nature would not obscure the thoughts of your friend who loves you.[6]

Galileo appreciated the gesture, soothed his dear friend with platitudes, but clearly harboured no thoughts of ever returning to Padua or Venice.

In September 1620, six months after Sagredo's premature passing, Galileo's 82-year-old mother, Madonna Giulia, died after a long period of physical and mental illness. It probably came as a relief to Galileo, who had suffered his mother for many long years. A year earlier his ever-thoughtful brother Michelangelo had written to him from Germany, where he now lived far from domestic responsibilities. 'I hear with no great surprise that our mother is being so dreadful,' he chirped. 'But then she is much aged, and soon there will be an end to all this quarrelling.'[7]

These four deaths affected Galileo emotionally, each in its own way and to varying degrees; but during this time two others close to him also died, and their passing had a significant impact on his future and the course his career was to take in subsequent years.

The first of these, that of Pope Paul V, came suddenly in January 1621. During a celebration to mark a Catholic victory in one of the most important battles of the Thirty Years War, the Battle of White Hill, the

70-year-old pontiff drank far too much wine and consumed too much rich food. He suffered a stroke and fell face first on to the dining table.

Galileo probably greeted the news with some relief. He had successfully played up to the pope (how could he have done otherwise?), but, like almost everyone in the Vatican, he had known the pontiff to be a megalomaniac who needed to be handled with extreme care. No one could guess accurately who would succeed him to the papacy, but Galileo and many others held the view that whoever it was they could not do a worse job than Paul.

The man who did succeed Paul V, Gregory XV, was on the papal throne for little more than two years, but he proved harmless enough, a frail old man who in his time changed nothing and offended few. With his untimely death in 1623 the way was open for Urban VIII; and, as we shall see, Urban (who was once known as Cardinal Maffeo Barberini), friend and admirer of Galileo, played a lead role in the story of the scientist's trial before the Inquisition in 1633, a decade after he took the tiara.

News of the death of Robert Bellarmine reached Galileo just as he was putting the finishing touches to *The Assayer* a few days after the cardinal passed away on 17 September 1621. The 78-year-old churchman had been out of circulation for some time, and Paul V's most senior cleric throughout his fifteen-year papacy had had little to do with Pope Gregory. Soon after Galileo had left Rome, in 1616, Bellarmine had begun to retreat from his high-profile position. Having grown too old to effectively hammer heretics, he spent the final years of his life in contemplation and writing on obscure theological subjects.

The deaths of Bellarmine and Pope Paul V gave Galileo renewed hope just when he was feeling most ragged. *The Assayer* was a source of deep satisfaction to him, but he was unhappy and frequently ill. He missed his friends: Sagredo was dead, and Paolo Sarpi, now 69 years old and ailing, was unable to travel far from Venice. Indeed, Galileo felt more lonely than he had ever felt.

To compound his misery, much of Europe was experiencing a succession of winters more extreme than anyone could remember. When the temperature dropped, Galileo's rheumatism suddenly became far worse and he found he could not conduct experiments; even writing was an agony. On top of this, war was spreading across Europe and plague struck with seemingly random vigour during the hot summers.

Amidst all this bleakness there remained one bright ray of light.

After the death of his mother and his closest friends, Galileo's relationship with his eldest daughter Virginia began to blossom. Virginia had adopted the name Maria Celeste when she took her vows, in October 1616, and she survived the harsh regime of life in the Convent of St Matthew by giving herself totally to her faith. With each passing year the worldly scientist and his daughter, the pious nun, drew closer.

Galileo finished *The Assayer* in the spring of 1623 and it was received enthusiastically by the Lynceans. For them it was nothing short of a manifesto for the 'new science' and a powerful weapon with which to pummel Jesuit arguments. The academy paid for the printing and publication of the book and, like its predecessors, it was received warmly by most philosophers and other intellectuals across Europe. Written in the vernacular, it enlightened where the Church wished to maintain darkness and confusion; and, as a consequence, it generated expected hostility.

With publication of his latest book Galileo felt again the urge to back up his words with a visit to Rome, where he could once more inspire, influence and excite. Writing to Cesi, he declared:

> I have great need of Your Excellency's advice (in whom more than anyone I trust) about carrying out my desire, or perhaps my duty, to come to kiss the feet of His Holiness. But I would like to do it at the right moment and I shall wait until you tell me so. I am turning over in my mind things of some importance for the learned world, and if they are not carried out in this marvellous combination of circumstances, there can be no hope in the future, at least as far as I can see, of ever finding such an opportunity.[8]

Cesi was immediately taken with the idea, and on 21 October he wrote to his friend urging him to set his plans in motion. 'Your coming here is necessary and will give much pleasure to His Holiness,' he responded. 'When he asked me when you were coming, I answered that an hour delay seemed to you like a thousand years. I added what I could about your devotion to him, and told him that you would soon bring him your book. He admires you, and is more than ever fond of you.'[9]

But even if to Galileo *an hour delay seemed like a thousand years*, because of illness and court commitments, plans for the trip met with delay upon delay. It was not until 22 April the following year that

Galileo finally entered Rome and took up residence at the home of his friend, a powerful and very wealthy lawyer, Mario Guiducci, who had just been elected to the prestigious position of consul to the Academy of Florence, one of the most highly regarded organisations of intellectual Italy.

Galileo immediately sensed that he had entered a city that was very different from the one he had left eight years earlier. He and many of his friends held high hopes for the new pope. He was a Florentine, an intellectual and a man who in his younger days had expressed a genuine interest in philosophy and the 'new science'. He was a great admirer of Galileo's work and had read everything the scientist had written. Furthermore, Galileo could trace back their friendship at least a dozen years.

Urban showed a favourable attitude towards Galileo during his stay in Rome and they had half a dozen meetings during the six-week visit. Some of these apparently lasted for an hour or more. It is also clear the two men spent some time discussing the ruling of the previous pope in 1616 and Paul's insistence that Galileo should not teach or write about the Copernican model. It peeved Urban that only in Italy had this rule been adhered to, not because he believed it should hold abroad but because he could see that it would cause Italian learning to slip behind. The idea that Protestant thinkers and scientists might take the reins of intellectual development away from his country, a place long considered the epicentre of the Renaissance, upset him.

Yet Urban was also astute, and he did not have the political will to alter past judgements. He knew that in the real world of Church politics, intellectual concerns cut little ice. Urban knew very well that Church doctrine was not a thing to be messed with lightly, and over such matters he listened to his advisers. There could be no overturning of earlier declarations, but, at the same time, Urban did not dissuade Galileo from thinking some more about Copernicus.

Thanks to his talks with Urban, Galileo left Rome in June a great deal wiser than when he had arrived. He had also acquired new friends and gained valuable influence. The showman in him had revelled in startling afresh the rich and powerful with the latest device that had come his way, an early model of the microscope, with which he studied insects, human hair and leaves. This new invention had drawn gasps of delight from the noblemen, cardinals and amateur philosophers who had been invited to peer into the eyepiece.

Of the microscope, Galileo had declared to his friend Prince Cesi:

I have observed many tiny animals with great admiration, among which the flea is quite horrible, the mosquito and the moth very beautiful, and I have seen with great pleasure how flies and other little animals can walk attached to mirrors upside down. You will have the opportunity of observing a large number of such particulars, and I shall be grateful if you would let me know about the more curious. In short, the greatness of nature, and the subtle and unspeakable care with which she works is a source of unending contemplation.[10]

He had also gained materially from the visit; acquiring an annual grant from the pope for his son Vincenzo, a gold medal, a painting and money, as well as an assurance that Urban's representative in Florence would see to it that conditions at his daughter's convent would be reviewed.

Most importantly, Galileo returned to Florence with a degree of clarity over Copernicus. The pope considered the Copernican theory in a similar way to many clerics: it was an interesting notion that might lead to some practical benefits, but it was only a hypothesis, a mind-game, a thought-experiment – nothing more. However, unlike Bellarmine and Pope Paul, this new pope appeared less keen to suppress the opinions of Copernicus's supporters. Urban could claim with honesty that he had never felt comfortable with the enthusiasm with which the Inquisition had muzzled science. Back in 1616, when the Congregation of the Index had withdrawn Copernicus's great book from circulation, he had objected to the attempts of his colleagues to declare *De Revolutionibus Orbium Coelestium* 'formally heretical'. It was he who at the time had pushed for and won a decision to commute the charge officially to 'false and contrary to Holy Scripture'. These were, of course, mere words, but to the theologians of Rome the phrasing used by the Congregation was a matter of great importance.

As Galileo left Rome, Cesi reported: 'His Holiness said that over the question of Copernicus the Holy Church had not condemned, nor would condemn, his opinion as heretical, but only as rash. So long as it is not demonstrated as true, it need not be feared.'[11] And on a more personal note, the pope had his secretary write a letter to be handed to the Grand Duke of Tuscany in which the pontiff announced: 'We have observed in him [Galileo] not only the literary distinction, but also the love of religion worthy of papal favour. We listened with pleasure to his learned demonstrations which add fresh renown to Florentine eloquence. His fame will shine on earth so long as Jupiter and his satellites shine in heaven.'[12]

Galileo took these comments to heart and, as he travelled north enjoying the warmth of the June sun and feeling rejuvenated and more inspired than he had felt in many years, the idea for a new book was beginning to take shape in his mind. This was to become the *Dialogue Concerning the Two Chief World Systems*, and it took Galileo over five years to complete.

The gestation of this new treatise was by no means an easy one. Galileo began the book in the autumn of 1624, but his concentration was broken constantly by a succession of illnesses, by family upheavals and by the devastation wrought by plague. For a period of over a year he stopped working on the book altogether and only picked up the threads again in the summer of 1626. By this point, many of his close friends had begun to assume the book would never be finished.

Galileo's illnesses came in different forms and they greatly reduced his productivity. When they struck most fiercely he found he could get little done. The best he could manage during the winter months was to prop himself up in a comfortable chair close to a roaring fire and dictate sections of his new work to an amanuensis.

If his poor health was not enough to slow him down, he was constantly put upon by his extended family. His brother Michelangelo had been a thorn in Galileo's side ever since they were young. He had married, sired children and gone from one poorly paid job to another as a court musician, all the time relying on his famous and wealthy sibling to help him out. This became especially exaggerated when the Thirty Years War (which had initially been contained within the German states) began to spread, in 1627, eventually drawing in Poland, England, Denmark, Holland and Spain. Soon Italy became something of a safe haven for Catholics.

In the summer of 1627, as Galileo was beginning the final third of his book, Michelangelo, who had been living with his family in Munich, wrote to him with less of a proposal than a declaration of intent. In his usual brash way he announced that he needed to bring his family to Florence because of the threat of the fighting and that Galileo's home would be perfect for them. 'This arrangement would be good for both of us,' he told his brother:

Your house will be well and faithfully governed, and I should be partly lightened of an expense which I do not know how to meet; for Chiara would take some of the children with her, who would be an amusement for you and a comfort to her. I do not suppose that you would feel the expense of one or two mouths more. At any rate, they will not cost you more than those you have about you now, who are not so near akin, and probably not so much in need of help as I am.[13]

Galileo could do little but acquiesce, and so, in July, the 63-year-old found his quiet life of contemplation in his home in the hills above Florence completely devastated by the arrival of the 'one or two mouths more' – Michelangelo, his wife Anna Chiara, their nanny and the couple's seven children, who ranged in age from the 9-month-old Maria to the 20-year-old Vincenzo. It was an arrangement that could not last long. By the end of the year Galileo had fled his own house to live with a friend in the city and only returned to Bellosguardo the following summer, when Michelangelo and his family had set off north after Catholic victories during the past year had made their old home safe once more.

After regaining the peace and quiet of Bellosguardo it took Galileo another year to complete the *Dialogue*, and by the autumn of 1629 it was ready for the publisher. Galileo had always placed great emphasis on literary style. Not for him the dry, impenetrable diatribe. He wanted people not just to read his words but to enjoy his storytelling. He wanted to influence as wide a readership as he possibly could. It was this wish that led him to write in Italian and to make his ideas as accessible as possible. With the *Dialogue* he again used the form of expression he had first employed with his earliest writings in Pisa, creating characters who would each take a point of view and argue over the topics encompassed in the book.

The *Dialogue* is set in Venice at the home of Galileo's old friend Sagredo, and the action takes place over the course of four days during which a collection of tenets of the new science are pitched against their Aristotelian counterparts and shown to be far sturdier and more forward-looking. There are three central characters in the book. Two of Galileo's dearest friends return from the grave: Gianfranceso Sagredo, who plays host and interested layperson, already half-convinced that Copernicus was right; and Filippo Salviati, who takes on the role of the confirmed Copernican and voice for Galileo's opinions.

The cast is completed by Simplicio, a naïve but likeable man who is really the fall guy whom Sagredo and Salviati tease. Based as it is on the Italian word for 'simpleton', Galileo's choice of the name was arch in the extreme; and although this member of the troupe was liked by most readers, it was this character and the words Galileo put into his mouth that was soon to cause the writer enormous trouble.

Galileo explained his intentions with these characters in the opening section of the book:

> Many years ago I was often to be found in the marvellous city of Venice, in discussions with Signore Giovanni Francesco Sagredo, a man of noble extraction and trenchant wit. From Florence came Signore Filippo Salviati, the least of whose glories were the eminence of his blood and the magnificence of his fortune. His was a sublime intellect which fed no more hungrily upon any pleasure than it did upon fine meditations. I often talked with these two of such matters in the presence of a certain Peripatetic philosopher whose greatest obstacle in apprehending the truth seemed to be the reputation he had acquired by his interpretations of Aristotle.
>
> Now, since bitter death has deprived Venice and Florence of those two great luminaries in the very meridian of their years, I have resolved to make their fame live on in these pages, so far as my poor abilities will permit, by introducing them as interlocutors in the present argument. (Nor shall the good Peripatetic lack a place; because of his excessive affection toward the Commentaries of Simplicius, I have thought fit to leave him under the name of the author he so much revered, without mentioning his own.) May it please those two great souls, ever venerable to my heart, to accept this public monument of my undying love. And may the memory of their eloquence assist me in delivering to posterity the promised reflections.

After his visit to Rome in 1624 Galileo felt he had been given some sort of licence to discuss Copernicanism once more. Although there is no written evidence to support the fact, it is likely that Galileo and Urban discussed the idea of a book in which both sides of the argument would be given equal voice, a discourse by the most respected scientist of the time in which the case for the Church's position was aired along with the views of Copernicus. But if this was the intention outlined by Urban at one of the meetings with Galileo (a way perhaps to begin to find common ground between Church and science and then move on), it was either misunderstood by Galileo or deliberately morphed by him into something altogether different. The *Dialogue Concerning the Two Chief World Systems* is an utterly partisan work in which Aristotelian cosmology is run out of town and the case for Copernicus made very clear.

In the first part of the book, 'Day One', Galileo tackles the Aristotelian notion of the perfect heavenly sphere – the idea that the heavens beyond the Earth are made of more refined material than the lumpen world in which we live. The main reason the Church cherished this idea was that it stopped in its tracks the argument that if the heavens were not perfect, it would be possible that life might exist on other worlds. The notion of extraterrestrial life raised all sorts of irreconcilable theological issues, not least of which was the matter of not knowing how such alien beings could have been saved by Our Lord.

Galileo dismissed this as nonsense and postulated (just as Bruno had done a generation earlier) that indeed there might be life on other worlds. Galileo's treatment of this subject was far more sophisticated than Bruno's, whose emphasis had been limited to the spiritual and metaphysical consequences of life on other planets. It was not, Galileo believed, a matter for the scientist to venture into the question of whether or not Christ had redeemed these creatures. All the scientist was interested in, he declared, was the *possibility* of extraterrestrial life. By using the examples of the Moon's craters and mountains and the presence of sunspots, Galileo argued that the ancient theory of a perfect heavenly sphere was untenable.

In part two of the *Dialogue*, the second day of the gathering at Sagredo's home, the three protagonists move on to a direct consideration of Copernicus and ponder the daily rotation of the Earth. On the third day, Sagredo, Salviati and Simplicio discuss the matter of the motion of the Earth around the Sun. In each of these sections of the book Salviati proposes the Copernican argument. He is often supported by Sagredo, who is sympathetic but relies upon Salviati's sound knowledge to back him up. Throughout these discussions, Simplicio offers resistance, but it is a resistance based entirely upon ignorance and he never gains a foothold; Galileo merely has him offering frail arguments that are readily swept away by the 'new science' espoused by the other two protagonists.

A good example of this is the exchange between Simplicio and Salviati when discussing the Aristotelian concept of a corruptible earth and an incorruptible, perfect heaven:

SIMPLICIO: On earth I continually see herbs, plants, animals generating and decaying; winds, rains, tempests, storms arising; in a word, the appearance of the Earth undergoing perpetual change. None of these changes are to be discerned in celestial bodies, whose positions and configurations correspond exactly with everything men remember, without the generation of anything new there or the corruption of anything old.

SALVIATI: But if you have to content yourself with these visible, or rather these seen experiences, you must consider China and America celestial bodies, since you surely have never seen in them these alterations which you see in Italy. Therefore, in your sense, they must be unalterable.

SIMPLICIO: Even if I have never seen such alterations in those places with my own senses, there are reliable accounts of them; besides which, since the rational should be the same for the whole or the part, those countries being a part of the Earth like ours, they must be alterable like this.

SALVIATI: But why have you not observed this, instead of reducing yourself to having to believe the tales of others? Why not see it with your own eyes?

SIMPLICIO: Because those countries are far from being exposed to view; they are so distant that our sight could not discover such alterations in them.

SALVIATI: Now see for yourself how you have inadvertently revealed the fallacy of your argument. You say that alterations which may be seen near at hand on Earth cannot be seen in America because of the great distance. Well, so much the less could they be seen in the Moon, which is many hundreds of times more distant. And if you believe in alterations in Mexico on the basis of news from there, what reports do you have from the Moon to convince you that there are no alterations there? From your not seeing alterations in heaven (where if any occurred you would not be able to see them by reason of the distance, and from whence no news is to be had), you cannot deduce that there are none, in the same way as from seeing and recognising them on Earth you correctly deduce that they do exist here.

SIMPLICIO: Among the changes that have taken place on Earth I can find some so great that if they had occurred on the Moon they could then well have been observed here below. From the oldest records we have it that formerly, at the Straits of Gibraltar, Abila and Calpe were joined together with some lesser mountains which held the ocean in check; but these mountains being separated by some cause, the opening admitted the sea, which flooded in so as to form the Mediterranean. When we consider the immensity of this, and the difference in appearance which must have been made in the water and land seen from afar, there is no doubt that such a change could easily have been seen by anyone then on the Moon. Just so would the inhabitants of Earth have discovered any such alteration in the Moon; yet there is no history of such a thing being seen. Hence there remains no basis for saying that anything in the heavenly bodies is alterable.

On 'Day Four', in the final section of the *Dialogue*, Galileo moves on to his theory of tides, and his belief that the tidal forces observed each day present clear evidence for the fact that the Earth is indeed moving. Galileo had been thinking deeply about the mechanism behind the tides for many years and had formulated a theory to explain the phenomenon. His earliest thinking on the subject probably dates from 1596, for a year later he wrote a letter to Kepler explaining his ideas as they were at that time.[14] Then, when Galileo had lived in Padua and made regular visits to Venice along the canal joining the two cities, he had observed the movement of water in buckets stored in the hold or on the deck; watching fascinated as it was slopped around by the movement of the boat. From this he had drawn an analogy with the movement of the oceans.

By 1616 Galileo had refined his notion of tidal movements to the point where he could write a short paper on the subject, 'Discourse on the Tides' (*'Discorso sul flusso e il reflusso del mare'*), which he sent in the form of a private letter to his friend Cardinal Orsini.[15] In this letter Galileo examines the ways water contained in a vase can move. He then extrapolated the concept to explain the tides experienced on Earth, linking them with the motion of the planet. Changes in the motions of the sea, he believed, could be effects of an irregularity in the Earth's motion. Based on this assumption, Galileo concluded that the movement of the Earth described by Copernicus was affected by two main circular motions. These were the annual revolution around the Sun and the diurnal rotation on the planet's axis. Owing to a cumulative effect of these motions there was an alteration in the surface speed of the Earth every twelve hours. For twelve hours a point on the surface would move eastwards (opposite to the global westward movement of the

Earth). For the other twelve hours of the day it would move westwards (the same direction as the annual motion). This motion caused a swelling and falling of water levels similar to that in a bucket slopping over into the bottom of a boat on a Venetian canal.

Although ingenious, this proposition was of course completely wrong and marks one of the few times Galileo grasped entirely the wrong end of the stick. It was realised by others in Galileo's lifetime that the rise and fall of the tides was actually a result of gravitational interaction between the Moon and the Earth and had absolutely nothing to do with the motion of the Earth in orbit about the Sun. Galileo never accepted this and went to his grave believing that the tides provided one of the best proofs of the Copernican theory.

In November 1629 Galileo began the laborious process of gaining papal approval for his new work. The book was to be published by the Lyncean Academy, who had handled *The Assayer*, and the official papal censor, Niccolo Riccardi, was a friend of the academy. Back in 1623 Riccardi had ensured that *The Assayer* passed through the system with little difficulty, so Galileo felt confident there would be no censorship problems with this new book.

In fact, such a laissez-faire attitude on Galileo's part was a big mistake. Riccardi himself had no personal objections to the book, but he did realise that Galileo was pushing the boundaries and that he had to operate within the rules. He suggested some revisions, and proposed that Galileo write a Preface and a Conclusion in which he was to make it abundantly clear that his work was pure speculation – that his espousal of the Copernican model was merely one side of the argument, one that was no better than the position taken by the theologians.

Galileo was not best pleased with these suggestions, but he under-stood the game. He wanted his work to reach as wide a readership as possible and he knew that to do this he would have to meet the demands of the papal office. He was also reassured by early reports from Rome indicating that Urban was thrilled by the parts of the *Dialogue* that had been read to him and that he had praised Galileo's wit and erudition.

In early May 1630, as Father Riccardi continued studying the *Dialogue*, while Galileo had still not offered him a suitable Preface and Conclusion, the scientist made a brief visit to Rome. His objective was to try to hurry his book through the censorship process by leaning on Father Riccardi, firing up his friends and supporters and exciting the pope enough to smooth the path for the *Dialogue*.

This time the trip proved an abject failure. The atmosphere in Rome had changed radically in the six years since his last visit, in 1624, and the pope was a very different man from the thoughtful conversationalist Galileo had been so encouraged by during his last trip. During the intervening years Urban had made the Vatican his own. True to the style of many a pope before and after him, he had first displayed his true self through nepotism, making his married brother Carlo the commander of the papal army and Carlo's son Francesco a cardinal. Later he adopted the robes of despotism. He ordered the exhuming of heretics who had died under interrogation so that their rotting corpses could be burned in public; he hounded poets and writers who were considered heretical, and even decreed that anyone found using snuff in church should face instant excommunication.

Immediately after his election, Urban's ego had begun to take over. In a fit of mock piety that must have shocked and embarrassed those in attendance, as the tiara was placed on his head, Urban had prostrated himself at the altar. Then, within days of ascending to the papacy he had begun to set himself up as a military leader as well as a spiritual guide for the devout, declaring: 'The judgement of one living pope is worth more than the maxims of a hundred dead ones.'[16] When a group of admirers and sycophants requested permission to commission a monument for him but advisers expressed doubts about the good taste of doing such a thing while he was alive, Urban snapped: 'Let them. I am not an ordinary pope.'[17]

By 1630 Urban had grown paranoid and introspective. Always a hypochondriac, he had taken to heart rumours that an astrological prediction had foretold his imminent death. As a result, he had sacked most of his staff, hired new guards and food-testers in case someone was trying to poison him, and on the very day the prophesy claimed was to be his last, he had locked himself in a room, allowed no one in and fasted until the danger had passed.

Meanwhile, the plague had spread almost the length and breadth of Italy, leaving hundreds of thousands of dead in its wake. Half the population of Milan had perished, a third of the population of Venice succumbed, and in Mantua, the worst-hit city in Italy, no few than three-quarters of the population had been taken by the disease.

In Rome, Galileo found few people beyond his immediate circle and the Lyncean Academy who were much interested in theological arguments or the thrusting proposals of the 'new science'. Indeed, death and disease, war and pestilence merely served to reinforce piety. What, after all, could science offer humanity as a defence against the ravages of the Black Death?

The pope granted Galileo one brief audience and the scientist's usual round of social engagements proved a disappointment. But worse was to follow after Galileo had returned home to Florence in late June 1630. As Riccardi continued to quibble over the *Dialogue*, Galileo learned that his friend and benefactor Prince Cesi had died at his home at Acquasparta, another victim of the plague.

At the time of his death, Cesi had been making ready for the publication of Galileo's masterpiece and expecting to hear from Riccardi that it had been cleared by the censors. But, unknown to most people, the Prince was almost broke and he had died intestate. As a result, the plans for publication of the *Dialogue* were now doubly wounded, first by Riccardi's resistance and then by the passing of the man who had been Galileo's greatest ally and most influential friend. With the prince's affairs in a mess, Galileo would have to find another patron for his work.

For Galileo, as 1630 turned into 1631, the world seemed to be falling apart around him. Dragged down by illness, watching impotent as so many died around him (including his own brother Michelangelo, who had left his vast family penniless), caught in the censor's net, on the one hand cut off from the support of the pope and on the other lost to the Lynceans, suddenly rudderless and bereft, he felt trapped and powerless. To add further to his misery, the ravages of the plague meant that communications across Europe were severely disrupted. Mail deliveries from Florence to Rome were unreliable and slow, so that Galileo's ongoing discourse with Riccardi over the corrections and refinements required by the Church was reduced to a slow trickle.

Throughout 1631 Galileo remained in limbo and only when the plague began to die down as colder weather arrived and life regained a semblance of normality was it finally agreed that he could publish his book in Florence. This still required the addition of a Preface and a Conclusion, both written by Riccardi, along with a formal report from the local censor in Tuscany; but at least it meant that the book would be read at last.

In February 1632, more than two years after the book had been finished and a fair copy made ready for the printers, *Dialogue Concerning the Two Chief World Systems* finally saw the light of day. Printed in Florence, copies were soon distributed across Europe, where it was devoured by the faithful of the 'new science' and acclaimed as a masterpiece by the many who had already grown to accept that the mechanism governing the universe had very little to do with the laws and postulates of ancient philosophers.

Early in 1632 a copy arrived in the offices of the pope, but he was too busy to pay it much attention. At the same time complimentary copies landed on the desks of Galileo's rich and powerful friends within the Church and beyond. Handsomely bound editions were transported to booksellers in all the great cities of the continent. In Rome, while the pope was too preoccupied with himself and his wars to read Galileo's latest offering, others, both supporters of Galileo and his bitter enemies, were not slow to explore the thoughts of the greatest intellectual of the age; and to both friends and foe the true nature of the book was revealed almost immediately.

Galileo's enemies could not fail to be taken with the author's skill and literary talents, but at the same time, as the many men who loathed him read the scientist's words, they could only sit back and marvel at how on earth Galileo had so far escaped censure. Indeed, such an apparent oversight by the Vatican must also have surprised Galileo's friends and supporters. To a few, his most energetic opponents, it was clear the scientist had either gone mad or was deliberately trying to provoke. To them it was evident that the *Dialogue* was a step too far. In private, some of these enemies even speculated that with this new book Galileo had signed his own death warrant. In this matter, at least, they were not far wrong.

12

Unholy Intrigue

In 1632 the first coffee shop in London opened, John Locke, Christopher Wren, Vermeer and Spinoza were born and Rembrandt painted *The Anatomy Lesson of Dr Nicolaas Tulp*. Meanwhile, for almost six months after publication of the *Dialogue* it seemed that there was to be no adverse reaction to it. Galileo, distracted by continued illness and already thinking of new ideas, might have felt relaxed about the nature of his work and that through a combination of his fame, his favour with the pope and his association with the Medici, the powers that be had turned a blind eye to anything that contradicted doctrine. But if Galileo was thinking along these lines he was very mistaken, for his enemies had already taken action.

It is not clear who was responsible for alerting the pope to what were quickly viewed as pernicious aspects to the new Galilean treatise. No documentary evidence or correspondence has survived to allow us to pin the blame accurately, but, based on what we already know of Galileo's enemies and rivalries, it takes little imagination to come up with a strong hypothesis. The trouble was almost certainly started by members of the Jesuit order.

The Jesuits fancied themselves as the intellectual wing of the Church. They experimented and conducted astronomical observations, and members of the order wrote learned books on scientific matters and the interface between science and religion. These were, of course, partisan works, which were then studied at the Collegio Romano and at other Jesuit institutions across Europe. But the real drive for all this activity was to formulate an alternative, Church-friendly science that refuted secular studies at every turn. The Jesuits took every opportunity available to gainsay Galileo. Just how important and intense this enmity became may be gleaned from a letter from an influential Jesuit at the

Collegio Romano, Father Christopher Grienberger, written in 1634, in which he pronounced: 'If Galileo had known how to keep the affection of the fathers of this college he would live in glory before the world and none of his misfortunes would have occurred, and he would have been able to write at his pleasure about any subject, even, I say, about the movements of the Earth.'[1] Galileo was particularly despised by two influential Jesuits: his old enemy Father Christopher Scheiner and the Professor of Mathematics at the Collegio Romano, Father Orazio Grassi.

Scheiner, we know from contemporary accounts, had not forgiven Galileo for the insults hurled at him over the years. Apparently, when he heard from a Galileo supporter that the *Dialogue* was a wonderful piece of work, he flew into a rage and went immediately to the nearest bookseller, where he offered five times the going rate for the book if it could be got for him with all haste.[2]

As for Grassi: if it were possible, he hated Galileo even more. Galileo had stirred up bad feeling amongst the Jesuits, and in particular he had recently sparked Grassi's anger by being openly critical of what he believed was the man's illogical philosophy. The best-known example of this appears in the *Dialogue*, where Galileo pokes fun at Grassi's belief that 'philosophy is a book of fiction created by one man, like the *Iliad* or the *Orlando Furioso*, books in which the last thing is whether what is written is true'. 'Signor Sarsi [Grassi's pseudonym], this is not the way matters stand,' Galileo retorts. 'Philosophy is written in that great book which ever lies before our eyes – I mean the universe – but we cannot understand it if we do not first learn the language and grasp the symbols in which it is written. It is written in mathematical language, and the symbols are triangles, circles and other geometrical figures, without whose help it is humanly impossible to comprehend a single word, and without which one wanders in vain in a dark labyrinth.'[3]

Grassi was evangelical and believed his opposition to Galileo was a divine cause. Eight years before the publication of the *Dialogue*, in 1624, he had told one of Galileo's friends in Rome, Mario Guiducci, that he was planning to write a book attacking *The Assayer*, which had been published the previous year. Furthermore, he had told Guiducci, he would expose what he considered heretical aspects of Galileo's book.[4] Then, in the same year, someone denounced Galileo to the Inquisition over the contents of *The Assayer*. This was done in the form of an anonymous written statement. Filed away quietly at the time, it would later play a key role in the drama of Galileo's trial and condemnation. The identity of this anonymous attacker remains a mystery, but it was almost certainly a high-ranking Jesuit with the ear of the Inquisition, quite possibly Father Orazio Grassi himself.

There is nothing in the way of hard evidence to link Grassi with the denouncing of Galileo over the *Dialogue* in 1632 or for his being the author of the written denouncement of Galileo to the Inquisition in 1624; but those close to Galileo had strong suspicions about who was behind both. In a private correspondence, Riccardi remarked to another associate of Galileo's: 'The Jesuits will persecute him [Galileo] bitterly.'[5] And Galileo himself observed in a letter to a friend in Paris: 'I hear from reliable sources that the Jesuit Fathers have managed to convince some very important persons that my book is execrable and more harmful to the Holy Church than the writings of Luther and Calvin. Thus I am sure it will be prohibited, despite the fact that to obtain the licence I went personally to Rome and delivered it into the hands of the Master of the Sacred Palace.'[6] A few months later, in another personal letter, he concluded: 'So you see that it is not because of this or that opinion that I have been and continue to be attacked, but because I am not liked by the Jesuits.'[7]

Mario Guiducci went so far as to call Galileo's clash with Grassi 'a war': 'I hear from all sides rumours of the war with which Grassi is threatening us to the point that I am tempted to believe that he has his reply ready,' he wrote in a letter to Galileo. 'On the other hand, I cannot see where he can attack us, since Count Virginio Malvezzi is virtually certain that he cannot gain a foothold against your position about the nature of heat, taste, smell and so on. The Count says that you must have written about that in order to give rise to a debate for which you must be armed to the teeth.'[8]

There is also the fact that, even after Galileo had been tried and sentenced, Grassi could still not let the matter rest, declaring: 'He [Galileo] has been ruined by himself. He was infatuated by his own genius, as he disdains the genius of others. It is not surprising that everyone conspires to injure him.'[9] This could be considered as simply a statement of the man's hatred for Galileo and it does not prove that he was behind the exposé in 1624 or 1632, but Grassi was certainly in the right place at the right time and in a position of influence. He also had plenty in the way of motive.

It was during the summer of 1632 that the many forces that were to shape the trial of Galileo each came into full effect. The persecution of

Galileo was the result of a complex brew of factors, some prosaic, others fundamental to Church and orthodoxy. It is clear Galileo's book appeared on the scene with extremely poor timing. The author was quite aware of this, but, after having spent so long forcing his treatise past the papal censors, he could not easily countenance any further hold-ups in publication. Yet 1632 was an inauspicious moment to publish the *Dialogue*, and his impatience definitely helped to activate political moves for Galileo to be investigated. However, an array of rather mundane personal elements also came together to contrive the great man's downfall.

First, let us consider how the political climate of the time worked against him. By 1632 the Thirty Years War had been fought for almost fourteen years and it had born witness to an astonishingly complex ebb and flow of military fortune. By 1630 the war had entered a new phase, which threatened to completely destabilise Europe when King Gustavus's Swedish army allied itself with France and invaded Protestant Germany. In May 1632, just a few months before the Galileo affair was to burst into the open, the city of Magdeburg was sacked and destroyed with a loss of at least twenty thousand of its people. This sent shock waves through Europe and served to encourage those who wished for the pope to intervene in the conflict.

Naturally, this had serious repercussions in Rome. Urban was the type of pope who took his temporal responsibilities, his position as a military leader and head of state, very seriously; but at the same time he was hampered by lack of funds. He was already unpopular with the people of Rome because he had increased taxes, and his military spending had pushed the Vatican into debt. The fact that the Holy Father had also lustily feathered his own nest and given jobs to the boys ever since having taken the tiara further eroded the purity of his image.

Urban was becoming evermore paranoid, and he trusted almost no one. Two months before the sacking of Magdeburg, in early March 1632, just as Galileo's *Dialogue* arrived in Rome, he and his supporters had become embroiled in an unseemly row with a group of rebellious Spanish cardinals led by Gaspare Borgia. Cardinal Borgia claimed that Urban was a coward for not getting directly involved in the war as an ally of Spain. The dispute, which reached its climax at a meeting of cardinals on 8 March, almost led to the exchange of blows and the Swiss Guard had to be called in to prevent the holy men from beating each other to a pulp.

This had unsettled Urban and he became even more nervous and isolated. He moved quickly to purge the Vatican of Spaniards, and then turned on a former pupil of Galileo's and a friend of the scientist, Monsignor Giovanni Ciampoli. Ciampoli had been rising fast through the Vatican hierarchy during the 1620s and had finally been appointed to the prestigious position of Secret Chamberlain and Secretary for the Correspondence with Princes. He was an arrogant and egotistical man who was undoubtedly very intelligent but had excelled through scheming and manipulation. He had a genuine fondness for Galileo and a deep respect for his ideas. For a long time he had been a very useful contact at the Vatican, but in March 1632 he had become embroiled in the political intrigue surrounding the rebellion of Spanish cardinals against Urban and a month later he was sent into exile, where he remained for the rest of his life.

It was into this somewhat fragile environment that Grassi, Scheiner or some other influential cleric who had access to the pope whispered a rumour that with his latest book, the *Dialogue*, Galileo had insulted the person of the Holy Father. The claims against Galileo were not simply based upon the fact that he had flaunted anti-Catholic ideologies, but that he had committed two other unforgivable sins. First, he had written a book that did not comply with what had been agreed in the many meetings between pope and scientist some years earlier. But second, and perhaps just as bad, was the fact that it was clear, even from a brief perusal of the *Dialogue*, that the author had placed Urban's sentiments and ideologies in the mouth of the fall guy of the piece, the likeable but none-too-bright Simplicio.

It was a cunning move on the part of whoever was responsible for denouncing Galileo. Urban's ridiculously bloated sense of self-worth, twinned with an acute paranoia, was well known in Rome. Galileo's denouncer was certainly aware that attacking Galileo over an issue of science would be hazardous and slow, and that it would have little chance of success; but making the matter one in which the honour and intellect of the pope were called into question – making it a personal issue – showed political skill and Machiavellian deviousness.

Of course it worked wonderfully. Urban, already feeling the strain from malcontent cardinals, creditors and invisible critics, was furious. In spite of all the praise and honour he had heaped on Galileo and in spite of the friendship he had shown the man, it took very little to convince him that he had been doubly betrayed. He believed Galileo had left Rome knowing what he should have written, and that he had chosen to compose something altogether different, an insidious tract.

Beyond that, the pope now believed the scientist had misrepresented him as a simpleton. He would pay for these sins.

Urban's immediate reaction was to create a Special Committee of Inquiry to investigate the precise nature of Galileo's work. 'We think that Galileo may have overstepped his instructions by asserting absolutely the Earth's motion and the Sun's immobility, thus deviating from hypothesis,' he declared.[10]

Next, he summoned the Tuscan ambassador, Francesco Niccolini, to the papal office. From this encounter Galileo heard the first reports about the trouble brewing in Rome. These were contained in a letter from Niccolini in which he informed the Grand Duke Ferdinand that the pope had 'exploded with anger; and that he could not have had a worse disposition towards "our poor Mr Galilei"'. And Urban's reasons were made clear: 'Galileo Galilei did not fear to make sport of me,' the pope had fumed. In conclusion, Niccolini warned: 'When His Holiness gets something into his head, that is the end of the matter, especially if one is opposing, threatening or defying him, since then he hardens and shows no respect to anyone . . . This is really going to be a troublesome affair.'[11]

A few days later Galileo learned that officers of the Inquisition had entered the premises of his Florentine printer Landini, ordered him to stop the production and distribution of the *Dialogue* and confiscated all materials pertaining to the book.

It was now obvious to Galileo that he had stirred up a hornets' nest. The pope was consumed with rage and had set in motion an inquiry, usually reserved for the most reviled heretics in Christendom; and in initiating this he had no shortage of willing helpers.

The papal censor, Father Riccardi, could easily have found himself in terrible trouble over his mishandling of the *Dialogue*; he might even have been held primarily responsible for its dissemination in 'uncorrected' form. But fortune shone upon him. For some reason, the pope concluded that Riccardi had been as duped by Galileo as he himself had been, and that he should bear no responsibility for the *Dialogue* slipping through the net. As proof of his satisfaction that Riccardi had acted honourably he made him head of the Special Committee of Inquiry to analyse Galileo's book, with the instruction to work with two other suitable theologians and report back as quickly as possible. Riccardi chose Agnostino Oregio, the pope's personal theologian, and a Jesuit, one Father Melchior Inchofer.

In spite of what the pope might have thought of Riccardi, the priest was still very much pro-Galileo. Naturally he kept his enthusiasm to himself, but he had some sympathy with the scientist's desire to allow freedom of intellectual investigation. It is likely Riccardi chose members of the Special Committee of Inquiry who he genuinely believed would look favourably upon Galileo without attracting suspicion. He may have been right about Oregio; but in choosing Inchofer he was quite misguided.

The 47-year-old Inchofer was a German priest who had risen rapidly through the ranks of theological academia to become the Professor of Theology at a Jesuit college in Messina, Sicily. He was vehemently anti-Copernican and anti-Galilean, but he also had an axe to grind. He was in Rome in 1632 upon the request of the Holy Office because he had written a book entitled *Epistolae B. Virginis Mariae ad Messanenses Veritas Vindicata* (*A Vindication of the Letter of the Blessed Virgin Mary to the People of Messina*), in which he had offered what he saw as 'proof' of the virgin birth; but in his tract he had overstepped the limits of orthodoxy by being *too* vigorously supportive of material evidence to support a point of faith.

As the evidence against Galileo was being collected and collated ready for what many within the Holy Office believed would be an important trial, Inchofer's own book was placed on the Index to await 'correction'. This had the effect of spurring him on to prove himself. As a consequence, he would do all he could to find every scrap of incriminating evidence that might be used against Galileo.

Some time during September 1632 Melchior Inchofer carried out a thorough investigation of the files kept on Galileo in the Vatican archives, and what he discovered there would become key elements in the trial to come.

The first document that came to Inchofer's attention was the declaration of 1616 (which was unsigned by either Galileo or Bellarmine), in which it was stated that Galileo agreed not to teach or to publicise any aspect of Copernicanism. This was the document contrived by the obsessive Dominican Commissary of the Inquisition Michelangelo Seghizzi. It was a damning piece of evidence and it became the centrepiece for the prosecution's case.

However, during the same search Inchofer stumbled upon a far more important document. This was the anonymous denunciation of Galileo's book *The Assayer*, lodged in 1624. In this the author claimed that Galileo described an atomic theory which cast doubt on the miracle of the Eucharist, a core principle of the Catholic faith. In so doing Galileo had, it was claimed, committed a far more serious act of heresy than that linked to his support for the Copernican model of the universe.

The Eucharist, as it is understood by Catholics, is an extremely odd doctrine, a blend of witchcraft, voodoo and medieval Christianity; but astonishingly, it is a doctrine – indeed a dogma – that remains a central pillar of Catholicism. With its roots in the solemn and deep meaning of the biblical Last Supper, it is such a cornerstone of the Faith that it is considered beyond questioning. St Augustine is said to have called the Eucharist 'a mystery that cannot reasonably be investigated';[12] while the historian Pietro Redondi has said of the Catholic obsession with the concept of transubstantiation (the mechanism behind the papal vision of the Eucharist): 'It has a long and difficult history, that of the conflict between reason and faith. In comparison, the opposition to the helio-centric astronomical truth seems like a short-lived, marginal episode.'[13]

For Catholics the Eucharist is not the symbolic ritual it is for Protestants. For Catholics the Eucharist is an event in which one unites with God, a ceremony in which the bread and the wine *become* the body and the blood of Christ: this is the essence of transubstantiation. For the Protestant, the bread and the wine merely *symbolise* or *represent* the body and the blood of Christ. For them, no transubstantiation occurs during communion; it is instead a sacred *ritual* and nothing more.

This might seem like a subtle distinction, but it is really one of the key points of difference between Roman Catholicism and Protest-antism. Indeed, it has been said that one could perhaps be Catholic and Copernican, but one could not be Catholic without respecting the Tridentine postulate of the Eucharist (the concept that the Holy Trinity interacts with the believer during communion).[14]

Transubstantiation was an invention of theologians of the twelfth and thirteenth centuries. According to these philosophers, led by the iconic St Thomas Aquinas, the explanation for it relies on an Aristote-lian atomic model. This states that all things have a dual nature ('substance' and 'accident'), and that these may be separated. 'Substance' is another word for 'soul', and 'accident' is a euphemism for 'body'. Another way of putting this is to say that 'substance' is a term used to describe what a given object *is* – the properties of the object that are essential to 'it' being 'it'. 'Accident' is the observable, physical characteristics of a thing.

Catholic doctrine holds that during Holy Communion, God replaces the 'substance' (or essence) of the bread and wine with Christ's body and blood, but because the 'accident' (the secondary qualities of the bread and wine) is unaffected, the bread and wine appear and taste as they normally would.

The atomic model described by Galileo in *The Assayer* gives an explanation for the structure of matter which makes it clear that transubstantiation is impossible. 'I think,' he writes, 'that tastes, odours, colours, and so on are no more than mere names so far as the object in which we locate them are concerned, and that they reside only in consciousness. If living creatures were removed, all these qualities would be wiped out and annihilated.'[15] Theologians believed in the power of names, words given to describe a thing. Galileo would have none of it. 'If their opinions and their voices have the power to call into existence the things they name, then I beg them to do me the favour of naming a lot of old hardware I have about the house "gold",' he chided.[16]

In *The Assayer* Galileo writes:

So I tell you, as soon as I conceive of a corporeal material or substance, I clearly feel pulled out of necessity to conceive that it is bounded or having this or that shape, that it is large or small in relation to others, that it is in this or that location, at this or that time, that it moves or is still, that it touches or does not touch another body, that it is one, few, or many, nor by any imagination can I separate it from these conditions; but that it be white or red, bitter or sweet, sounding or mute, of a pleasant or unpleasant smell, I do not feel compelled in the mind to apprehend it necessarily accompanied by such conditions.

Galileo's atomic theory was, of course, anti-Aristotelian and entirely radical. He conceived the idea that all substances had properties such as taste and colour because they were made of particular invisible particles (atoms or molecules), and most crucially that if they were changed into other substances their characteristics also changed. This principle lies at the core of *The Assayer*, but it is also a philosophy he reiterates in his *Dialogue*, when he has the character Salviati (who is the author's mouthpiece) declare: 'I have never been able to understand fully this transmutation of substance whereby matter has been so transformed that one must say it has been totally destroyed and nothing of its previous being remains in it, and that another body, very different from it, is produced.'

Both these statements are clear denials of the Thomist principle of transubstantiation, and they were highly inflammatory because they attacked the Faith during a period in history when members of the Church were feeling vulnerable and defensive. In his *Summa Theologica* of 1264 Thomas Aquinas had made the doctrine of transubstantiation clear; there could be no argument: this was how the universe operated. During the years 1545 to 1563 the Council of Trent elevated the doctrine of transubstantiation to a new level. In an official statement it was declared: 'If any deny that, in the venerable sacrament of the Eucharist, the whole of Christ is contained within each species and within each portion of each species after it has shared out let him be anathema.'

'Let him be anathema' – those words were favourites of the Inquisition. Those who disagreed with them were not only 'wrong', they were 'evil', 'antichristian', fit only for the flames. To make it clear to the laity what was meant by Aquinas's deluded metaphysics, the clerics of the Council of Trent encapsulated the notion in what they at least perceived to be a clear, succinct statement of Faith: 'The accidents cannot adhere in the body and blood of Christ . . . above the order of nature they sustain themselves, supported by nothing else' (in other words, the observable characteristics of the bread and wine were unchanged when the Holy Spirit miraculously replaced the 'substance' of these things). They then added a barefaced lie: 'This has been the uniform and constant belief of the Catholic Church,' they announced. In fact it had only been contrived by human beings less than three centuries earlier.[17]

The Jesuits were particularly conscientious in attacking any opposition to the concept of transubstantiation and they tried to root out any suggestion of an alternative theory of matter by stopping any talk of atomism. In August 1632, just as Galileo's *Dialogue* was facing censure, the Jesuit leaders issued an 'internal statement' meant only for high-ranking officials of the order, which expressly forbade the teaching and dissemination of any form of atomic theory.[18] The man behind this, the most powerful intellectual guide of the Jesuits during this period, was Father Orazio Grassi.

As we have seen, back in 1624 Grassi had been engaged in an intense rivalry with Galileo and he held a powerful ecclesiastical position: the Chair of Mathematics at the Jesuit College in Rome. It is quite possible he convinced himself that by composing a suitably worded and entirely anonymous attack on Galileo's heretical propositions in *The Assayer* he would cause his enemy enormous harm. The denouncement began with false humility, asking for advice:

Having in past days perused Signor Galileo Galilei's book entitled *The Assayer*, I have come to consider a doctrine already taught by certain ancient philosophers and effectively rejected by Aristotle, but renewed by the same Signor Galilei. And having decided to compare it with the true and undoubted Rule of revealed doctrines, I have found that in the Light of that Lantern which by the exercise and merit of our faith shines out indeed in murky places, and which more securely and more certainly than any natural evidence illuminates us, this doctrine appears false, or even (which I do not judge) very difficult and dangerous. So that he who receives the Rule as true must not falter in speech and in the judgement of more serious matters, I have therefore thought to propose it to you, Very Reverend Father, and beg you, as I am doing, to tell me its meaning, which will serve as my warning.

A few paragraphs on, the author makes his point abundantly clear:

Now, if one admits this philosophy of accidents as true, it seems to me, that makes greatly difficult the existence of the accidents of the bread and wine which in the Most Holy Sacrament are separated from their substance; since finding again therein the terms, and the objects of touch, sight, taste, etc., one will also have to say according to this doctrine that there are the very tiny particles with which the substance of the bread first moved our senses, which if they were ever substantial, it follows that in the Sacrament there are substantial parts of bread and wine, which is the error condemned by the Sacred Tridentine Council, Session 13, Canon 2.[19]

This condemnation of Galileo's *The Assayer* was ignored for almost a decade. We do not know precisely why; it might have been studied and deemed too dangerous to bring to public attention, or it may simply have fallen into the hands of someone sympathetic to Galileo's cause. But its existence was certainly known to some of those close to Galileo in 1624. Around the time of his letter to Galileo (quoted earlier) in which he mentioned Grassi's interest in writing a book attacking *The Assayer*, Mario Guiducci had written to Prince Cesi, the leader of the Lynceans. In this he had informed Cesi:

Some months ago at the Congregation of the Holy Office, a pious person proposed to prohibit or correct *The Assayer*, charging that it praised the doctrine of Copernicus with respect to the Earth's motion: as to which matter a cardinal assumed the task of informing himself about the situation and reporting it; and by good fortune he happened to hand over the case to Father Guevara, father general of some sort of Theatines, who I believe are called Minims, and this father then went to France with the Signor Cardinal Legate. He read the work diligently and, having enjoyed it very much, praised and celebrated it greatly to that cardinal, and besides put on paper certain defences, according to which that doctrine of motion, even if it were held, did not seem to him to be condemnable; and so the matter quieted down for the moment.[20]

This letter is very strange, and at first it appears to make little sense. Either Guiducci was writing to Cesi in code, or he did not know the true nature of the written attack on Galileo and was merely aware some influential figure had made some form of denunciation to the Inquisition. This possibility is supported by Guiducci's references to Galileo's treatment of Copernicanism and the motion of the Earth. There is no mention of Copernicanism or celestial mechanics in *The Assayer*.

Almost ten years later, with Galileo in a very different stage of his career and under ecclesiastic threat, Inchofer unearthed the revealing statement on *The Assayer* that had possibly come from Grassi's pen. At that moment he must have thought he had struck a seam of the purest gold, for in his hands lay unequivocal evidence to send the egotistical, jumped-up Galileo to the stake.

As we shall see, in thinking this Inchofer was being overly optimistic and naïve to the political complexities of the situation in which he was now suddenly, intimately involved. Staggeringly, after its brief moment in the clear light of a Holy Office inquiry, this document (now known to historians as G3) disappeared once more into the archives and was only unearthed again 350 years later, in 1982, by the Galileo scholar Pietro Redondi.

G3 is a pivotal document in the story of Galileo's persecution and subsequent trial. Redondi discovered the document (written in Italian) in the palace of the Holy Office, which stands next to St Peter's Square while he was researching another historical matter. The Records (*Protocolli*) of the Congregation of the Index are filed using capital letters, A, AA, B, BB, etc. The document G3 was located in volume EE and covered sheets 292 (recto and verso) and sheet 293.*

*No one is quite sure why it has been called G3, though it might be in reference to there being three pages and the document being about Galileo.

Redondi was immediately excited by its contents, and the following year he published a new theory concerning the reason for Galileo's trial. This appeared in the 1983 book *Galileo Heretic*, which offered an alternative analysis of the reasons he was put on trial. I shall consider this theory in detail in the next chapter.

Back in 1632, after having studied the claims made in the document today called G3, the keen and conscientious Inchofer wrote a full and detailed report, which he submitted to the Holy Office as part of his broader conclusion concerning Galileo's *Dialogue* for the Special Committee of Inquiry. This document also had its moment in the sun before being sealed up in the vaults of the Vatican. Today known as document EE291, it was not discovered until 1999, when another Italian historian, Mariano Artigas, working with the same volume (EE) as studied by Redondi, came across another document, this time written in Latin and covering two pages, sheet 291 recto and half of 291 verso (hence the name EE291). Redondi, it transpires, had missed this document, even though it lay only one page behind the material comprising G3. This was because, in 1982, he had been forbidden from viewing it; but by 1999 the rules had relaxed and Artigas was allowed access to the entire volume.

Inchofer's full report on G3 (the document EE291) reads as follows:

I saw the discourse of the Lyncean [Inchofer's name for Galileo throughout the document] and I realised that it was the philosophy of someone who does not stick to the true philosophy. Whether this be through error or ignorance, it is always rash.

1. He errs in the first place, in denying primary and secondary qualities even in bodies that act on external matter, as when he denies that heat inheres in the fire that acts on us to warm us.
2. He errs when he says that it is not possible to conceptually separate corporeal substances from the accidental properties that modify them, such as quantity and those that follow quantity. Such an opinion is absolutely contrary to faith, for instance in the case of the Eucharist, where quantity is not only really distinguished from substance but, moreover, exists separately.
3. He errs when he says that taste, smell, and colour are pure names, or are like extrinsic denominations taken from bodies that can have sensations, so that if these bodies were destroyed the accidental properties would also be removed and annihilated, especially since

they are said to be distinct from the primary, true, and real accidents. From this error two others follow: 1. That bodies that have the same quantity and the same figure will have the same taste, smell, etc. 2. That the bodies that lose their smell and taste will also lose their quantity and their figure, which, in the Lyncean's imagination, are not distinguished from taste, odour, etc.

4. He errs in calling actions the sensations of a living body which is acted upon by some external object, for instance when it is tickled by a feather or some other body. But this can be excused by the philosopher's lack of sophistication.

5. He errs when he claims that the cause of smell and taste is the same as that of tickling, which is caused by external agents since tickling is felt by the patient according to the disposition of his organic body, so that the sensation is accidentally related to whatever acts on the individual. But tastes and smells proceed from the qualities of objects and result from the way they are mixed. Likewise the organ of sensation in a given individual is accidentally disposed in this or that way so that one person feels more or less than another one according to these different dispositions.

6. He errs when he says, for example, that a heated iron can only warm sentient beings, for any object, placed before a fire, will receive heat as long as it is a 'mixed' body, and not composed of some fifth essence. And I say that the same happens whenever a body, placed next to a substance that acts by sensible qualities, receives the same qualities as that substance.

7. It immediately follows from the opinion of this author that in the Eucharist the accidental properties do not remain without the substance of the bread. This is evident for the accidental properties are said to act on the organ of sensation by being divided into very small particles which, since they are not the same as quantity (otherwise they would only act on the sense of touch) must be parts of the substance. And this can only be the substance of bread, for what else could it be? The same follows no less clearly from the statement that posits that the parts of the substance are distinct from dimensional quantity but not really distinct from the substance.

8. It also follows immediately that in the Eucharist there remain no other accidental qualities beyond quantity, figure, etc., because taste and smell are mere words if they are not related to the senses,

as the Lyncean erroneously believes. Therefore the accidental properties are absolutely not distinct from quantity, figure, etc.

If the author understands the smallest particles as sensible species, he will find some supporters in ancient philosophy, but he will have to affirm many things that are absurd and contrary to the Faith. This seems enough for now and, in the light of this, matters could be further investigated by the Holy Office.[21]

The Special Committee of Inquiry met five times during the two weeks following its creation in the first week of September 1632. On Thursday, 23 September, within twenty-four hours of their fifth and last meeting, the three clerics took their findings to a meeting of the Holy Office presided over by the pope. What they had to say must immediately have created confusion and no small sense of alarm. Urban had rushed into a full-frontal attack on Galileo and his accursed book because it had angered him and because he believed it to be politically expedient to do so. Now, thanks to Inchofer, he had too much on the man. If he put Galileo on trial as an arch-heretic, a man who dared using his new scientific ideas to question the nature of the Eucharist, he might be opening up a Pandora's box. The last thing the pope wanted was to draw attention to the mechanism of transubstantiation. Indeed, he could think of nothing more dangerous.

The Strong Arm of the Church

Just as the three members of the Special Committee of Inquiry into Galileo's work were reporting their findings linking *The Assayer* to the Eucharist, they also informed the pope that, in their opinion, the author of *The Dialogue Concerning the Two Chief World Systems* had erred in nine other distinct ways.

Top of their list was their belief that Galileo had been deceitful with the Roman censor and had not informed the relevant parties of the injunction against him dating back to 1616. The other eight points of conflict included having the Church's Preface to the book printed in a different font from the rest of the manuscript so that Galileo could distance himself from it; that he *frequently* deviated from the idea of using the Copernican model purely as a hypothesis; that the author tried to pretend he was giving a balanced account but was in fact clearly supportive of the Copernican model as fact; and that, in matters of mathematics and natural philosophy, he tried to claim that human knowledge can be equal to God's.

And here we come to a crossroads. From this point on we may consider two alternative scenarios to describe the machinations behind Galileo's trial. The first is the traditional one whereby Galileo was tried simply because he had openly defied the Church and had supported the Copernican theory (even though, officially, Copernicus's treatise *De Revolutionibus Orbium Coelestium* was 'false and contrary to Holy Scripture' and not strictly 'heretical').

However, the fact that Pope Urban VIII and the Inquisition were in possession of the document now known as G3 means that doubt must be cast on these transgressions having been the only reasons for the trial. Their existence means that the papal machinations in dealing with Galileo could have been far more complex than has been believed until recent times. This latter scenario is the central tenet of Pietro Redondi's theory (mentioned in the last chapter) and I believe it gives a far more convincing description of the events leading to Galileo's trial and sentence than that offered by traditional accounts. The well-known story of how Galileo was tried for disobedience and support of Copernicus has been mulled over and written about for centuries, but in the following pages I will present the case for a more complex description first proposed by Redondi in the early 1980s.

Presented with the conclusions of his committee in 1632, it was clear to the pope what must be done. The key to the prosecution would be that Galileo had deliberately defied the commands of the Church not to teach or write in support of Copernicanism unless his work was treated merely as a hypothesis, and there could be absolutely no mention of Galileo's much greater heresy: his conclusions about the nature of the atomic world and its ramifications for the miracle of the Eucharist. This was because the slightest suggestion the traditional Thomist description of transubstantiation might be fallible would be seized upon for their own ends by the many enemies of Rome.

A few days after this crucial meeting in the Vatican, Pope Urban dispatched a written summons to Galileo, ordering him to appear before the Inquisition in Rome, without delay. But delay was exactly what Galileo did do. Whether he was simply shocked by the call to the Vatican, or genuinely too ill to travel, he seems to have been paralysed into inaction.

He was certainly traumatised by Urban's response to the *Dialogue*, and his first reaction was to write to fellow Lyncean and trusted friend, the pope's nephew Cardinal Francesco Barberini. In this *cri de cœur* we can sense Galileo's desperation and barely suppressed fury:

Both my friends and I foresaw that my recently published *Dialogue* would find detractors [he began]. Of this we were assured by the fate of other works of mine previously printed, and because it seems this generally happens with doctrines which distinctly depart from common and inveterate opinions. But that the hatred of some men against me and my writings should have had the power to convince the most holy minds of the superiors that this book of mine is unworthy of publication was truly unexpected. Whenever I think of it, the fruits of all my studies and labours over so many years, which had in the past brought my name to the ears of men of letters with no little fame, are

now converted into grave blemishes on my reputation, giving a foothold to my enemies that they may rise up against my friends and say
that finally I have deserved to be ordered before the tribunal of the
Holy Office, a thing that happens only because of the most grave
delinquencies. This affects me in such a way that it makes me detest all
the time I have spent in those studies, by means of which I hoped and
aspired to separate myself somewhat from the trite and popular thinking of scholars; and by making me regret that I have exposed to the
world a part of my compositions, it causes me to wish to suppress and
condemn to the flames those which remain in my hands, entirely
satiating the umbrage of my enemies, to whom my thoughts are so
troublesome.[1]

He was now 68 years old and had been worn down by the struggle to
get his book published. Most importantly, though, the stress of learning
that this very same work had now exposed him to what would inevitably be, as the Tuscan ambassador Niccolini had recently put it
euphemistically, 'a troublesome affair', must have been incredibly hard
to bear.

He had many friends, and some advised him to flee Italy, to relocate
to Germany or Holland. These were largely Protestant states, and
Holland especially was famed for its tolerance of religious minorities
and ideologies. Even though Galileo was a Catholic, he would have
been received in either country as a hero, an avenging master perhaps;
and from there he might really have been able to change people's
thinking. But Galileo probably never took these suggestions seriously.
He was an Italian and he had long believed he could influence the
intellectual world from the inside. Furthermore, his daughters, whom
he loved and visited often, lived close to his home near Florence. They
were wedded to Christ and he could not take them with him.

One friend whom Galileo rather naïvely believed could help him
significantly was his patron, the grand duke. Such hopes, though, were
misplaced. Ferdinand liked Galileo, but he was afraid of the pope, who
had made the pecking order in Italy very clear when, during the spring
of that year, he had snatched Urbino after the ruler of the region,
Francesco della Rovere, had died suddenly. This territory should have
returned to Medici control, but Ferdinand was young and weak and
still very much under the influence of his extremely pious grandmother.
She was very fond of Galileo but not entirely approving of his philosophies. There can be no doubt that Ferdinand assisted Galileo as much

as he dared, but he had no sway at all over papal decisions and was really limited to trying to make Galileo's life as materially comfortable as possible during his ordeal. It was through his intermediary, the Tuscan ambassador to Rome, that Ferdinand kept open a line of communication with Urban that led to Galileo being treated with unique consideration by the papal office.

Indeed, the entire process in which Galileo was about to play a key role was quite different from any other trial contrived by the Holy Office. We must recall just how famous and important a figure Galileo was. He was a national treasure, famed for his genius and known across Europe for his discoveries and inventions, and this certainly influenced the behaviour of the Inquisition.

The usual procedures of the Inquisition were clinical and brutal. The best point of comparison is the treatment meted out to Giordano Bruno some three decades earlier. He had been imprisoned in a stinking, rat-infested cell and subjected to repeated torture. After arriving in Rome, Galileo was housed in palatial quarters and provided with all the creature comforts he could wish for. Additionally, he was able to communicate with the outside world through the Tuscan ambassador; but, in terms of due process, Galileo was subject to the same strictures as any other prisoner of the Inquisition. He was not told the nature of the charges brought against him, nor was he informed who had brought those charges. He was also forbidden to communicate his ideologies to anyone other than his prosecutors.

Through the final months of 1632 Galileo continued to plead ill health as a reason for delaying his journey to Rome. He produced doctor's certificates to prove his case and the ministers of the grand duke wrote letters to the Vatican to quell papal suspicions. He also made a reasonable case for the fact that travel was hampered by plague. But by the end of December the pope had had enough of excuses. On the thirtieth he sent a messenger to Tuscany to tell Galileo that if he did not leave for Rome immediately he would have him dragged there in chains.

Even then a further seven weeks passed before Galileo finally made it to the Palazzo Firenze, the ambassadorial palace in which Ferdinand had arranged for Galileo to stay. Much of the delay had been no fault of Galileo's. Thanks to the plague, he had been held up at Ponte a Centino, a small town on the border between Tuscany and the papal states, where he was kept in quarantine for twenty-two days and fed on a diet of eggs, bread and wine. By the time he reached Rome he was feeling surprisingly well. Perhaps some of the old fighting spirit of his younger days had returned, or else he had simply come to terms with uncertainty, accepting that ahead lay perils he could not avoid.

Galileo's arrival in Rome was entirely different from any other of his many visits to the city. The ambassador received him as an honoured guest and gave him the best rooms in the palace, but he was confined to the Palazzo Firenze and was only allowed approved visitors. This time there were no grand dinners, no celebrated evenings at the homes of the rich and famous, no awe-inspiring demonstrations of new devices. Galileo's first day in Rome was a bleak and chilly Sunday, the first of Lent, 13 February 1633, two days before his sixty-ninth birthday.

And then he was simply left to stew. This was a deliberate ploy of Urban's designed to undermine Galileo's mental state. February passed into March and March into April, and all the while Galileo was confined to the Palazzo Firenze and its grounds. During the long days he paced the flower-bordered paths of the palace gardens while at night he wandered the corridors, unable to sleep.

He was confined, but Ambassador Niccolini was not, and he met the pope several times during the two months his ward was held at the Tuscan embassy. At each meeting Niccolini tried to soften the mood of the pontiff, but Urban was immovable. He could be accommodating when it came to Galileo's personal requirements – allowing him to see some friends, allowing him the freedom of the palace grounds – each act of leniency offered as a kindness to the grand duke; but over matters of doctrine, or the question of Galileo's clear disobedience, Urban's views were unshakable.

As a consequence, any attempt Niccolini made to resolve the matter without a trial fell on deaf ears. The ambassador was the mouthpiece for the grand duke, who was attempting to soften the pope's stance through his intermediary; but the pope had the bit between his teeth and was resolute. 'There is no way out,' he told Niccolini, 'and may God forgive Galileo for meddling in these subjects. There is an argument that no one has ever been able to answer, namely that God, who is omnipotent, can do anything. And if he is omnipotent, who can bind him?'[2]

It is possible that the further delay in the proceedings against Galileo was due to continued debate within the Holy Office over the question of how the case should be conducted. The order of 1616 seemed to make it clear that in writing the *Dialogue* Galileo had been openly defiant, but most of the key players of seventeen years earlier were now dead; Bellarmine, Paul V and the scabrous Seghizzi were now silent on the matter; and, of course, the document describing the strictures on Galileo was unsigned by either the man at the centre of the dispute or Cardinal Bellarmine. Furthermore, it was unclear where Galileo himself stood over the cause of the trial and the judgements of the prosecution. Would he be compliant?

All the while, Niccolini was trying, with only limited success, to calm down Galileo and to help him prepare for what was now the inevitable: a trial before the Inquisition. 'We are dealing with the Congregation of the Holy Office, whose goings-on are so secret and none of those members opens his mouth because of the censures that are in force,' he told him bluntly.[3]

Galileo's daughter Maria Celeste also played her part in reassuring her father. She wrote to him every Saturday and Galileo was attentive in his responses. A typical letter from her arrived in Rome on 5 March, in which she wrote: 'I rejoice and ever again I thank blessed God hearing that your affairs thus far proceed with such tranquillity and silence, which bodes well for a happy and prosperous outcome, as I have always hoped would come with divine help and by the intercession of the most holy Blessed Virgin.'[4]

But the wait in Rome and the clear resolution of Urban had the effect of hardening Galileo's mood. Niccolini rightly saw this as incredibly dangerous. Writing to the grand duke, he reported with some alarm how he had been unsuccessful in trying to get Galileo to be more flexible:

> I begged him, in the interests of a quick resolution, not to bother maintaining them [his scientific views] and to agree to what they want him to hold or believe about the Earth's motion. He was extremely distressed by this, and since yesterday I see him so depressed that I fear greatly for his life. I will try to obtain permission for him to keep a servant and have other conveniences. We all want to cheer him up, and we seek the assistance of friends and those who play a role in these deliberations because he really deserves to be helped. Everyone in the embassy is extremely fond of him and feels the greatest sorrow.[5]

Imagining how Galileo must have felt is no easy task. He had been forced into a gilded cage, but we must remember he was a very proud and self-assured man. He was a member of the Lyncean Academy, a radical group which believed that the religious should face up to the challenges of the 'new science', that suppression of the intellect was a sin greater than anything Rome could claim for the pious. But Galileo was growing old. He had lost none of his mental prowess, but he was tired, and he did not want to be in Rome to fight the clergy. The days when he would gladly have stood up to declare his beliefs to all who would listen were passing; now he would rather be enjoying the quiet of his home in Tuscany and writing more books that might make his philosophies clearer. He simply could not accept the position in which he now found himself: he had done everything possible to secure papal permission to publish the *Dialogue*, and he had played by the rules. Bellarmine had not forced him into complete silence over Copernicus, and he had been encouraged to write his latest work by Urban himself.

The first hearing before the Inquisition took place on Tuesday, 12 April at the Palace of the Holy Office on the south side of St Peter's. Galileo was escorted from the embassy by an armed guard and taken to a small, plain room. Inside there was nothing but a wooden table and two chairs. The prisoner was obliged to stand while the two Inquisitors, Commissioner Vincenzo Maculano and his assistant, Prosecutor Carlo Sinceri, were seated. On the table there was a set of papers and a copy of the *Dialogue*, which throughout the hearing was referred to as 'Exhibit A'.

We know the precise nature of this hearing and those that followed because a detailed record of everything that was said and done was kept for the Inquisition records. Throughout the hearings (there were four altogether) Commissioner Maculano put his questions to Galileo in Latin and in the third person. The answers came back in Italian in the first person, which adds a fitting element of dislocation to the exchange. It begins:

> Summoned, there appeared personally in Rome at the palace of the Holy Office, in the usual quarters of the Reverend Father Commissary, fully in the presence of the Reverend Father Vincenzo Maculano of Firenzuola, Commissary General, and of his assistant Reverend Father Carlo Sinceri, Prosecutor of the Holy Office, Galileo, son of the late Vincenzo Galilei, Florentine, seventy years old [*sic*], who, having taken a formal oath to tell the truth, was asked by the Fathers the following:

> Q: By what means and how long ago did he come to Rome.
> A: I arrived in Rome the first Sunday of Lent, and I came in a litter.

Q: Whether he came of his own accord, or was called, or was ordered by someone to come to Rome, and by whom.

A: In Florence the Father Inquisitor ordered me to Rome to present myself to the Holy Office, this being an injunction by the officials of the Holy Office.

Q: Whether he knows or can guess the reason why he was ordered to Rome.

A: I imagine that the reason why I have been ordered to present myself to the Holy Office in Rome is to account for my recently printed book. I imagine this because of the injunction to the printer and myself, a few days before I was ordered to come to Rome; not to issue any more of these books; and because the printer was ordered by the Father Inquisitor to send the original manuscript of my book to the Holy Office in Rome.

Q: That he explain the character of the book on account of which he thinks he was ordered to come to Rome.

A: It is a book written in dialogue form. It treats of the constitution of the world, that is, of the two chief systems, and the arrangement of the heavens and the elements.

Q: Whether, if he were shown the said book, he is prepared to identify it as his.

A: I hope so; I hope that if the book is shown to me I should recognise it. And having been shown one of the books printed in Florence in 1632, whose title is *Dialogue of Galileo Galilei Lyncean etc.*, which examines the two systems of the world, and having looked at it and inspected it carefully, he said: I know this book very well; it is one of those printed in Florence; and I acknowledge it as mine and written by me.

Q: Whether he likewise acknowledges each and every thing contained in the said book as his.

A: I know this book shown to me, for it is one of those printed in Florence; and I acknowledge all it contains as having been written by me.

Q: When and where he wrote the said book, and how long it took him.

A: In regard to the place, I wrote it in Florence, beginning ten or twelve years ago; and it must have taken me seven or eight years, but not continuously.

Q: Whether he was in Rome other times, especially in the year 1616, and for what occasion.

A: I was in Rome in the year 1616. I was here in the second year of His

Holiness Urban VIII's pontificate; and I was here three years ago, the occasion being that I wanted to have my book printed. The occasion for my being in Rome in the year 1616 was that, having heard objections to Nicolaus Copernicus's opinion on the Earth's motion, the Sun's stability, and the arrangement of the heavenly spheres, in order to be sure of holding only holy and Catholic opinions, I came to hear what was proper to hold in regard to this topic.

Q: Whether he came of his own accord or was summoned, the reason for the summons, and with whom he discussed the above-mentioned topics.

A: In 1616 I came to Rome of my own accord, without being summoned, for the reason I mentioned. In Rome I discussed this matter with some cardinals who oversaw the Holy Office at that time, especially with Cardinals Bellarmine, Aracoeli, San Eusebio, Bonsi, and d'Ascoli.

Q: What specifically he discussed with the above-mentioned cardinals.

A: The occasion for discussing with the said cardinals was that they wanted to be informed about Copernicus's doctrine, his book being very difficult to understand for those who are not professional mathematicians and astronomers. In particular they wanted to understand the arrangement of the heavenly spheres according to Copernicus's hypothesis, how he places the Sun at the centre of the planets' orbits, how around the Sun he places next the orbit of Mercury, around the latter that of Venus, then the Moon around the Earth, and around this Mars, Jupiter, and Saturn; and in regard to motion, he makes the Sun stationary at the centre and the Earth turn on itself and around the Sun, that is, on itself with the diurnal motion and around the Sun with the annual motion.

Q: Since, as he says, he came to Rome to be able to have the resolution and the truth regarding the above, what then was decided about this matter.

A: Regarding the controversy which centred on the above-mentioned opinion of the Sun's stability and Earth's motion, it was decided by the Holy Congregation of the Index that this opinion, taken absolutely, is anathema and is to be admitted only hypothetically, in the way that Copernicus takes it.

Q: Whether he was then notified of the said decision, and by whom.

A: I was indeed notified of the said decision of the Congregation of the Index, and I was notified by Lord Cardinal Bellarmine.

Q: What the Most Eminent Bellarmine told him about the said decision, whether he said anything else about the matter, and if so, what.

A: Lord Cardinal Bellarmine told me that Copernicus's opinion could be held hypothetically, as Copernicus himself had held it. His Eminence knew that I held it hypothetically, namely in the way that Copernicus held it, as you can see from an answer by the same Lord Cardinal to a letter of Father Master Paolo Antonio Foscarini, Provincial of the Carmelites; I have a copy of this, and in it one finds these words: 'I say that it seems to me that Your Paternity and Mr Galileo are proceeding prudently by limiting yourselves to speaking hypothetically and not absolutely.' This letter by the said Lord Cardinal is dated 12 April 1615. Moreover, he told me that otherwise, namely taken absolutely, the opinion could be neither held nor defended.

Q: What was decided and then made known to him precisely in the month of February 1616.

A: In the month of February 1616, Lord Cardinal Bellarmine told me that since Copernicus's opinion, taken absolutely, was contrary to Holy Scripture, it could be neither held nor defended, but it could be taken and used hypothetically. In conformity with this I keep a certificate by Lord Cardinal Bellarmine himself, dated 26 May 1616, in which he says that Copernicus's opinion cannot be held or defended, being against Holy Scripture. I present a copy of this certificate. And he showed a sheet of paper with twelve lines of writing on one side only, beginning 'We, Robert Cardinal Bellarmine, have' and ending 'on this 26th day of May 1616,' signed 'The same mentioned above, Robert Cardinal Bellarmine.' This evidence was accepted and marked with the letter B. Then he added: I have the original of this certificate with me in Rome, and it is written all in the hand of the above-mentioned Lord Cardinal Bellarmine.

Q: Whether, when he was notified of the above-mentioned matters, there were others present, and who they were.

A: When Lord Cardinal Bellarmine notified me of what I mentioned regarding Copernicus's opinion, there were some Dominican Fathers present, but I did not know them nor have I seen them since.

Q: Whether at that time, in the presence of those Fathers, he was given any injunction either by them or by someone else concerning the same matter, and if so, what.

A: As I remember it, the affair took place in the following way. One morning Lord Cardinal Bellarmine sent for me, and he told me a certain detail that I should like to speak to the ear of His Holiness before telling others; but then at the end he told me that Copernicus's opinion could not be held or defended, being contrary to Holy Scripture. I do not recall whether those Dominican Fathers were there at first or came afterward; nor do I recall whether they were present when the Lord Cardinal told me that the said opinion could not be held. Finally, it may be that I was given an injunction not to hold or defend the said opinion, but I do not recall it since this is something of many years ago.

Q: Whether, if one were to read to him what he was then told and ordered with injunction, he would remember that.

A: I do not recall that I was told anything else, nor can I know whether I shall remember what was then told me, even if it is read to me. I am saying freely what I recall because I claim I have not violated that injunction, the said opinion of the Earth's motion and Sun's stability.

Q: And having been told that the said injunction, given to him then in the presence of witnesses, states that he cannot in any way whatever hold, defend, or teach the said opinion, he was asked whether he remembers how and by whom he was so ordered.

A: I do not recall that this injunction was given me any other way than orally by Lord Cardinal Bellarmine. I do remember that the injunction was that I could not hold or defend, and maybe even that I could not teach. I do not recall, further, that there was the phrase in any way whatever, but maybe there was; in fact, I did not think about it or keep it in mind, having received a few months thereafter Lord Cardinal Bellarmine's certificate dated 26 May which I have presented and in which is explained the order given to me not to hold or defend the said opinion. Regarding the other two phrases in the said injunction now mentioned, namely not to teach and in any way whatever, I did not retain them in my memory, I think because they are not contained in the said certificate, which I relied upon and kept as a reminder.

Q: Whether, after the issuing of the said injunction, he obtained any permission to write the book identified by himself, which he later sent to the printer.

A: After the above-mentioned injunction I did not seek permission to write the above-mentioned book which I have identified, because

I do not think that by writing this book I was contradicting at all the injunction given me not to hold, defend, or teach the said opinion, instead I believe I was refuting it.

Q: Whether he obtained permission for printing the same book, by whom, and whether for himself or for someone else.

A: To obtain permission to print the above-mentioned book, although I was receiving profitable offers from France, Germany, and Venice, I refused them and spontaneously. I came to Rome three years ago to place it into the hands of the chief censor, the Master of the Sacred Palace, giving him absolute authority to add, delete, and change as he saw fit. After having it examined very diligently by his associate Father Visconti, the Master of the Sacred Palace reviewed it again himself and licensed it; that is, having approved the book, he gave me permission but ordered to have the book printed in Rome. Since, in view of the approaching summer, I wanted to go back home to avoid the danger of getting sick, having been away all of May and June, we agreed that I was to return here the following autumn.

While I was in Florence, the plague struck and commerce was halted; so, seeing that I could not come to Rome, by correspondence I requested of the same Master of the Sacred Palace permission for the book to be printed in Florence. He communicated to me that he would want to review my original manuscript, and that therefore I should send it to him.

Despite having used every possible care and having contacted even the highest secretaries of the Grand Duke and the directors of the postal service, to try to send the said original safely, I received no assurance that this could be done, and it certainly would have been damaged, washed out, or burned, such was the strictness at the borders. I related this to the same Father Master Giacinto Stefani, a Dominican, professor of Scared Scripture at the University of Florence, preacher for the Most Serene Highnesses, and consultant to the Holy Office. The book was handed over by me to the Father Inquisitor of Florence and by the Father Inquisitor to the above-mentioned Father Giacinto Stefani; the latter returned it to the Father Inquisitor, who sent it to Mr Niccolò dell' Antella, reviewer of books to be printed for the Most Serene Highness of Florence; the printer, Landini, received it from this Mr Niccolò and, having negotiated with the Father Inquisitor, printed it, observing strictly every order given by the Father Master of the Sacred Palace.

Q: Whether, when he asked the above-mentioned Master of the Sacred Palace for permission to print the above-mentioned book, he revealed to the same Most Reverend Father Master the injunction previously given to him concerning the directive of the Holy Congregation, mentioned above.

A: When I asked him for permission to print the book, I did not say anything to the Father Master of the Sacred Palace about the above-mentioned injunction because I did not judge it necessary, having no fears since with the said book I had neither held nor defended the opinion of the Earth's motion and Sun's stability. I had instead shown the contrary of Copernicus's opinion and shown that Copernicus's reasons are invalid and inconclusive.

With this the deposition ended, and he was assigned a certain room in the dormitory of the officials, in the Palace of the Holy Office, in lieu of prison, with the injunction not to leave it without special permission, under penalty to be decided by the Holy Congregation; and he was ordered to sign below and was sworn to silence.

I, Galileo Galilei, have testified as above.[6]

This first hearing laid the foundations of the dispute. The inquisitors had been instructed to gather information from Galileo, but a more important objective was to ascertain the stance the man would take. Would he be completely compliant or was he so arrogant and assured that he would resist?

It is clear from this transcript that Galileo was in no mood to comply with the demands of the Holy Office. Indeed, at times his answers are almost flippant. He was still in a defensive frame of mind, and it is obvious that at this stage he had no idea of the hidden agenda behind the trail. All he had to go on was his own suspicions and the fragmentary information from friends leaked to him via the ambassador. But for Galileo at this time the most disturbing aspect of the hearing came with the final announcement. He had believed he was to return to the Tuscan embassy, but instead he was now being taken to a suite of rooms in the Palace of the Inquisition. This may have been a shock, but it was cushioned by more papal leniency. Thanks to the intervention of Ferdinand, Galileo was not to be treated like any other prisoner and left to survive on a subsistence diet in the dungeons of the Castel Sant' Angelo. Instead, his own prosecutor, Father Sinceri, had offered to vacate the rooms he normally occupied so that the famous prisoner would be comfortable.

He could not complain about the lavish quarters in which he was held or the fine foods served to him by servants; it was simply the fact of his imprisonment that disturbed Galileo so much. At the home of the ambassador he could at least pretend there was little wrong – that he still had his freedom and that this entire matter would be quickly resolved. Now, he was being held in a real prison, albeit a very comfortable one. He could not even deceive himself that he could walk out through the gates of the palace unmolested.

Writing to him immediately after this first hearing, Maria Celeste, who appears to have remained in no doubt that her father was innocent and that his call to Rome was due to nothing more than a 'misunderstanding', tried to lift his spirits:

Signor Geri [the grand duke's secretary] informed me of the conditions imposed on you on account of your affair [she wrote]. Sire, alas that you are detained in the chamber of the Holy Office; on the one hand this gives me great distress, convinced as I am that you find yourself with scant peace of mind, and perhaps also deprived of all bodily comforts: on the other hand, considering the need for events to reach this stage, in order for the authorities to dismiss you, as well as the kindliness with which everyone there has treated you up till now, and above all the justice of the cause and your innocence in this instance, I console myself and cling to the expectation of a happy and prosperous triumph, with the help of blessed God, to Whom my heart never ceases to cry out, commending you with all the love and trust it contains.

The only thing for you to do now is to guard your good spirits [she continued], taking care not to jeopardise your health with excessive worry, but to direct your thoughts and hopes to God, Who, like a tender, loving father, never abandons those who confide in Him and appeal to Him for help in time of need. Dearest lord father, I wanted to write to you now, to tell you I partake in your torments, so as to make them lighter for you to bear: I have given no hint of these difficulties to anyone else, wanting to keep the unpleasant news to myself, and to speak to the others only of your pleasures and satisfactions. Thus we are all awaiting your return, eager to enjoy your conversation again with delight.

And who knows, Sire, if while I sit writing, you may not already find yourself released from your predicament and free of all concerns? Thus may it please the Lord, Who must be the One to console you, and in Whose care I leave you.[7]

The first hearing had not helped to simplify the situation. It was quite apparent that Galileo was not going to fall to his knees in repentance without some encouragement. Commissioner Maculano was an intelligent and cunning man on the rise, and he was one of perhaps only half a dozen individuals, including the three members of the Special Committee of Inquiry, who were aware of the broader agenda.

Since the beginning of April Pope Urban had been staying at his country estate of Castel Gandolfo and had missed several meetings of the Holy Office. At one such meeting, on 28 April, Maculano made the bold suggestion that Galileo should now be informed of the bigger picture. He believed he should be told of the document we know as G3 and Inchofer's report (EE291), and should be made to understand the dangerous nature of his own theories. Thus informed of a simple truth, Maculano believed, Galileo would be led to confess to his crimes and to admit that he had been in error. If he did not do this he should be tortured until he submitted. In short, Galileo should be offered a way out. If he could admit to the lesser offences of disobedience and contradicting doctrine, he would be punished with imprisonment under house arrest. If he challenged this – if he objected in any way or, most importantly, if he ever again made any mention of his ideas concerning atomic theory – he would face the ultimate punishment.

This was a very unusual idea because it broke with the normal protocol of the Inquisition – the policy of never informing the suspect of the charges brought against them; but, unorthodox as Maculano's proposal may have seemed, the Inquisition record of the proceedings against Galileo shows that it was in fact agreed to by the other churchmen at the meeting.[8] Leaving the meeting, Maculano went directly to Galileo's rooms at the Palace of the Inquisition. The old man had been ill in bed for four days with a fever and was suffering from severe stress. Maculano suggested a gentle walk through the gardens of the palace, and on this stroll he laid out his proposal to Galileo, explaining the find in the archive and the concerns of the Holy Office. Maculano was brutally frank. If Galileo decided not to cooperate: 'It would', he informed him, 'become necessary to apply greater rigour to the administration of justice and less regard for the ramifications of this business'.[9] In other words, Galileo had no real choice: comply, or else.

Giordano Bruno had chosen to defy attempts by Pope Clement VIII to cajole him into a confession, but Bruno had been a visionary of a different hue from Galileo. He had been prepared for self-sacrifice, and believed that his destiny was to change religion, to make it a better thing. Galileo harboured no such pretensions or fantasies. He wished for the cardinals to understand his philosophical ideas and to accommodate the new rationality for which he was the leading spokesman; but he had no intention of dying for this cause. It is hard to imagine him pausing for a heartbeat before accepting Maculano's proposal.

Almost four centuries on, it is impossible to know whether Galileo had any inkling the clergy had realised the importance of his atomic model before Commissioner Maculano visited him on 28 April 1633; but, crucially, it offered a way out of the horrible nightmare into which he had been cast since the previous August. He would be allowed to live, to continue working. All he had to do was keep quiet about his atomic theory and not provoke the paranoia of the Church.

Maculano was thrilled by his own cleverness and wrote immediately to the pope:

I hope His Holiness will be satisfied. In this matter, the case can now be brought to a speedy conclusion. The tribunal will maintain its reputation. The culprit may be treated with mercy. Whatever the final outcome, he will be thankful for the favour which has been given him. Tomorrow I will obtain his confession. After that I will question him about his intention and allow him to present a defence. That done, he can be granted imprisonment in his own house, as Your Eminence has suggested.[10]

Two days later, on 30 April, Galileo made his second appearance before Maculano and Sinceri, and the report of the meeting describes a very different encounter from the first one held eighteen days earlier. The official account begins:

Called personally to the Hall of the Congregations, in the presence and with the assistance of those mentioned above and of myself, the above-mentioned Galileo Galilei, who has since then petitioned to be heard, having sworn an oath to tell the truth, was asked by the Fathers the following:

Q: That he state whatever he wished to say.

A: For several days I have been thinking continuously and directly about the interrogations I underwent on the 16th of this month and in particular about the question whether sixteen years ago I had been prohibited, by order of the Holy Office, from holding, defending, and teaching in any way whatever the opinion, then condemned, of the Earth's motion and Sun's stability. It dawned on me to reread my printed *Dialogue*, which over the last three years I had not even looked at. I wanted to check very carefully whether, against my purest intention, through my oversight, there might have fallen from my pen not only something enabling readers or superiors to infer a defect of disobedience on my part, but also other details through which one might think of me as a transgressor of the orders of the Holy Church. Being at liberty, through the generous approval of superiors, to send one of my servants for errands, I managed to get a copy of my book, and I started to read it with the greatest concentration and to examine it in the most detailed manner.

Not having seen it for so long, I found it almost a new book by another author. Now, I freely confess that it appeared to me in several places to be written in such a way that a reader, not aware of my intention, would have had reason to believe that the arguments for the false side, which I intended to confute, were so stated as to be capable of convincing because of their power, rather than being easy to answer. In particular, two arguments, one based on sunspots and the other on the tides, are presented favourably to the reader as being strong and powerful, more than would seem proper for someone who deemed them to be inconclusive and wanted to confute them, as indeed I inwardly and truly wish to do and do hold them to be inconclusive and refutable.

As an excuse for myself, within myself, for having fallen into an error so foreign to my intention, I was not completely satisfied with saying that when one presents arguments for the opposite side with the intention of confuting them, they must be explained in the fairest way and not be made out of straw to the disadvantage of the opponent, especially when one is writing in dialogue form. Being dissatisfied with this excuse, as I said, I resorted to that of the natural gratification everyone feels for his own subtleties and for showing himself to be cleverer than the average man, by finding ingenious and apparent arguments even in favour of false propositions.

Nevertheless, even though, to use Cicero's words, 'I am more desirous of glory than is suitable' – if I had to write out the same arguments now, there is no doubt I would weaken them in such a way that they could not appear to exhibit a force which they really and essentially lack. My error then was, and I confess it, one of vain ambition, pure ignorance, and carelessness. This is as much as I need to say on this occasion, and it occurred to me as I reread my book.

With this, having obtained his signature, and having sworn him to silence, the Fathers formally concluded the hearing.

I, Galileo Galilei, have testified as above.

According to the report, Galileo was then led from the room, but as he was escorted along the corridor he asked to be taken back to the courtroom. He felt that his replies had been insufficiently plain and he wished to make his position absolutely clear. He told his interrogators:

For greater confirmation that I neither did hold nor do hold as true the condemned opinion of the Earth's motion and Sun's stability, if, as I desire, I am granted the possibility and the time to prove it more clearly, I am ready to do so. The occasion for it is readily available since in the book already published the speakers agree that after a certain time they should meet again to discuss various physical problems other than the subject already dealt with. Hence, with this pretext to add one or two other days, I promise to reconsider the arguments already presented in favour of the said false and condemned opinion and to confute them in the clearest way that the blessed God will enable me to do. So I beg this Holy Tribunal to co-operate with me towards this good resolution, by granting me the permission to put it into practice.

And again he signed: 'I, Galileo Galilei, affirm the above.'

Quite how genuine Galileo was being in making this statement is unknowable. It could have sprung simply from fear, exhaustion, or a clear desire to absolve himself as best he could. It might also have been a genuine request to alter the balance of the *Dialogue* to offer a stronger voice to Simplicio, the case for the theologians.

Ten days later, on 10 May, a third hearing was convened. This time Galileo was told to present his written defence to the Inquisitors.

Galileo Galilei mentioned above; and, called before his Paternity, the same Father Commissary gave him a deadline of eight days to present his defence, if he wanted and intended to do it.

Having heard this, he said: I understand what Your Paternity has told me. In reply I say that I do want to present something in my defence, namely in order to show the sincerity and purity of my intention, not at all to excuse my having transgressed in some ways, as I have already said. I present the following statement, together with a certificate by the late Most Eminent Lord Cardinal Bellarmine, written with his own hand by the Lord Cardinal himself, of which I earlier presented a copy by my hand. For the rest I rely in every way on the usual mercy and clemency of this Tribunal.

Galileo then read out his defence:

In an earlier interrogation, I was asked whether I had informed the Most Reverend Father Master of the Sacred Palace about the private injunction issued to me sixteen years ago by order of the Holy Office: 'not to hold, defend, or teach in any way whatever', the opinion of the Earth's motion and Sun's stability and I answered 'No'. Since I was not asked the reason why I did not inform him, I did not have the opportunity to say anything else. Now it seems to me necessary to mention it, in order to prove the absolute purity of my mind, which is always averse to using simulation.

I say, then, that at that time some of my enemies were spreading the rumour that I had been called by the Lord Cardinal Bellarmine in order to abandon some opinions and doctrines of mine, that I had had to abjure, that I had also received punishments for them, etc., and so I was forced to resort to His Eminence and to beg him to give me a certificate explaining why I had been called. I received this certificate, written by his own hand, and it is what I attach to the present statement.

In it one clearly sees that I was only told not to hold or defend Copernicus's doctrine of the Earth's motion and Sun's stability; but one cannot see any trace that, besides this general pronouncement applicable to all, I was given any other special order. Having the reminder of this authentic certificate, hand-written by the one who issued the order himself, I did not try later to give any other thought to the words used to give me the said injunction, to the effect that one cannot defend or hold, etc.; thus, the two phrases besides 'holding' and 'defending' which I hear are contained in the injunction given to me and recorded, that is, 'teaching' and 'in any way whatever', struck me as new. I do not think I should be mistrusted about the fact that in the course of fourteen or sixteen years I lost any memory of them, especially since I had no need to give the matter thought, having such a valid reminder in writing. Now, when those two phrases are removed and we retain only the other two mentioned in the attached certificate, there is no reason to doubt that the order contained in it is the same as the injunction issued by the decree of the Holy Congregation of the Index. From this I feel very reasonably excused for not notifying the Father Master of the Sacred Palace of the injunction given to me in private, the latter being the same as the one of the Congregation of the Index.

Given that my book was not subject to more stringent censures than those required by the decree of the Index, I followed the surest and most effective way to protect it and purge it of any trace of blemish. It seems to me that this is clear, since I handed it over to the supreme Inquisitor at a time when many books on the same subjects were being prohibited solely on account of the above-mentioned decree.

From the things I am saying, I think I can firmly hope that the idea of my having knowingly and willingly disobeyed the orders given me will be given no credence by the Most Eminent and Most Prudent Lord judges. Thus, those flaws that can be seen scattered throughout my book were not introduced through the cunning of an insincere intention, but rather through the vain ambition and satisfaction of appearing clever above and beyond the average among popular writers; this was an inadvertent result of my writing, as I confessed in another deposition of mine. I am ready to make amends and compensate for this flaw by every possible means, whenever I may be either ordered or allowed by Their Most Eminent Lordships.

Finally, I am left with asking you to consider the pitiable state of health to which I am reduced, owing to ten months of constant mental distress, and the discomforts of a long and tiresome journey in the most awful season and at the age of seventy; I feel I have lost the years which my previous state of health promised me.

I am encouraged to do this by the faith I have in the clemency and kindness of heart of the Most Eminent Lordships, my judges; and I hope that if their sense of justice perceives anything lacking among so many ailments as adequate punishment for my crimes, they will, I beg them, condone it out of regard for my declining old age, which I humbly also ask them to consider. Equally, I want them to consider my honour and reputation against the slanders of those who despise me, and I hope that when the latter insist on disparaging my reputation, the Most Eminent Lordships my judges will take it as evidence why it became necessary for me to obtain from the Most Eminent Lord Cardinal Bellarmine the certificate attached herewith.

As a special favour from the pope, after this hearing Galileo was returned to the embassy, where he was allowed to reside for the rest of the trial. He was exhausted by his ordeal and immediately took to his sickbed. The ambassador, Niccolini, was clearly concerned for his guest and in a letter to the grand duke he reported that Galileo had returned from the latest hearing 'half-dead'.

There was a long delay between this hearing and Galileo's final appearance before Maculano and Sinceri. The main reason for this was simple logistics: the pope did not return to Rome from his holiday home until 20 May, and when he did, he was preoccupied with military concerns. The first opportunity he had to attend a meeting of the Holy Office to discuss the Galileo affair was Thursday, 16 June. At this meeting it was decided that Galileo should appear one last time before his judges in order to clarify his opinions again.

At this meeting of the Holy Office it was also decided just what should be done with Galileo. Three weeks earlier, on 22 May, his *Dialogue* had been placed on the Index, an act which in itself was enormously upsetting and depressing for the author. But the pope wanted to see Galileo suffer. He could not simply allow him to return to his work unscathed and unfettered. The gathered cardinals concluded that Galileo must be publicly humiliated and then imprisoned for life.

The report of the trial tells us that on 21 June, three days after the meeting of the Holy Office, the prisoner was brought again to the Palace of the Holy Office and made to stand before his inquisitors, where he swore to tell the truth and was asked by the Fathers the following:

Q: Whether he had anything to say.
A: I have nothing to say.
Q: Whether he holds or has held, and for how long, that the Sun is the centre of the world and the Earth is not the centre of the world but moves also with diurnal motion.

A: A long time ago, that is, before the decision of the Holy Congregation of the Index, and before I was issued that injunction, I was undecided and regarded the two opinions, those of Ptolemy and Copernicus, as disputable, because either the one or the other could be true in nature. But after the above-mentioned decision, assured by the prudence of the authorities, all my uncertainty stopped, and I held, as I still hold, as true and undoubted Ptolemy's opinion, namely the stability of the Earth and the motion of the Sun.

Q: Having been told that he is presumed to have held the said opinion after that time, from the manner and procedure in which the said opinion is discussed and defended in the book he published after that time, indeed from the very fact that he wrote and published the said book, therefore he was asked to freely tell the truth whether he holds or has held that opinion.

A: In regard to my writing of the *Dialogue* already published, I did not do so because I held Copernicus's opinion to be true. Instead, deeming only to be doing a beneficial service, I explained the physical and astronomical reasons that can be advanced for one side and for the other; I tried to show that none of these, neither those in favour of this opinion or that, had the strength of a conclusive proof and that therefore to proceed with certainty one had to resort to the determination of more subtle doctrines, as one can see in many places in the *Dialogue*. So for my part I conclude that I do not hold and, after the determination of the authorities, I have not held the condemned opinion.

Q: Having been told that from the book itself and the reasons advanced for the affirmative side, namely that the Earth moves and the Sun is motionless, he is presumed, as it was stated, that he holds Copernicus's opinion, or at least that he held it at the time, therefore he was told that unless he decided to proffer the truth, one would have recourse to the remedies of the law and to appropriate steps against him.

A: I do not hold this opinion of Copernicus, and I have not held it after being ordered by injunction to abandon it. For the rest, here I am in your hands; do as you please.

Q: And he was told to tell the truth; otherwise one would have recourse to torture.

A: I am here to obey, but I have not held this opinion after the determination was made, as I said.

And since nothing else could be done for the execution of the decision, after he signed he was sent to his place.

I, Galileo Galilei, have testified as above.

At last the affair was almost over. Just one more symbolic act remained: Galileo was to be called before a gathering of cardinals in a room adjoining the Church of Santa Maria Sopra Minerva, where he would be made to recant publicly. It was all vaudeville, of course – a show.

Dressed in a penitent's white robe, Galileo was led into the room. Before him, seated in a semicircle, were eight cardinals along with their assistants and a miscellany of witnesses. Three officials – Cardinal Laudivio Zacchia, Cardinal Gaspare Borgia and Francesco Barberini – had either refused to attend or were indisposed. It is possible that Borgia refused to attend simply out of spite towards Urban, with whom he had recently clashed. Most notable, however, was the absence of Francesco Barberini, Galileo's closest friend in Rome and fellow member of the Lynceans. It is quite likely that he simply could not bring himself to attend, to sit impassively as Galileo was forced to humiliate himself.

Galileo was told to kneel to hear the clerical condemnation and the sentence of the Holy See:

Whereas you, Galileo, son of the late Vincenzo Galilei, Florentine, aged seventy years [it began], were in the year 1615 denounced to this Holy Office for holding as true the false doctrine taught by some that the Sun is the centre of the world and immovable and that the Earth moves, and also with a diurnal motion; for having disciples to whom you taught the same doctrine; for holding correspondence with certain mathematicians of Germany concerning the same; for having printed certain letters, entitled *On the Sunspots*, wherein you developed the same doctrine as true; and for replying to the objections from the Holy Scriptures, which from time to time were urged against it, by interpreting the said Scriptures according to your own meaning: and whereas there was thereupon produced the copy of a document in the form of a letter, purporting to be written by you to one formerly your disciple, and in this divers propositions are set forth, following the position of Copernicus, which are contrary to the true sense and authority of Holy Scripture.

This Holy Tribunal being therefore of intention to proceed against the trouble and mischief thence resulting, which went on increasing to the prejudice of the Holy Faith, by command of His Holiness and of the Most Eminent Lords Cardinals of this supreme and universal Inquisition, the two propositions of the stability of the Sun and the motion of the Earth were by the theological Qualifiers qualified as follows:

The proposition that the Sun is the centre of the world and does not move from its place is absurd and false philosophically and formally heretical, because it is expressly contrary to Holy Scripture.*

The proposition that the Earth is not the centre of the world and immovable but that it moves, and also with a diurnal motion, is equally absurd and false philosophically and theologically considered at least erroneous in faith.

But whereas it was desired at that time to deal leniently with you, it was decreed at the Holy Congregation held before His Holiness on the twenty-fifth of February, 1616, that his Eminence the Lord Cardinal Bellarmine should order you to abandon altogether the said false doctrine and, in the event of your refusal, that an injunction should be imposed upon you by the Commissary of the Holy Office to give up the said doctrine and not to teach it to others, not to defend it, nor even to discuss it; and that failing your acquiescence in this injunction, that you should be imprisoned. In execution of this decree, on the following day at the palace of and in the presence of the Cardinal Bellarmine, after being informed and warned in a friendly way by the same Lord Cardinal, you were given an injunction by the then Father Commissary of the Holy Office in the presence of a notary and witnesses to the effect that you must completely abandon the said false opinion, and that in the future you could neither hold, nor defend, nor teach it in any way whatever, either orally or in writing; having promised to obey, you were dismissed.

Furthermore, in order to completely eliminate such a pernicious doctrine, and not let it creep any further to the great detriment of Catholic truth, the Holy Congregation of the Index issued a decree which prohibited books which treat of this and declaring the doctrine itself to be false and wholly contrary to the divine and Holy Scripture.

And whereas a book has appeared here lately, printed in Florence last year, whose inscription showed that you were the author, the title

---

*It is interesting to note the insistence upon the words 'formally heretical'. Copernicus's *De Revolutionibus Orbium Coelestium* was officially prescribed as merely 'false and contrary to Holy Scripture'. This was thanks to the intervention of Cardinal Barberini, who, in 1616 (seven years before he became Pope Urban VIII), had persuaded the Inquisition to make clear this distinction.

being *Dialogue by Galileo Galilei on the Two Chief World Systems, Ptolemaic and Copernican*; and whereas the Holy Congregation was informed that with the printing of this book the false opinion of the Earth's motion and the Sun's stability was being disseminated and taking hold more and more every day, the said book was diligently examined and found to violate explicitly the above-mentioned injunction given to you; for in the same book you have defended the said opinion already condemned and so declared to your face, although in the said book you try by means of various subterfuges to give the impression of leaving it undecided and labelled as probable; this is still a very serious error since there is no way an opinion declared and defined contrary to divine Scripture may be probable.

Therefore, by our order you were summoned to this Holy Office, where, examined under oath, you acknowledged the book as written and published by you. You confessed that about ten or twelve years ago after having been given the injunction mentioned above, you began writing the said book, and that then you asked for permission to print it without explaining to those who gave you such permission that you were under the injunction of not holding, defending, or teaching such a doctrine in any way whatever.

Likewise, you confessed that in several places the exposition of the said book is expressed in such a way that a reader could get the idea that the arguments given for the false side were effective enough to be capable of convincing, rather than being easy to refute. Your excuses for having committed an error, as you said so foreign from your intention, were that you had written in dialogue form, and everyone feels a natural satisfaction for one's own subtleties and showing oneself cleverer than the average man by finding ingenious and apparently probable arguments even in favour of false propositions.

Having been given suitable terms to present your defence, you produced a certificate in the handwriting of the most Eminent Lord Cardinal Bellarmine, which you said you obtained to defend yourself from the accusations of your enemies, who were claiming that you had abjured and had been punished by the Holy Office. This certificate says that you had neither abjured nor been punished, but only that you had been notified of the declaration made by His Holiness and published by the Holy Congregation of the Index, whose content is that the doctrine of the Earth's motion and Sun's stability is contrary to Holy Scripture and so can be neither supported nor held. Because this certificate does not contain the two phrases of the injunction, namely 'to teach' and 'in any way whatever', one is supposed to believe that in the course of fourteen or sixteen years you had lost any recollection of them, and that for this same reason you had been silent about the injunction when you applied for the licence to publish the book.

Furthermore, one is supposed to believe that you point out all of this not to excuse the error, but in order to have it attributed to conceited ambition rather than to malice. However, the said certificate you produced in your defence aggravates your case further since, while it says that the said opinion is contrary to Holy Scripture, yet you dared to treat of it, defend it, and show it as probable; nor are you helped by the licence you artfully and cunningly extorted since you did not mention the injunction you were under.

Because we did not think you had said the whole truth about your intention, we deemed it necessary to proceed against you by a rigorous examination. Here you answered in a Catholic manner, though without prejudice to the above-mentioned matters confessed by you and deduced against you about your intention.

Therefore, having seen and seriously considered the merits of your case, together with the above-mentioned confessions and excuses and with any other reasonable matter worth seeing and considering, we have come to the final sentence against you given below.

Therefore, invoking the most Holy name of Our Lord Jesus Christ and his most glorious Mother, ever Virgin Mary; and sitting as a tribunal, with the advice and counsel of the Reverend Masters of Sacred Theology and the Doctors of both laws, our consultants; in this written opinion we pronounce final judgement on the case pending before us between the Magnificent Carlo Sinceri, Doctor of both laws, and Prosecuting Attorney of this Holy Office, on one side, and you the above-mentioned Galileo Galilei, the culprit here present, examined, tried, and confessed as above, on the other side:

We say, pronounce, sentence and declare that you, Galileo, by reason of these things which have been detailed in the trial and which you have confessed already, have rendered yourself according to this Holy Office vehemently suspect of heresy, namely of having held and believed a doctrine that is false and contrary to the divine and Holy Scripture: namely that the Sun is the centre of the world and does not move from east to west, and that one may hold and defend as probable an opinion after it has been declared and defined contrary to Holy Scripture. Consequently, you have incurred all the censures and penalties enjoined and promulgated by the sacred Canons and all particular and general laws against such delinquents. We are willing to absolve you from them provided that first, with a sincere heart and unfeigned faith, in our presence you abjure, curse and detest the said errors and heresies, and every other error and heresy contrary to the Catholic and Apostolic Church in the manner and form we will prescribe to you.

Furthermore, so that this grievous and pernicious error and transgression of yours may not go altogether unpunished, and so that you will be more cautious in future, and an example for others to abstain from delinquencies of this sort, we order that the book *Dialogue of Galileo Galilei* be prohibited by public edict.

We condemn you to formal imprisonment in this Holy Office at our pleasure. As a salutary penance we impose on you to recite the seven penitential psalms once a week for the next three years. And we reserve to ourselves the power of moderating, commuting, or taking off, the whole or part of the said penalties and penances.

This we say, pronounce, sentence, declare, order and reserve by this or any other better manner or form that we reasonably can or shall think of. So we the undersigned Cardinals pronounce:

F. Cardinal of Ascoli
B. Cardinal Gessi
G. Cardinal Bentivoglio
F. Cardinal Verospi
Fr. D. Cardinal of Cremona
M. Cardinal Ginetti
Fr. Ant. s Cardinal of. S. Onofrio.

Silence fell in the room.

Galileo's mind must have been reeling. This announcement spoke of formal imprisonment; he would be cast into the dungeons of Castel Sant'Angelo, where he would surely die before many days could pass.

Before he had time to properly digest this, one of the assistants to the cardinals stepped forward to hand the prisoner a prepared statement. Galileo read it through and baulked. He could not utter these words. The statement included two declarations he would never contemplate. The first was that he had obtained the papal imprimatur by deception, the second, that he had lapsed in his behaviour as a good Catholic.

At that moment a succession of painful images must have swept through his mind. On the one hand he lived again the frustrations of trying to clear his book for publication through official channels and the constant hampering of his goals. On the other was the vision of his daughter Maria Celeste, his devout child who loved and respected him. What would she think if he declared to the world and to history that he had not acted as a good Catholic? Beyond this was Galileo's own sense of self-worth. He viewed himself as a good Catholic and he had always done so. Furthermore, as far as he was concerned, he had obtained the papal imprimatur by entirely honest means.

Galileo stood his ground and refused to read the statement until it had been corrected. It is impossible to say what might have happened if the cardinals had refused to budge. But it is likely that none of them could have made a unilateral decision to halt the proceedings – an act that would certainly have attracted papal wrath and might have jeopardised the careful schemes of the Holy Office.

The statement was duly altered and Galileo made his final statement before the Inquisition:

I, Galileo Galilei, son of the late Vincenzo Galilei, Florentine, aged seventy years, arraigned personally before this tribunal, and kneeling before you, most Eminent and Reverend Lord Cardinals, Inquisitors general against heretical depravity throughout the whole Christian Republic, having before my eyes and touching with my hands, the Holy Gospels – swear that I have always believed, do now believe, and by God's help will for the future believe, all that is held, preached, and taught by the Holy Catholic and Apostolic Roman Church. But whereas – after an injunction had been judicially intimated to me by this Holy Office, to the effect that I must altogether abandon the false opinion that the Sun is the centre of the world and immovable, and that the earth is not the centre of the world, and moves, and that I must not hold, defend, or teach in any way whatsoever, verbally or in writing, the said doctrine, and after it had been notified to me that the said doctrine was contrary to Holy Scripture – I wrote and printed a book in which I discuss this doctrine already condemned, and adduced arguments of great cogency in its favour, without presenting any solution of these; and for this cause I have been pronounced by the Holy Office to be vehemently suspected of heresy, that is to say, of having held and believed that the Sun is the centre of the world and immovable, and that the Earth is not the centre and moves.

Therefore, desiring to remove from the minds of your Eminences, and of all faithful Christians, this strong suspicion, reasonably conceived against me, with sincere heart and unfeigned faith I abjure, curse, and detest the aforesaid errors and heresies, and generally every other error and sect whatsoever contrary to the said Holy Church; and I swear that in the future I will never again say or assert, verbally or in writing, anything that might furnish occasion for a similar suspicion regarding me; but that should I know any heretic, or person suspected of heresy, I will denounce him to this Holy Office, or to the Inquisitor of the place where I may be. Further, I swear and promise to fulfil and observe in their integrity all penances that have been, or that shall be, imposed upon me by this Holy Office. And, in the event of my contravening, (which God forbid) any of these my promises, protestations, and oaths, I submit myself to all the pains and penalties imposed and promulgated in the sacred canons and other constitutions, general and particular, against such delinquents. So help me God, and these His Holy Gospels, which I touch with my hands.

I, the said Galileo Galilei, have abjured, sworn, promised, and bound myself as above; and in witness of the truth thereof I have with my own hand subscribed the present document of my abjuration, and recited it word for word at Rome, in the Convent of Minerva, this twenty-second day of June, 1633.

I, Galileo Galilei, have abjured as above with my own hand.

With this statement complete, the prisoner was led from the room and escorted to the Palace of the Inquisition.

According to legend, as he was being escorted away, his fate sealed, Galileo whispered: 'And yet it does move.' Although this is probably no more than a myth, such a comment would certainly have been in character.

14

Gagged

Immediately the trial was over the pope commuted Galileo's sentence, first to imprisonment at the embassy and then to house arrest in Tuscany. But just as the Church authorities were showing Galileo comparative leniency in this way, they were ruthless in their treatment of his intellectual presence. With one hand the pope saved the scientist from the Inquisition dungeons, while with the other he gagged him and tried to eradicate his influence.

As word of Galileo's recantation and subsequent sentence spread through Italy and beyond, the Holy Office sent written instructions to their inquisitors in every major town and city in the country to warn academics under their jurisdiction to heed the example of Galileo. An accompanying letter explained: 'These documents are sent to you so that you may make it known to your vicars, and that all professors of philosophy and mathematics may know of it; that they may know why the Church proceeded against the said Galileo and recognise the gravity of his error in order that they may avoid it and thus not incur the penalties which they would have to suffer in case they fell into the same.'[1]

As well as this, the Vatican actively encouraged compliant academics to publish anti-Galilean tracts. One of these was *Against the Author of The Two Chief World Systems* written by the Professor of Mathematics at the University of Pisa, Scipione Chiaramonti, whom Galileo had poked fun at in his *Dialogue*. In this risible little book, which Chiaramonti dedicated to Urban VIII, he declared: 'Animals . . . move, have limbs and muscles; the Earth has no limbs or muscles, therefore it does not move. It is angels who make Saturn, Jupiter, the Sun, etc., turn round. If the Earth revolves, it must also have an angel in the centre to set it in motion; but only devils live there; it would therefore be a devil who would impart motion to the Earth.'[2]

Another highly critical and quite irrational attack came in a book called *Anticopernicus Catholicus* by Girogo Polacco, in which the author helpfully made it clear where Galileo had gone wrong:

> The Scripture always represents the Earth as at rest, and the Sun and Moon as in motion; or, if these latter bodies are ever represented as at rest, Scripture represents this as the result of a great miracle . . . These writings [Galileo's] must be prohibited, because they teach certain principles about the position and motion of the terrestrial globe repugnant to Holy Scripture and to the Catholic interpretation of it, not as hypotheses but as established facts . . . The planets, the Sun, the fixed stars, all belong to one species, namely, that of stars. It seems, therefore, to be a grievous wrong to place the Earth, which is a sink of impurity, among these heavenly bodies, which are pure and divine things.

Finally he asks: 'If we concede the motion of the Earth, why is it that an arrow shot into the air falls back to the same spot, while the Earth and all things on it have in the meantime moved very rapidly toward the east? Who does not see that great confusion would result from this motion?'[3]

Another individual who continued to attack Galileo and needed no prompting from Urban and his associates was Christopher Scheiner. His book *Prodromus pro Sole Mobili et Terra Stabili contra Galilaeum a Galileis* (*Introductory Treatise in Favour of a Moving Sun and a Stable Earth against Galileo Galilei*) was published in 1650; but it made little impact and, unlike the *Dialogue*, it has since been almost entirely lost to history.

Galileo could not respond to these criticisms; it was a one-way affair in which C-list academics could rip strips off their favourite hate figure with impunity. The old man appears to have taken it all resignedly, writing to a friend in France: 'It is advisable for me to succumb. I must remain silent about the attacks that have rained down on me in such number, in order to suppress the Copernican doctrine and publicise my innocence. It is also advisable that I swallow the sneers, the sarcasms, the insults.'[4] But Galileo did have some news to make him feel better. As his detractors were seeking to demean his work, copies of the *Dialogue* became hot property. The Church had decreed that all copies should be burned and anyone owning a copy should hand it over to the local Inquisitor's office. But within months of Galileo's sentence, the book was changing hands for six times its original price, and new editions were beginning to appear outside Italy.

Meanwhile, Galileo's family and close friends were quick to contain the damage done by the Church. It was several days before Maria Celeste learned of her father's fate and in the interim she had not known if he was to be executed, imprisoned in the Vatican or set free. When she learned of his sentence, she allowed Geri Bocchineri, the brother-in-law of Galileo's son Vincenzo and a high-ranking local civil servant who was very fond of Galileo, to go through the scientist's vacated house and remove anything that might incriminate. In a letter Maria Celeste wrote her father on 13 July 1633 she explained: 'Signor Geri was here one morning, during the time we suspected you to be in the greatest danger, Sire, and he and Signor Aggiunti went to your house and did what had to be done . . . seeming to me at the time well conceived and essential, to avoid some worse disaster that might befall you, wherefore I knew not how to refuse him the keys and freedom to do what he intended, seeing his tremendous zeal in serving your interests, Sire.'[5]

It is impossible to say what the family may have considered incriminating. Bocchineri was no scientist, but he had been very interested in the work of his illustrious relative and might well have known enough to destroy any books of a radical nature in Galileo's library along with any unpublished thoughts on Copernicanism and other contentious ideas. It is also possible that a swathe of correspondence, particularly anything linked with the Lynceans, was put to the flame. In private and within their correspondence, the group had been very open over a raft of controversial subjects. These things were never intended for public consumption and much of it would probably have horrified men like the pope.

As the Church set about dismantling Galileo's reputation and credibility, the man at the centre of this messy dispute was expelled from Rome, never to return. The pope had arranged for Galileo to stay in Siena in the care of the archbishop of the city, Ascanio Piccolomini. Piccolomini, an aristocrat and a man of some learning, had actually lobbied to have Galileo stay at his palace in Siena. The archbishop was a powerful man and obviously in favour with the pontiff, but his own thinking over theology and cosmology could not have been more different from that of the traditionalists of the Holy Office.

Galileo arrived in Siena in early July and stayed five months. In that time he was treated as a most honoured guest rather than a heretic despised by the Church. Piccolomini, who had been for a short time a student of Galileo's thirty years earlier (when he was teaching the young Medici heir Cosimo in 1605), was extremely fond of the old man and was privately appalled at his treatment in Rome. He made it his personal ambition to try to roll back the years of abuse Galileo had suffered and to invigorate him, to fill him with new life and enthusiasm for natural history.

In this Piccolomini did a remarkable job considering how much Galileo's self-esteem had been battered and his opinions shredded by far lesser men. In a short space of time the archbishop had turned his home into a salon, a meeting place for many of the most respected and honoured philosophers, artists, writers and poets of the region, drawn there to meet the greatest sage of the new age of natural philosophy; and Galileo, of course, loved the attention: it was an environment in which he thrived.

His life was also enlivened by a regular exchange of letters with Maria Celeste, which helped to lift him from the misery of the past months. On 16 July, she wrote: 'When you were in Rome, Sire, I said to myself: if I have the grace of your leaving that place and coming as far as Siena I will be satisfied, for then I can almost say that you are in your own house. And now I am not content, but find myself longing to again have you here closer.'[6]

The very homeliness and affection of Maria Celeste's letters and the unconditional love she had for her father warmed the old man's heart. Of the family duties she was performing, she wrote:

> If nothing else, I will first see to these other disbursements, in the event you are not here to take care of them yourself, Sire, which I suspect on account of the excessive heat that is upon us.
>
> The lemons that hung in the garden all dropped, the last few remaining ones were sold, and from the 2 lire they brought I had three masses said for you, Sire, on my own initiative . . . And here, sending you love with all my heart, I pray Our Lord to bless you.[7]

By the autumn he had begun to consider ideas for new books, works he knew would not be published in any Catholic country but which he nevertheless believed he should write for posterity. He needed to do this even if many of his contemporaries and countrymen could not tolerate what he had to say about the nature of the universe. When he was not taking part in lively debate or being introduced to dignitaries and the well-heeled curious, Galileo spent time alone in the study put aside for him by Piccolomini trying to recapture the times of contemplation he had enjoyed before his arrest and defilement.

One of the visiting illuminati, a French poet named Saint-Amant, later wrote of a brief encounter with Galileo and Piccolomini and reported how the scientist was living a luxurious lifestyle amongst the rich tapestries and fine furniture of the archbishop's home, and how the two men were often engaged in intense discussion ranging over an assortment of high-minded subjects.

Of course, not everyone was pleased to see Galileo in Siena and it was inevitable that before long some jealous bigot would do the obvious thing and denounce their archbishop to the Inquisition. The anonymous exposé told how Galileo had disseminated, in Siena, 'ideas that are not quite Catholic with the support of the Archbishop, his host, who has told several people that Galileo was unjustly sentenced by this Holy Congregation, that he is the first man in the world, that he will live for ever in his writings even if they are prohibited, and that he is followed by all the best modern minds. And since such seeds sown by a prelate might bear pernicious fruit, I hereby report them.'[8]

Galileo had been very happy in Siena, but he longed for his own home and to see Maria Celeste again. This desire had been exaggerated after he learned that she was very ill. His beloved daughter was one of the few remaining bright aspects to his life and he wanted to make up for their time apart.

But all his petitions to the Holy Office to allow him to return to Florence had fallen on deaf ears – until, that is, the Vatican learned that Piccolomini had been treating his prisoner with what they considered improper kindness; and so, ironically, the spite of Piccolomini's denouncer had an effect that was presumably quite unexpected. Within weeks Galileo was making his farewells to the archbishop and the city of Siena and was once more on the road, returning home to a small house outside Florence that he had acquired immediately before his enforced trip to Rome almost a year earlier.

Meanwhile, the Inquisition made sure it covered its tracks over the real reason for Galileo's show trial. Galileo's friend Giovanni Ciampoli, who had fallen out of favour with Urban over a political matter just before Galileo's arrest, was one of the few men who had also been aware of the subterfuge surrounding the Galileo affair. He was never allowed to return to Rome and served in a succession of obscure outposts of papal influence, ending his days in the remote city of Jesi, in Poland. But before leaving Rome he had succeeded in having copies made in secret of all the correspondence he had been responsible for in his role as papal secretary. This included letters between Galileo and the papal office and secret correspondence between cardinals, in which reference was made to Galileo's *Assayer* and its importance in the case against him.

Shortly after his arrival in Jesi, Ciampoli was befriended by King Ladislao of Poland, the most tolerant Catholic monarch in Europe. When Ciampoli died, in 1643, he left his entire archive and library, including documents linked to the Galileo affair, to Ladislao. A few weeks after his death this archive, consisting of a dozen boxes of material, was due to be transported to a mountain repository in the north of Poland when functionaries of the Holy Office flanked by an armed escort entered the palace of the Governor of Jesi, where Ciampoli's documents were being stored, and had them removed. Rather than the documents being secured away in Poland, they were taken with all haste south, where papal interests ensured they immediately disappeared into the darkest recesses of the Vatican library, and where they probably reside still today, untouchable even in the twenty-first century.

Another major player in the Galileo affair, Father Orazio Grassi, also became a victim of papal intrigue. As Galileo's trial was drawing to a close, Grassi, who was a powerful figure in the Vatican and a much-admired academic, was removed from his position at the Collegio Romano and exiled from Rome. No official reason was ever given for this. Within a few months he found a position at the College of Genoa, but he was never allowed to publish a single word again.

The villa in which Galileo spent the rest of his life was situated in the tiny village of Arcetri and called Il Gioiello, meaning 'Little Jewel'. Built in the fourteenth century and remodelled in the sixteenth, it still stands today. The village itself was no more than a mile or two from the centre of Florence and is today a wealthy suburb of the city. Galileo took out the lease on the property in September 1632, just at the time he was called to Rome to face charges over his *Dialogue*. It was an ideal spot in which to live out the remaining years of his life, and it was close to the convent in San Matteo where Maria Celeste had lived since 1615.

By the time Galileo saw his daughter again she was ailing. She had written to him in Siena telling of her frail state of health, but since then she had gone into a rapid decline. Even so, she did everything she could to welcome home her father. 'There are two pigeons in the dovecote,' she told him in a letter he received just before leaving Siena, 'waiting for you to come and eat them. The beans in the garden wait for you to gather them. Your tower is lamenting your long absence.'[9]

The past year had placed an enormous strain on Maria Celeste, not least because, as a devout Catholic, she must have harboured fears that her beloved father had in some way acted heretically. There must have been many times during that year when she struggled to resolve the conflict between paternal love and her religious feelings, the two most powerful forces guiding her. Maria Celeste found a solution by concluding that her father was innocent of any crime against the Faith; the troubles he faced stemmed from a terrible misunderstanding that had simply slipped out of control.

While Galileo was still in Siena he had written to his daughter to tell her that he would soon be taking the road home. From her sickbed, Maria Celeste had replied: 'I do not think that I shall live to see that hour. Yet may God grant that it be for the best.'[10]

She knew she was gravely ill, but perhaps she found renewed strength from her love for her father so that she could survive long enough to see him again. By then, just before Christmas 1633, the region was in the grip of winter. Living in a freezing-cold convent without proper medical care and surviving on an inadequate diet did nothing to help Maria Celeste recover. She died on 2 April, just as spring began to emerge from the chill. She was thirty-three.

Galileo was devastated. 'I feel immense sadness and melancholy,' he told his relative Geri Bocchineri, 'together with extreme inappetite; I am hateful to myself, and continually hear my beloved daughter calling to me.'[11]

During the past two years Galileo's world had been turned upside down. He had gone from being a man celebrated and respected throughout Italy to a pariah of the Faith, banned from publishing anything ever again, his work condemned; and now his daughter, less than half his own age, was dead. He had loved Maria Celeste more than he had loved anyone. All his old friends were now gone – Salviati, Sagredo and Cesi. Sarpi had perished a decade earlier, loathed by Rome just as, now, he was. Another lost one was Kepler – he had died in 1630; and with the passing of Prince Cesi, his champion and sponsor, the bonds that had held together the Lyncean Academy began to loosen, so that he quickly lost touch with his friends in the group.

In February 1634 Galileo turned seventy. It was not a time for celebration: he was still bereft over the loss of his daughter; and the pain kept coming. In April, his brother's widow, Chiara Galilei, and four of their children – three daughters and a son – came to live with Galileo at Il Gioiello. Within weeks they were all dead from the plague.

That spring and summer Galileo was shrouded in depression; but the bitterness that lay in the pit of his stomach, a feeling that would last until the day he died, was also a powerful stimulant. He could have lain down and died, and if he had done so he would still be regarded today as one of the greats, for he had achieved more in one lifetime than most men could claim in a thousand. But he was not yet done. His innate stubbornness, his bloody-minded determination and the utterly unshakable conviction that he had been entirely right and his enemies entirely wrong gave him the strength to carry on thinking, and to keep working. He had one last great work to offer the world, *The Discourses on Two New Sciences*, the treatise Galileo himself considered his most important.

Not only were the two new sciences of the title really new; they each acted as a foundation for later developments made by those who followed Galileo. The first 'new science' was a study of the macro-scale properties of matter. Galileo had begun to explore the microcosmic or atomic world in *The Assayer*, but in this new book he offered a modern interpretation of the large-scale properties of materials. As with all his works, it was based upon careful experimentation and analysis of what he observed. He investigated the strengths of metals and other substances, conducted experiments on elasticity and cohesive forces, and then drew original conclusions about the limits of size and proportion for objects made from different materials.

> Nature cannot make trees of immeasurable size [he wrote], because their branches would eventually fall of their own weight; and likewise it would be impossible to fashion skeletons for men, horses or other animals which could exist and carry out their functions proportionally when such animals were increased to immense height . . . It follows that when bodies are diminished, their strengths do not diminish proportionally; rather, in very small bodies the strength grows in greater ratio, and I believe that a little dog might carry on his back

two or three dogs the same size, whereas I doubt if a horse could carry one horse his size.[12]

This research was to prove useful for experimenters of the next century, who would take Galileo's mathematical analysis of such things as tensile strength and viscosity, along with the generalisations he drew from his experiments, to lay the very earliest foundations of what would become the post-Industrial Revolution world, the era of technology.

The second 'new science' considered by Galileo was the motion of bodies – what became the branch of physics known as dynamics. This had, of course, been a subject studied long before by the Greeks, and Aristotle had had plenty to say on the subject. But Galileo, with a lifetime of experience behind him from his days studying pendulums and falling balls in Pisa to his most recent work in Arcetri, was the first to create concrete mathematical generalisations from specific experimental results.

Galileo's work on dynamics also provided an infrastructure for those who followed him. The most notable of these was, of course, Isaac Newton, who owed an enormous debt to Galileo's work on motion. Half a century after Galileo's death, Newton extrapolated from the ideas laid down in *The Discourses on Two New Sciences* and produced his *Principia Mathematica*, the template for the Industrial Revolution.

The Discourses was finished early in 1637. As anti-Aristotelian as anything Galileo had written, this new treatise contained nothing that would conflict with orthodoxy in the way the *Dialogue* or *The Assayer* did; but even so, Galileo was completely silenced and unable to publish in Italy. One associate commented blithely that if Galileo had wanted to publish a new edition of the Lord's Prayer, he would have been banned from doing so. To a friend, Galileo complained:

You have read my writings and from them you have certainly understood which was the true and real motive that caused, under the lying mask of religion, this war against me that continually restrains and undercuts me in all directions, so that neither can help come to me from outside nor can I go forth to defend myself, there having been issued an express order to all Inquisitors that they should not allow any of my works to be reprinted which have been printed many years ago or grant permission to any new work that I would print . . . a most rigorous and general order, I say, against all my works, *omnia edita et edenda* [everything published and everything I might have published in the future]; so that it is left to me only to succumb in silence under the flood of attacks, exposés, derision and insult coming from all sides.[13]

Yet, although the views of Galileo and everything he produced were anathema to the Church, his work was valued by intellectuals. Indeed, amongst the literate of Europe the opinion of Urban and his associates was in the minority. Unfortunately, in Italy and other Catholic states, it was the opinion of the orthodox that held sway; but in France Galileo's many supporters were keen to see the *Discourses* published and in Holland, where he was viewed as an anti-papal hero, publishers would soon be even more excited about obtaining the rights to produce the first edition.

Whilst writing the *Discourses*, Galileo had been corresponding with two trusted associates in France. The first of these was Elia Diodati, who had many contacts in the publishing world and had been responsible for finding a French publisher for the *Dialogue*. The other was the aristocrat and scholar François de Noailles, who had been campaigning to have Galileo released from house arrest ever since he was first sentenced.

The Count de Noailles placed the *Discourses* with the publisher Louis Elzevir in the Netherlands and it first appeared there in 1638. Galileo dedicated the book to his friend as thanks for his efforts. And for the Preface they contrived a lengthy statement in which Galileo feigned surprise that the book was published at all and claimed it had somehow leaked out to the world without his knowing:

> I recognise as resulting from Your Excellency's magnanimity the disposition you have been pleased to make of this work of mine, notwithstanding the fact that I myself, as you know, being confused and dismayed by ill fortune of my other works, had resolved not to put before the public any more of my labours. Yet in order that they might not remain completely buried, I was persuaded to leave a manuscript copy in some place, that it might be known at least to those who understood the subjects of which I treat. And thus having chosen, as the best and loftiest such place, to put this into Your Excellency's hands, I felt certain that you, out of your special affection for me, would take to heart the preservation of my studies and labours. Hence,

during your passage through this place on your return from your Roman embassy, when I was privileged to greet you in person (as I had so often greeted you before by letters) I had occasion to present to you the copy that I then had ready of these two works. You benignly showed yourself very much pleased to have them, to be willing to keep them securely, and by sharing them in France with any friend of yours who is apt in these sciences, to show that although I remain silent, I do not therefore pass my life in entire idleness.

I was later preparing some other copies, to send to Germany, Flanders, England, Spain, and perhaps also to some place in Italy, when I was notified by the Elzevirs that they had these works of mine in press, and that I must therefore decide about the dedication and send them promptly my thoughts on that subject. From this unexpected and astonishing news, I concluded that it had been Your Excellency's wish to elevate and spread my name, by sharing various of my writings, that accounted for their having come into the hands of those printers who, being engaged in the publication of other works of mine, wished to honour me by bringing these also into light at their handsome and elaborate press . . . Now that matters have arrived at this stage it is certainly reasonable that, in some conspicuous way, I should show myself grateful by recognising Your Excellency's generous affection. For it is you who have thought to increase my fame by having these works spread their wings freely under an open sky, when it appeared to me that my reputation must surely remain confined within narrow spaces.[14]

In this we can see at work Galileo's dark sense of humour. He could not have imagined for a minute that the readers of his book in the Vatican would believe the words sincere, but there was little they could do about it without causing an unseemly fuss that was not really worth the effort.

The *Discourses* was a wonderful way for Galileo to conclude his illustrious career and it also served as a great snub to Rome. By 1638 Galileo was more popular as a writer, thinker and anti-Establishment hero than he ever would have been before Urban's persecution. In trying to gag the man, the Jesuits who loathed him and the papal cabal who bullied him merely achieved the opposite.

As Galileo's friend François de Noailles was finding a publisher for the *Discourses*, Galileo was going blind. It began with an infection of the right eye, which went untreated because the Inquisition constantly refused to grant him permission to travel into Florence for medical treatment. This infection then spread to his left eye, so that over a period of three months his world gradually darkened and faded to black.

Galileo continued experimenting and observing for as long as he could. One of his final written accounts was of observations he made of the lunar surface from which he could conclude that the Moon wobbled in its orbit around the Earth. After that, he was forced to rely on the observations of assistants, who also acted as secretaries to whom he dictated notes.

The two most notable of these helpers were Vincenzo Viviani, a young researcher who went on to write the first biography of his mentor, the *Life of Galileo*. The accuracy of much of what Viviani wrote is questionable, but his book is the only account of the scientist's life written by someone who actually knew him. The other assistant was Evangelista Torricelli, then in his early thirties and on the cusp of his own illustrious career. Ironically, soon after Galileo's death, Torricelli found himself in hot water over his anti-doctrinal description of the vacuum (how, after all, could there be such a thing as a vacuum if God is everywhere?). He survived papal censure and later succeeded Galileo at the Tuscan court as grand-ducal mathematician. His greatest achievement was the elucidation of a law describing the rate of flow of a liquid through an opening, now known as Torricelli's law.

Galileo's son Vincenzo, to whom the old man had grown close since the death of Maria Celeste, wrote a rather rose-tinted description of his father during his final days. He was, he reported,

of jovial aspect, in particular in old age, of proper and square stature, of robust and strong complexion, as such that is necessary to support the really Atlantic efforts he endured in the endless celestial observations. His eloquence and expressiveness were admirable; talking seriously he was extremely rich of sentences and deep concepts; in these pleasing discourses he did not lack wit and jokes. He was easily angered but more easily calmed. He had an extraordinary memory, so that, in addition to the many things connected to his studies, he had in mind a great quantity of poetry and in particular the better part of *Orlando Furioso*, his favourite among the poems of whose author [Ariosto] he praised above all the Latin and Tuscan poets. His most detested vice was the lie, maybe because with the help of the mathematical science he knew the beauty of the Truth too well.[15]

The last two months of Galileo's life were miserable, however. As well as being totally blind, he suffered from a collection of illnesses including arthritis, a hernia and the kidney disease that eventually killed him. But almost until the last day of his life he continued to dictate ideas to his amanuensis, often surprising Torricelli and Viviani with his radical and innovative insights. To a friend he wrote:

> I have in mind a great many miscellaneous problems and questions, partly quite new and partly different from or contrary to those commonly received, of which I could make a book more curious than the others written by me; but my condition, besides blindness on top of other serious indispositions and a decrepit age of seventy-five years, will not permit me to occupy myself in study. I shall therefore remain silent, and so pass what remains to me of my laborious life, satisfying myself in the pleasure I feel from the discoveries of other pilgrim minds.[16]

But at the same time, his bitterness towards the Church grew stronger with each passing day, and as the physical pain grew and he knew his life was ebbing away, the work of his pen, which had so readily lashed his opponents, became positively corrosive. A letter in reply to one from a Tuscan dignitary who had written to Galileo quietly supporting the Copernican model serves as an example: 'The falsity of the Copernican system must not on any account be doubted, especially by us Catholics, who have the supreme authority of Holy Scripture interpreted by the greatest masters in theology,' he wrote. 'These masters assure us of the fixity of the Earth and the movement of the Sun around it. That most sound argument, taken from the omnipotence of God, renders false the conjectures of Copernicus.'[17]

Some wishful thinkers would have us believe Galileo was converted at the last to the opinion of the Church, but this is very unlikely indeed; he was merely hitting back in the only way left to him.[18] Such sarcasm represented the last bitter punches of a man (who knew he had been wronged) living out his final days.

Galileo died on the evening of 8 January 1642 in the room in which he had spent most of the past eight years. With him were his faithful assistant Viviani and his son Vincenzo. A few days later an associate of Cardinal Francesco Barberini, one of the few men in the Vatican who had stayed loyal to the scientist wrote: 'Today the news has come of the loss of Signor Galilei, which touches not just Florence but the whole world, and our whole century which from this divine man has received more splendour than from almost all the other ordinary philosophers. Now, envy ceasing, the sublimity of that intellect will begin to be known, which will serve all posterity as guide in the search for truth.'[19]

15

Phoenix Rising

Ferdinand de' Medici, the well-meaning but rather feeble Grand Duke of Tuscany, wanted to bury the great Galileo with all due honours in the main basilica of the Church of Santa Croce, where a suitable monument could be erected at his own expense, to commemorate the man's achievements. The plans for all this were well under way when Ferdinand received a crisply worded letter from Urban VIII: Galileo, the pope declared, must be buried as an ordinary citizen without pomp or ceremony, in the novices' chapel, and there was to be no monument.

The letter directed to Ferdinand via his ambassador in Rome, Francesco Niccolini, stated that 'the Holy See had heard that the Grand Duke might have thought to have a tomb erected in Santa Croce . . . it would not be a good example to the world for you [Ferdinand] to do so . . . as that man had been here before the Holy Office for a very false and erroneous opinion, which he had also impressed upon many others, there giving rise to a universal scandal against Christianity by means of a damned doctrine.'[1]

Galileo's burial was attended by a tiny group: his son Vincenzo, Viviani and Evangelista Torricelli, along with the curate of Galileo's local church in Arcetri. The grand duke and his entire family remained obediently in Pisa. This was nothing more than another spiteful act on the part of Urban and his cardinals – a further attempt to rewrite history and to remove Galileo from the record book; but, of course, they had no real chance of succeeding in this aim. They won immediate victories by bullying and pressurising people like Galileo, but time has worn down the power of the Church's obstinacy, and as it has faded, Galileo's memory and all that he stood for have shone brighter.

There were many who loved and admired Galileo. Viviani was incensed by the treatment meted out to his dead mentor and he vowed to have a monument to the master erected at an appropriate spot; but although Viviani became the executor of Galileo's work, he had no money of his own with which to fulfil his dream.

It helped that Urban VIII died just two years after Galileo in 1644, because Viviani then received some financial support from Ferdinand, who paid for two busts of Galileo, one bronze and one marble. But when Ferdinand died, in 1670, Viviani received little interest from the grand duke's successor, Cosimo III, who turned out to be one of the worst rulers of the Medici dynasty, squandering much of the family fortune and making himself extremely unpopular by increasing taxes to line his own pockets.

Viviani did everything he could. He erected a plaque on the wall of the novices' chapel to commemorate Galileo's life and he even paid for another, larger one to be placed on the side of his own house. But he died childless in 1703 and his estate passed to a nephew, who had absolutely no interest in the long-dead scientist who had so inspired his uncle. Instead, the job of bringing Vincenzo Viviani's dream to fruition fell to a wealthy Florentine senator, Giovanni Battista Clemente de Nelli, who bought the Viviani estate. In 1737 he financed the construction of a grand monument to one of the most famous of his countrymen a few years shy of a century after his death.

Galileo's mausoleum was constructed so that the scientist's remains could be moved at last from the novices' chapel to the main basilica, where he could be interred with the rest of his family.

On 12 March 1737 a small group of distinguished Florentines gathered in the novices' chapel of the Church of Santa Croce to exhume the body of Galileo. Breaking into the small room under the campanile they found three coffins. One, the most recent addition, was the coffin of Viviani, who had requested in his will to be buried with his hero. This was removed and placed in the new mausoleum. The first of the other coffins was opened to reveal the skeleton of an old man; the other was found to contain the remains of a much smaller person, clearly female: Galileo's daughter Maria Celeste. With great ceremony these two bodies were brought into the chapel, where a vertebra, three fingers and a tooth were removed from Galileo's corpse. The coffins were then taken to the main basilica and placed where they had long belonged.

One of Galileo's fingers was immediately placed in an urn and, as the jar was sealed, a solemn epitaph was read by one of the congregation, Tomasso Perelli. Today this odd relic may be viewed by the public in the collection of the Institute and Museum of the History of

Science of Florence, while Galileo's vertebra is in the possession of the University of Padua.

Perhaps more important than the Church's insistence on suppressing any celebration of Galileo's life was its continued effort to suffocate interest in the scientist's work. Galileo's books remained on the Index of Prohibited Books until 1835 (the Index itself was only retired during the 1960s); and even as late as 1744 the publication of Galileo's *Complete Works* was censored by the Church. For this edition the Sacred Congregation for the Doctrine of the Faith insisted that Galileo's *Letter to Christina* and *Letter to Castelli*, in which he gave his views on the relationship between science and theology, should both be omitted. Furthermore, the *Dialogue* had to be printed out of sequence in volume IV of the collection and was to be accompanied by Galileo's abjuration before the Inquisition in 1633 along with a disclaimer that the Copernican model described was merely a hypothesis. This edition appeared a generation after the death of Sir Isaac Newton, during the height of the Enlightenment and only forty years before the start of the Industrial Revolution.

The story beyond Italy was very different. In France, England and the Netherlands, Galileo was revered as a great scientist. Newton realised the importance of his predecessor and mentioned him in his *Principia Mathematica*. His science was based on the sturdy foundations laid by Galileo. In particular, he followed Galileo's example by relying heavily on what he observed from experiments and he applied the scientific method pioneered by Galileo – to produce a general rule from a specific set of observations or experiences, encasing the entire thing with mathematical rigour. In spite of the fact that Galileo's works were on the papal index, they had reached England (a largely Protestant realm) by the 1640s and Newton had read his entire works before going to Cambridge in 1661. Galileo was a model and an inspiration for the future Lucasian Professor, but Newton was not the sort of man who liked to admit to any influences of the many great figures who preceded him and so he did not give Galileo the public credit he deserved.

Voltaire, a man who idolised Newton and embodied the Enlightenment, wrote of Galileo's trial:

> The persecutors were the party that happened to be mistaken. Those who enjoined the penance upon Galileo were more mistaken still. Every inquisitor ought to be overwhelmed by a feeling of shame in the deepest recesses of his soul at the very sight of one of the spheres of

Copernicus. Yet, if Newton had been born in Portugal, and any Dominican had discovered a heresy in his inverse ratio of the squares of distances, he would without hesitation have been clothed in a 'san-benito' and burned as a sacrifice acceptable to God at an 'auto-da-fé'.²

Outside Italy, interest in Galileo began to grow long before his death, and as I mentioned earlier, the trial before the Inquisition merely made him more famous and added to his mystique. Scientists and philosophers from non-Catholic states cherished his advanced ideas, but there was also a Protestant element who wished to emphasise Galileo's challenge to orthodoxy. To these people, the man was a martyr.

It is hard, though, to empathise with such anti-papal opinions, because both Martin Luther and John Calvin were extremely backward in their appreciation of science and had no time for Copernicanism. Luther called the 'new science' 'the over-witty notions of a fool, for does not Joshua 10 plainly say that the Sun, not the Earth, stood still?' If anything, Calvin was even more of a brutal philistine. In 1553 he had the medic and writer Michael Severetus roasted over a spit until he died after two hours because he had the nerve to suggest that blood was pumped through the body by the heart. About Copernicus, Calvin merely quoted Psalm 93:1: 'The Earth is set firmly in place and cannot be moved . . .' 'Who, then,' he insisted, 'will dare to place the authority of this man Copernicus above Holy Scriptures?'

When Galileo was imprisoned in Arcetri, he was allowed very few visitors and those who did come to see him had to be vetted by Rome. However, the eyes of the Inquisition could not be everywhere at once and we know of at least two famous men whose visits were certainly clandestine. The first of these was the English philosopher and atheist Thomas Hobbes, whose own masterpiece, *Leviathan* (1651), so shocked Protestants everywhere that, like Galileo, he was branded a heretic. Hobbes gained much from Galileo and claimed the scientist had inspired the notion at the heart of *Leviathan* that human beings and human life may be studied as mathematical entities.

The other celebrity visitor in Galileo's waning years in Arcetri was the English poet John Milton, who is considered by many to be second only to Shakespeare in the pantheon of great English literary figures. Milton was appalled by the way Rome had treated Galileo and he was one of the first to suggest that the intellectual development of Italy and other Catholic states would be adversely affected by papal persecution of free thinking. In 1644, two years after Galileo's death, Milton wrote an essay entitled *Areopagitica* in which he recalled:

> I have sat [in Italy] among their learned men and been counted happy to be born in such a place of philosophical freedom as they supposed England was, while they themselves did nothing but bemoan the servile condition into which learning amongst them was brought; that this was it which had damped the glory of Italian wits, that nothing had been there written now these many years but flattery and fustian. There it was that I found and visited the famous Galileo, grown old, a prisoner of the Inquisition.

Milton may have been one of the first to realise that the backward perception of Rome would slow cultural development, but many others have echoed these sentiments, believing that the silencing of Galileo caused science in Italy to fall behind other European countries from the 1630s until perhaps the nineteenth century. One scholar has remarked: 'The pope paralysed scientific life in Italy. The centre of the new research came to the Protestant countries in the North.'[3] Others, though, claim that this was merely a result of shifting national fortunes, a natural social process and not directly related to the Galileo affair.

It is true to say that the great flowering of culture between the thirteenth and seventeenth centuries, which was centred on Italy, declined in that part of Europe soon after Galileo's trial. The cutting edge of learning and the evolution of thought moved west to England and France and north to Holland and Germany, leaving behind the countries that were truly in the grip of Catholic dogma. It is unreasonable to assume that this was entirely due to the censorship of the Church; but there is no coincidence in the fact that until Rome's grip on the evolution of the intellect loosened, in the nineteenth century, Catholic philosophers and scientists could not write freely in their own countries. Instead, the outpourings of their minds could only be made public abroad, and this served to enrich further the development of ideas in those states where intellectual freedom was nurtured, even if the founders of Protestantism had been anti-intellectual bigots.

But Galileo's ideas could not be suppressed for ever. What the Church most feared about the man came back to haunt it; three hundred years after his death, another icon, Albert Einstein, could say of the man: 'The discovery and use of scientific reasoning by Galileo was one of the most important achievements in the history of human thought, and marks the beginning of physics.'[4]

A further illustration and perhaps an apt final word on Galileo's legacy is the avowal of Archbishop Ascanio Piccolomini of Siena (quoted in the last chapter), who, according to an informant to the Inquisition, had declared: 'He [Galileo] is the first man in the world, that he will live for ever in his writings even if they are prohibited, and that he is followed by all the best modern minds.'[5]

Galileo's science did bear what the Church would consider 'pernicious fruit', and does 'live for ever in his writings'. Indeed, while Urban, Grassi, Scheiner, Paul V and even Bellarmine have been largely forgotten by all but the devout, their works gathering dust and now almost entirely unread, Galileo is seen as the progenitor of the scientific age, one of the founders of the modern world.

16

Twenty-First-Century Witchcraft
(The Flesh, the Blood, the Bread and the Wine)

For the Catholic Church, transubstantiation and the Eucharist remain supreme obsessions. In centuries past the Holy Office did everything it could to protect the sanctity of the Roman interpretation of the Eucharist and the occult notions of 'substance' and 'accident'. And they had a good reason: this interpretation is what distinguishes Catholicism from other forms of Christian belief. Today the Church still holds rigidly to the notions of Aquinas, a monk who, eight hundred years ago, decided that his model of the universe was the correct one. Catholics continue to hold the orthodox view because they believe Aquinas was given divine guidance and that therefore his reasoning was infallible; but the reason for maintaining the Catholic interpretation of the Eucharist has changed. The Church no longer fears the encroachment of Protestantism, but in a world that is becoming increasingly secular it needs to offer a stable faith-based platform for the devout.

Many of the papers relating to the trial of Galileo were kept secret until the late twentieth century. Some documents pertaining to Galileo's treatment before the trial were opened in 1849, and in the late 1860s Giacomo Manzoni, who was Minister of Finances for the short-lived Roman Republic, and Silvestro Gherardi, Minister of Public Education, used some of the archive materials to research a book published in 1870. This had the title *The Trial of Galileo Reseen through Documents from a New Source*. Later, the Prefect of the Secret Vatican Archive, Gaetano Marini, wrote a book for public consumption in which selected excerpts from the archives were examined.

In 1880 parts of the secret archives were opened for a brief time by Pope Leo XIII, and the scholar Antonio Favaro began his work on the *National Edition of the Works of Galileo*; but, like all his predecessors,

Favaro was given only limited access to the records and the release of information was (and continues to be) carefully controlled.

In 1941 the Pontifical Academy of Sciences commissioned a biography of Galileo to commemorate the 300th anniversary of his death. The author chosen for the task was Monsignor Pio Paschini, who was Professor of Church History in Rome at the Pontifical Lateran University; but when Paschini delivered his book for papal approval it was rejected on the grounds that his account was unfairly critical of the Jesuits and their role in the Galileo affair. The book, entitled *Vita e Opere di Galileo Galilei*, only saw the light of day more than twenty years later, in 1965, after it had been 'corrected' by the Holy See.[1]

The obsessional stance of the Roman Church over the Galileo affair is clear to see in its continuing resistance to the work of Galileo and in the insistence of the Holy Office that the actions of the Church in 1633 were justified. When he was simply Cardinal Joseph Ratzinger, the successor to John Paul II, Pope Benedict XVI, once declared: 'At the time of Galileo the Church remained much more faithful to reason than Galileo himself. The process against Galileo was reasonable and just.'[2] So evidently, even today, the deception, the chimera created by Urban and his lieutenants remains an essential element of the Galileo affair.

In July 1981, some three years after becoming pope, John Paul II established an investigative body called the Galileo Commission to reopen the case against the scientist and to try to come to a set of definitive conclusions about the events of 350 years earlier. The pope was genuine in his desire to have Galileo's case investigated, and there is no coincidence in the fact that, although he was by then the head of the world Church, he was also a Pole, and Nicolaus Copernicus had been a Pole. Furthermore, John Paul had always been interested in science. Indeed, he remained fascinated with the relationship between science and religion throughout his papacy and was always keen to talk to the world's most accomplished scientists.

Two years before creating the commission to investigate the Galileo affair, during an address before the Pontifical Academy of Sciences, on 10 November 1979, to celebrate the 100th anniversary of the birth of Einstein, John Paul II gave his personal opinion on the Galileo affair:

The greatness of Galileo is known to everyone, like that of Einstein, but unlike the latter . . . the former had to suffer a great deal – we cannot conceal the fact – at the hands of men and organisms of the

Church . . . I hope that theologians, scholars and historians, animated by a spirit of sincere collaboration, will study the Galileo case more deeply and, in a loyal recognition of wrongs from whatever side they come, will dispel the mistrust that still opposes, in many minds, a fruitful concord between the Church and the world. I give all my support to this task, which will be able to honour the truth of faith and of science and open the door to future collaboration.[3]

When John Paul established the Galileo Commission (a group comprising eight theologians headed by Cardinal Gabriel-Marie Garrone), he proffered the explicit instruction that 'the work be carried out without delays and that it lead to concrete results'. Not surprisingly, perhaps, the commission accomplished neither of these goals. Its report was only announced publicly on 31 October 1992 and published in *L'Osservatore Romano* on 4 November the same year, more than eleven years after the group had been brought together. Furthermore, its conclusions were anything but concrete.

The findings of the Galileo Commission were announced by Pope John Paul during an audience given to the Pontifical Academy of Sciences, and this was reported widely around the world (including an amusing article in the *New York Times* in which it was noted that the Church had finally admitted Galileo was right and that the Earth did indeed move). By 1992 the Vatican could no longer cling to the notion that the Earth was stationary at the centre of the universe; but nor could it admit it had been wrong about Galileo. The best the pope could offer was that in 1633 there had been a 'tragic mutual incomprehension'. John Paul declared:

From the beginning of the Age of Enlightenment down to our own day, the Galileo case has been a sort of myth, in which the image fabricated out of the events was quite far removed from reality. In this perspective, the Galileo case was the symbol of the Church's supposed rejection of scientific progress, or of dogmatic obscurantism opposed to the free search for truth. This myth has played a considerable cultural role. It has helped to anchor a number of scientists of good faith in the idea that there was an incompatibility between the spirit of science and its rules of research on one hand and the Christian faith on the other.[4]

This is a cleverly worded statement, which tries to have us believe that a regrettable misunderstanding led to the conflict between Galileo and the Church. But the most cunning aspect of this statement is the way the entire affair is described as a 'myth', for by using this word the pope and his cardinals were attempting to lull the faithful into accepting the notion that what happened to Galileo was not a cut-and-dried historical event reported for posterity in trial documents and letters, but a semi-fictionalised story – a parable, perhaps.

After setting this tone, the pope then went on to describe the findings of the Galileo Commission. These may be boiled down to three particular points:

1. Galileo did not seem to understand that the Copernican model was merely a hypothesis. He had no proof to support his heliocentric world view and was therefore betraying the very scientific method he was espousing.
2. The theologians of the time did not correctly understand the nature of Scripture.
3. When the proofs of Copernicanism were established, the Church was quick to accept these and to admit implicitly that it had erred in condemning the model.

Let us consider each of these points in turn.

First, Galileo's apparent lack of scientific rigour. This claim constitutes a scandalous twisting of the facts. To begin with, the Church was never interested in the scientific meaning of Copernicanism; at no point was science argued over. There were no scientists on the committee who investigated Galileo's *Dialogue*, and although Bellarmine and Barberini were both interested in science, neither of them was trained in the subject.

Most importantly, Galileo was fully cognisant of the fact that the Church treated Copernicanism as a hypothesis; but in both of Galileo's official encounters with the Holy See (with Bellarmine and Seghizzi in 1616 and during the trial of 1633), accuser and accused considered the meaning of 'hypothesis' in very different ways. To the Church the use of the word 'hypothesis' provided a way out of accepting new scientific ideas; Copernicanism could be swept under the carpet because it had not been proved conclusively. For Galileo, a hypothesis was simply a working model, a step on the road to the establishment of a world-view.

In considering this difference we really strike at the heart of how the Church and science approach matters in ways that are entirely contradictory. It is quite wrong to criticise anyone of the seventeenth century or earlier for not having accepted Copernicus because to them it simply 'seemed wrong'. The logical conclusion to be drawn about the mechanism of the cosmos is that the Sun does in fact orbit the Earth, because, after all, we see this happen – the Sun rising each day in the east and setting in the west. It is the Sun that appears to move, not us.

However, although it is unjust to criticise anyone who held this view because of what they experienced in their daily life, the Church has received just opprobrium for its position over Copernicus, because it did not challenge the heliocentric model on scientific grounds. The Church attacked Galileo and Copernicus simply because the views of these men offered an alternative to Vatican dogma. It was not interested in logical conclusions or the merits and demerits of one particular theory over another. It merely insisted it was right and all opponents were wrong.

What this amounts to is a difference in motive, and therein lies the real distinction between science and the Church: scientists are motivated by a desire to know and to understand; religious advocates are motivated by fear. As a monk in Brecht's play *Galileo* puts it:

> They [the laity] have been assured that God's eye is always on them – probingly, even anxiously – that the whole drama of the world is constructed around them so that they, the performers, may prove themselves in their greater or lesser roles. What would my people say if I told them they happen to be on a small knob of stone twisting endlessly through the void round a second-rate star? What would be the value then of so much patience? I can see how betrayed and deceived they will feel. So nobody's eye is on us, they'll say. Have we got to look after ourselves, old, uneducated, and worn out as we are? Our poverty has no meaning: hunger is no trial of strength, it's merely not having eaten: effort is no virtue, it's just bending and carrying.[5]

But, even if we ignore this difference in interpretation, the conclusion of the Galileo Commission is disingenuous because, although Galileo could not offer concrete proof that Copernicus was right (and actually believed incorrectly that the phenomenon of the tides was proof of the Copernican model), he did have some very compelling evidence to support heliocentrism. These included his many observations of the Jovian system, the phases of Venus and the regular procession of sunspots across the face of the Sun. All of these were studiously ignored by the Inquisition.

Now let's turn to the second claim, that the theologians of the time did not know how properly to interpret Scripture. What is meant by this is that the theologians of the Vatican in the seventeenth century took every aspect of God's Word literally and did not see anything in the Bible as being open to interpretation. Pope John Paul II summed this up in his speech by saying: 'The problem posed by theologians of that age was, therefore, that of the incompatibility between helio-centrism and Scripture. Thus, the new science, with its methods and the freedom of research which they implied, obliged theologians to examine their own criteria of Scriptural interpretation. Most of them did not know how to do so.'[6]

It is important to note that the commission is careful never to name names. Nowhere in its account is any blame for the affair placed at the door of any clergyman involved, nor is any responsibility placed with the Holy Office or the Inquisition. Those who formulated the ban on Copernicanism and Galilean science are merely referred to as 'theologians'. More importantly, this claim by the pope is actually untrue. Theologians of the time were quite aware of the idea of interpretation. In fact, such ideas had been discussed in detail since the time of Augustine and scriptural interpretation was part of the curriculum in all colleges of theology.

The final item in the commission's list – 'When the proofs of Copernicanism were established, the Church was quick to accept these and to admit implicitly that it had erred in condemning the model' – is also a complete whitewash. By placing this statement in a declaration concerning the Galileo trial, the implication is that, 'having erred in condemning the [Copernican] model', the Church has laid to rest the entire matter of Galileo's persecution, the trial and his punishment. This is quite untrue. The statement above refers to the Vatican im-primatur granted by Pope Pius VII to a book entitled *Elements of Optics and Astronomy* by Canon Giuseppe Settele in 1822. In this book the author explains the Copernican model and offers proof that it is true and not a mere hypothesis. But Copernicus's own treatise, *De Revolutionibus*, and all of Galileo's works, remained on the Index of Prohibited Books until 1835, thirteen years after this publication.

The imprimatur of 1822 was organised by the Commissary of the Holy Office, but he quickly realised that allowing this publication might compromise the good name of the Holy See, because if the Church admitted Copernicus had been right, then it should also posthumously pardon Galileo. To prevent this from happening, the

Commissary concocted a very imaginative response. Copernicus, he said, had actually been wrong because he had described the orbits of the planets as circular whereas they are, in fact, ellipses. So there was no need to revoke a decree that had rejected what was actually incorrect at the time (in 1616 and in 1633).[7]

In a less formal context than the report of the Galileo Commission other apologists have made some remarkable statements to try to extricate the Vatican from the ideological mess it created in 1633. My favourite comes from the anonymous author of a piece published in 2004 entitled 'The Galileo Controversy' on a website called 'Catholic Answers'. In this piece he declares:

> It is a good thing that the Church did not rush to embrace Galileo's views, because it turned out that his ideas were not entirely correct, either. Galileo believed that the Sun was not just the fixed centre of the solar system but the fixed centre of the universe. We now know that the sun is not the centre of the universe and that it *does* move – it simply orbits the centre of the galaxy rather than the Earth . . . Had the Catholic Church rushed to endorse Galileo's views – and there were many in the Church who were quite favourable to them – the Church would have embraced what modern science has disproved.

This article carries the imprimatur of Robert H. Brom, the Bishop of San Diego.

But let us put to one side the content of the report of the Galileo Commission, and ignore the lies and half-truths contained within it. If we do this we are still left with two oddities associated with the investigation. The first of these is the striking way in which the address made by John Paul II in 1992 is so much harder in tone compared with his statement of 1979. In the earlier statement the pope talked of a 'fruitful concord', and even hinted that the Church might have been unfair in its treatment of the scientist. After having received the report of the commission, thirteen years later, the pope's scriptwriter created the chimera of 'mutual incomprehension' and 'the Galileo myth', and the blame for the entire affair was placed, in large part with Galileo, and in smaller part with faceless 'theologians'.

The second peculiarity is the fact that the commission took eleven years to reach its conclusions. This has been explained away by the Vatican as being a result of continuing ill health through the 1980s of one of the key members of the commission, its president, Cardinal

Gabriel-Marie Garrone, who died in 1994. This, though, has about
it the same ring of falsity as the commission's conclusions about
Copernicus and Galileo.

But if the official line of the Vatican is open to question, what could
be the real reason for the delay in publicising the findings of the Galileo
Commission? For a possible answer to this we need to recall that the
entire matter of Copernicus, the heliocentric versus the geocentric
model and the question of hypothesis versus provable fact were quite
possibly decoys. There is evidence to show that Galileo's real crime was
that the atomic theory he described in *The Assayer* threatened to damage
the orthodox depiction of the Eucharist. To save his life, he struck a
deal with the Vatican authorities to say nothing more about his model
for the structure of matter and to allow the entire focus of the trial and
his persecution to rest on the question of Copernicanism.

This fact was only revealed by historians, searching through the
archives, who unearthed the documents G3 (in 1982) and EE291 (in
1999). In all likelihood, no one in the Vatican of the 1980s was even
aware of the true story behind the persecution of Galileo Galilei. What
then happened was an almost exact repeat of history. In 1633 Inchofer
stumbled upon the document later known as G3 and wrote his report
EE291. Some three and a half centuries later the commission created by
John Paul II brought to light the real foundation of the dispute between
the most important scientist of the early seventeenth century and the
Roman Church.

If this is true, in the reaction of the commission and in the pope's
announcement we see the Church in its true colours. Today the Vatican
is as frightened as ever by the possibility that the laity might be
educated by those not confined by bigotry and dogma. Ratzinger
made this clear before he became the head of the Church: 'The
Eucharist is God,' he proclaimed, unequivocally.

The orthodox Roman Catholic depiction of the Eucharist has not
changed since Aquinas invented it and, because of this, Catholic belief
in witchcraft remains fundamental. As Ratzinger, who at the time was
head of the Sacred Congregation of the Doctrine of the Faith (the
modern-day Inquisition) said in 2002:

> The ancient Church . . . rightly understood the word orthodoxy not to
> mean right doctrine but to mean the authentic adoration and glorifi-
> cation of God . . . It is truly the one, identical Lord, whom we receive
> in the Eucharist . . . we all 'eat' the same person . . . we are confronted

by the word transubstantiation. The bread becomes . . . his body. The bread of the earth becomes the bread of God . . . The Lord . . . wishes to transform the bread . . . into . . . his body . . . The Lord himself becomes present.[8]

Because of such beliefs it is unlikely Galileo will ever be 'forgiven' by the Church, and the sordid details of the case may never be revealed to the public.

Appendix I: The Key Characters in Galileo's Life

Cardinal Francesco Barberini (1597–1679)
Cardinal Francesco Barberini was the nephew of Pope Urban VIII. He was a close and devoted friend of Galileo's and he may have refused to sign the documents condemning Galileo at his trial (it is not certain that he was otherwise disposed). Paradoxically, Barberini was an occultist and a member of the Lyncean Academy. He was Galileo's staunchest supporter in Rome and it may have been through his influence that Galileo was treated with some leniency by the cardinal's uncle. It was Francesco Barberini who successfully petitioned the pope to allow Galileo to be transferred to the custody of the Archbishop of Sienna.

Cardinal (later Saint) Robert Bellarmine (1542–1621)
Known as the 'Hammer of Heretics', Cardinal Robert Bellarmine was considered to be one of the most vigorously evangelical Catholics of the period. He was interested in science, but placed Roman doctrine above all things. Bellarmine was largely responsible for the hounding of Giordano Bruno and instrumental in his torture and execution in 1600. He may also have been involved behind the scenes in the Gunpowder Plot of 1605. In his role as Pope Paul V's right-hand man he warned Galileo against pursuing Copernicanism as anything more than a hypothesis. He died aged 78 in 1621 and was canonised in 1930.

Camillo Borghese (1550–1621)
Born to a wealthy Sienese family, he became Paul V in May 1605. Paul was pope during the early stages of Galileo's persecution but had been dead a decade by the time of the trial. He treated Galileo with favour but deferred on most theological matters to Bellarmine.

Giordano Bruno (1548–1600)
Bruno was a radical natural philosopher who held extreme views concerning science and religion. He was a Dominican priest who was expelled from his order and excommunicated *in absentia*. Hounded by the Church, he was finally captured in Venice in 1592 and executed in Rome in February 1600. Although

his work had little influence upon Galileo's own, Bruno's cruel fate offered a deadly precedent.

Tommaso Caccini (1574–1648)
Father Tommaso Caccini was a Dominican monk and the initiator of Galileo's first struggle with Rome. On 20 December 1614 he preached a sermon in Florence that condemned mathematics and alleged that Copernicanism was either heretical or very close to it. The following March, Caccini testified against Galileo before the Tribunal of the Inquisition. His accusations were shown to be unfounded, but his actions precipitated the persecution of Galileo and instigated the trial that followed.

After playing his role in gaining Galileo's admonition in 1616, Caccini managed to earn the enmity of the powerful Pope Paul V and was forced to leave Rome. He spent his later years as Prior of San Marco in Florence.

Benedetto Castelli (1578–1643)
Father Castelli was Galileo's favourite pupil. The two often exchanged warm letters on matters ranging from scientific topics to the quality of wine. A letter from Castelli describing his conversation with the Grand Duchess Christina sparked the earliest truly aggressive ecclesiastical attacks on Galileo in December 1614. Castelli was a fine scientist who did much to help Galileo's experimental technique. He became a respected mathematician and was given the title Father Mathematician of His Holiness. In this role he tried to help Galileo during the early stages of the latter's trial, in 1633; but, suspecting the close links between the two men, the pope ordered Castelli to be sent to Brescia, in Lombardy, until the trial was over.

Prince Federico Cesi (1585–1630)
The Cesi family belonged to the high aristocracy of Rome and the Papal States. Originating in the little town of Cesi, near Rome, its incredible wealth came primarily from the Church. At the age of eighteen Cesi founded the Lyncean Academy. Other early members of the group included the mathematician Francesco Stelluti and the physician Johannes Eck. The members lived communally in Cesi's house, where he provided them with books and laboratory equipment. He died a few years before Galileo's trial, his help and presence sorely missed by the scientist.

Giovanni Ciampoli (1589–1643)
Ciampoli was a good friend of Galileo's. He was an exceptional scholar but possessed a maverick and unorthodox mind. Ciampoli was helpful with Galileo's earliest battles with the Church because he had the ear of the pope, but he later fell into disfavour. He was exiled and died in Poland a year after Galileo.

Nicolaus Copernicus (1473–1543)
Copernicus was born into a Polish middle-class family. He studied at the universities in Krakow, Bologna, Padua and Ferrara, developing strong

backgrounds in mathematics, medicine and Church law. He spent most of his life leading a sheltered academic existence as a canon in the cathedral of Frauenburg.

Beginning in the first years of the sixteenth century, he conducted detailed naked-eye astronomical studies. After two decades of observations he formulated what has become known as the heliocentric model, in which the Earth orbits the Sun. His book *The Revolutions of the Heavenly Spheres* was published days before his death in 1543 but was only seen as a controversial work more than seventy years later, in 1616. Copernicus's work laid the foundations of modern astronomy and led to Galileo's trial and persecution.

Giulia Galilei (Galileo's mother) (1538–1620)

Little is known of Giulia Galilei. She was born Giulia di Cosimo Ammananti into the equivalent of an upper-middle-class family and married Vincenzo in 1562. She gave birth to seven children, but only four of them survived into adulthood. During the last thirty years of her life she lived sporadically with Galileo, her eldest. She is reported to have been an affectionate mother to Galileo, but apparently loathed her son's mistress and the mother of his three children, Marina Gamba.

Vincenzo Galilei (Galileo's father) (c.1525–91)

Vincenzo was a musician and composer who held quite radical ideas about composition and is credited with being one of the originators of the operatic form. Vincenzo was not very successful in his career and he earned little, dying in debt. But he is regarded by posterity as an original thinker in the field of music theory. For the time in which he lived, he travelled widely and learned a great deal about non-European music which he incorporated into his own works. His most accomplished treatise is *Dialogue on Ancient and Modern Music*, published in 1579.

Virginia Galilei (1600–34)

Born in Padua on 12 August 1600. Virginia's mother, Marina Gamba, was Galileo's mistress. When Galileo moved to Florence, in 1610, he took Virginia and his other daughter, Livia (1601–59), with him, leaving his son Vincenzo (only 4 years old) with his mother for several years.

Virginia and Livia were placed in the convent of St Matthew run by the Poor Clares, where they spent the rest of their lives. Sister Maria Celeste, as Virginia became, was very close to her father and they shared an exchange of intimate and revealing letters. About 120 letters from Maria Celeste to her father, written between 1623 and 1634, have survived. She died on 2 April 1634, less than four months after Galileo's return to Arcetri.

Marina Gamba (1579–1619)

Galileo never married the former prostitute Marina Gamba, but they had three children: Virginia (1600), Livia (1601) and Vincenzo (1606). In none of the three baptismal records is Galileo named as the father.

She married Giovanni Bartoluzzi three years after Galileo left Padua.

Galileo succeeded in having his son Vincenzo legitimated by the Grand Duke of Tuscany, but for most of their lives Galileo and Vincenzo did not get on. This changed after Galileo's trial and during the final years of the scientist's life father and son grew close.

Johannes Kepler (1571–1630)

Kepler was born in Weil der Stadt, Württemburg, in the Holy Roman Empire. He was a sickly child and his parents were poor, but his evident intelligence earned him a scholarship to the University of Tübingen to study for the Lutheran ministry. He soon became interested in astronomy and made it his career, moving to Prague to work with the renowned Danish astronomer Tycho Brahe. He inherited Tycho's post as Imperial Mathematician in 1601. In 1609 he published *Astronomia Nova*, delineating his discoveries, which are now called Kepler's first two laws of planetary motion. In 1612 Lutherans were forced out of Prague and Kepler moved on to Linz, where his wife and two sons died. In 1619 he published *Harmonices Mundi*, in which he describes his 'third law'. He died in Regensburg in 1630 while on a journey from his home in Sagan to collect a debt.

Grand Duchess Christina de' Medici (1565–1637)

Christina of Lorraine was the granddaughter of Catherine de' Medici, Queen of France; she was well disposed towards Galileo. She married Ferdinand I de' Medici, Grand Duke of Tuscany, in 1589 and they had eight children. The eldest son, Cosimo II, ascended to the throne upon his father's death in 1609. Christina was influential in the running of Tuscany until her death at the age of seventy-two while Galileo was imprisoned in Arcetri.

Gianvincenzio Pinelli (1535–1601)

A very wealthy Paduan intellectual, Pinelli gathered together some of the finest minds of his age at his salon in Padua. His guests included Galileo, Sarpi, Bellarmine, Bruno and many others. He was also famed for his extensive library. Upon his death this, along with his other possessions, was shipped to his family home in Naples. On the way the ship was attacked by pirates and most of Pinelli's magnificent collection was lost when it was thrown into the sea. Only a small sample survives to this day.

Gianfrancesco Sagredo (1573–1620)

After Maria Celeste (Galileo's eldest child) Sagredo perhaps came closest to Galileo. He was born into a very wealthy Venetian family and became something of a playboy. However, he was also very intelligent and learned, and he adored Galileo. In 1608 Sagredo took up a diplomatic post in Aleppo, Syria, where he served until 1611, by which time Galileo had moved back to Florence. They remained close friends and wrote to each other frequently. Galileo was devastated by Sagredo's death from the plague in 1620.

Filippo Salviati (1582–1614)

An aristocrat and friend of Galileo's. The scientist's *Three Letters on Solar Spots* was dedicated to Salviati and Galileo used him as a character in his *Dialogue Concerning the Two Chief World Systems*. Salviati was a fellow member of the Lyncean Academy and after the scientist moved to Florence in 1610, he helped him a great deal with his experiments. He died in a brawl in a bar in Barcelona.

Paolo Sarpi (1552–1623)

Sarpi was a Venetian cleric, theologian, historian and scientist. During a struggle for authority between Pope Paul V and the Venetian Republic, Sarpi was instrumental in guiding the republic against the pressures of the Vatican. He was a good friend of Galileo's and deeply interested in his work. In 1606 an attempt on Sarpi's life failed, but he was seriously injured. Today Paolo Sarpi is best remembered as the author of the *History of the Council of Trent*, the first detailed account of the inner workings of the council that did so much to define and consolidate the Catholic Church after the Reformation. To modern free-thinkers Sarpi is considered a leading anti-papal figure and he is still hated by Catholics. Almost four centuries after the man's death the *Catholic Encyclopedia* describes him as a hypocrite 'devoid of authority'.

Pope Urban VIII (formerly Cardinal Maffeo Barberini) (1568–1644)

Born into a wealthy Florentine family, Maffeo Barberini was an intellectual and interested in science. He became a cardinal in 1606 and with the death of Pope Gregory XV, in 1623, he ascended to the papacy. Urban was keen to enlarge papal territory but never committed forces to the Thirty Years War. He outlived Galileo by just over two years. He was so unpopular that when news of his death was announced, the people of Rome ripped down the statue of him in the Vatican.

Vincenzo Viviani (1622–1703)

Viviani was Galileo's amanuensis and his first biographer. He was a fine scientist in his own right and had studied mathematics before being appointed by Grand Duke Ferdinand II in 1639 as Galileo's helper at Arcetri. In 1647 Viviani became a lecturer at the Accademia dell' Arte del Disegno in Florence and he was later appointed as engineer with the Uffiziali dei Fiumi. In 1666 Ferdinand II made Viviani Mathematician to the Grand Duke. Starting in 1655, he edited the first collected edition of Galileo's works. He died in 1703 and was buried with Galileo in the Church of Santa Croce. The lunar crater Viviani is named after him.

Appendix II: 'Letter to the Grand Duchess Christina of Tuscany' (1615) by Galileo Galilei

To the Most Serene Grand Duchess Mother:

Some years ago, as Your Serene Highness well knows, I discovered in the heavens many things that had not been seen before our own age. The novelty of these things, as well as some consequences which followed from them in contradiction to the physical notions commonly held among academic philosophers, stirred up against me no small number of professors as if I had placed these things in the sky with my own hands in order to upset nature and overturn the sciences. They seemed to forget that the increase of known truths stimulates the investigation, establishment and growth of the arts; not their diminution or destruction.

Showing a greater fondness for their own opinions than for truth, they sought to deny and disprove the new things which, if they had cared to look for themselves, their own senses would have demonstrated to them. To this end they hurled various charges and published numerous writings filled with vain arguments, and they made the grave mistake of sprinkling these with passages taken from places in the Bible which they had failed to understand properly, and which were ill-suited to their purposes.

The reason produced for condemning the opinion that the Earth moves and the Sun stands still was that in many places in the Bible one may read that the Sun moves and the Earth stands still. Since the Bible cannot err; it follows as a necessary consequence that anyone takes an erroneous and heretical position who maintains that the Sun is inherently motionless and the Earth movable.

With regard to this argument, I think in the first place that it is very pious to say and prudent to affirm that the Holy Bible can never speak untruth, whenever its true meaning is understood. But I believe nobody will deny that it is often very abstruse, and may say things which are quite different from what its bare words signify. Hence, in expounding the Bible, if one were always to confine oneself to the unadorned grammatical meaning, one might fall into error. Not only contradictions and propositions far from true might thus be made to appear in the Bible, but even grave heresies and follies. Thus it would be necessary to assign to God feet,

260

hands and eyes, as well as corporeal and human affections, such as anger, repentance, hatred, and sometimes even the forgetting of things past and ignorance of those to come. These propositions uttered by the Holy Ghost were set down in that manner by the sacred scribes in order to accommodate them to the capacities of the common people, who are rude and unlearned. For the sake of those who deserve to be separated from the herd, it is necessary that wise expositors should produce the true senses of such passages, together with the special reasons for which they were set down in these words. This doctrine is so widespread and so definite with all theologians that it would be superfluous to adduce evidence for it.

Hence I think that I may reasonably conclude that whenever the Bible has occasion to speak of any physical conclusion (especially those which are very abstruse and hard to understand), the rule has been observed of avoiding confusion in the minds of the common people which would render them contumacious toward the higher mysteries. Now the Bible, merely to condescend to popular capacity, has not hesitated to obscure some very important pronouncements, attributing to God himself some qualities extremely remote from (and even contrary to) His essence. Who, then, would positively declare that this principle has been set aside, and the Bible has confined itself rigorously to the bare and restricted sense of its words, when speaking but casually of the Earth, of water, of the Sun, or of any other created thing? Especially in view of the fact that these things in no way concern the primary purpose of the sacred writings, which is the service of God and the salvation of souls — matters infinitely beyond the comprehension of the common people.

This being granted, I think that in discussions of physical problems we ought to begin not from the authority of scriptural passages but from sense experiences and necessary demonstrations; for the Holy Bible and the phenomena of Nature proceed alike from the divine Word the former as the dictate of the Holy Ghost and the latter as the observant executrix of God's commands. It is necessary for the Bible, in order to be accommodated to the understanding of every man, to speak many things which appear to differ from the absolute truth so far as the bare meaning of the words is concerned. But Nature, on the other hand, is inexorable and immutable; she never transgresses the laws imposed upon her, or cares a whit whether her abstruse reasons and methods of operation are understandable to men. For that reason it appears that nothing physical which sense experience sets before our eyes, or which necessary demonstrations prove to us, ought to be called into question (much less condemned) upon the testimony of biblical passages which may have some different meaning beneath their words. For the Bible is not chained in every expression to conditions as strict as those which govern all physical effects; nor is God any less excellently revealed in Nature's actions than in the sacred statements of the Bible. Perhaps this is what Tertullian meant by these words: 'We conclude that God is known first through Nature, and then again, more particularly, by doctrine, by Nature in His works, and by doctrine in His revealed word.'

From this I do not mean to infer that we need not have an extraordinary esteem for the passages of Holy Scripture. On the contrary, having arrived at any certainties in physics, we ought to utilise these as the most appropriate aids in the true exposition of the Bible and in the investigation of those meanings which are necessarily contained therein, for these must be concordant with demonstrated truths. I should judge that the authority of the Bible was designed to persuade men of those articles and propositions which, surpassing all human reasoning, could not be made credible by science, or by any other means than through the very mouth of the Holy Spirit.

Yet even in those propositions which are not matters of faith, this authority ought to be preferred over that of all human writings which are supported only by bare assertions or probable arguments, and not set forth in a demonstrative way. This I hold to be necessary and proper to the same extent that divine wisdom surpasses all human judgement and conjecture.

But I do not feel obliged to believe that the same God who has endowed us with sense, reason and intellect has intended us to forego their use and by some other means to give us knowledge which we can attain by them. He would not require us to deny sense and reason in physical matters which are set before our eyes and minds by direct experience or necessary demonstrations. This must be especially true in those sciences of which but the faintest trace (and that consisting of conclusions) is to be found in the Bible. Of astronomy, for instance, so little is found that none of the planets except Venus are so much as mentioned, and this only once or twice under the name of 'Lucifer'. If the sacred scribes had had any intention of teaching people certain arrangements and motions of the heavenly bodies, or had they wished us to derive such knowledge from the Bible, then in my opinion they would not have spoken of these matters so sparingly in comparison with the infinite number of admirable conclusions which are demonstrated in that science. Far from pretending to teach us the constitution and motions of the heavens and other stars, with their shapes, magnitudes and distances, the authors of the Bible intentionally forbore to speak of these things, though all were quite well known to them. Such is the opinion of the holiest and most learned Fathers, and in St Augustine we find the following words:

'It is likewise commonly asked what we may believe about the form and shape of the heavens according to the Scriptures, for many contend much about these matters. But with superior prudence our authors have forborne to speak of this, as in no way furthering the student with respect to a blessed life, and, more important still, as taking up much of that time which should be spent in holy exercises. What is it to me whether heaven, like a sphere, surrounds the Earth on all sides as a mass balanced in the centre of the universe, or whether like a dish it merely covers and overcasts the Earth? Belief in Scripture is urged rather for the reason we have often mentioned; that is, in order that no one, through ignorance of divine passages, finding anything in our Bibles or hearing anything cited from them of such a nature as may seem to oppose manifest conclusions, should be induced to suspect their truth when they teach, relate, and deliver more profitable matters. Hence let it be said briefly, touching the form of heaven, that our authors knew the truth but the Holy Spirit did not desire that men should learn things that are useful to no one for salvation . . .'

Now if the Holy Spirit has purposely neglected to teach us propositions of this sort as irrelevant to the highest goal (that is, to our salvation), how can anyone affirm that it is obligatory to take sides on them, that one belief is required by faith, while the other side is erroneous? Can an opinion be heretical and yet have no concern with the salvation of souls? Can the Holy Ghost be asserted not to have intended teaching us something that does concern our salvation? I would say here something that was heard from an ecclesiastic of the most eminent degree: 'That the intention of the Holy Ghost is to teach us how one goes to heaven, not how heaven goes.'

References

INTRODUCTION
1. Steven Weinberg, cited in 'The Public Square' by Richard John Neuhaus, *First Things*, February 2000, p. 92.

CHAPTER 1: LIKE FATHER, LIKE SON
1. *Le Opere di Galileo Galilei*, vol. XVIII (Barbera, Firenze, 1968–71), p. 445.
2. Antonio Favaro, *Atti e Memorie della R. Accademia di scienze, lettere ed arti in Padova*, vol. XXIV (1908), pp. 6–8.
3. Sherwood Taylor, *Galileo and the Freedom of Thought* (London, 1938), p. 1.
4. D. P. Walker, *Studies in Musical Science in the Late Renaissance* (London, 1978), p. 45.
5. Vincenzio Viviani, *Racconto istorico della vita del Sig. Galileo Galilei*.
6. William Stukeley, *Memoirs of Sir Isaac Newton's Life*, ed. A. Hastings White (Taylor and Francis, London, 1936), p. 44.
7. Archivio di Stato di Pisa, Comune D. 66, pp. 73t, 74r. Riassumo alcune osservazioni di N.Caturegli, di cui vedi l'articolo di nota 11.
8. Angelo Maria Bandini, *Commentariorum de vita et scriptis Joannis Bapt Dini patricii florentini ecc* (Firenze, 1755).
9. N. Caturegli, *La scula media in Pisa* (Bollettino Storico, Pisano, 1936).
10. Vincenzio Viviani, *Racconto istorico della vita del Sig. Galileo Galilei*.
11. Ibid.
12. Friar Diego Franchi of Genoa, Archive of St Mary of Vallombrosa, Florence.
13. N. Caturegli, *La scula media in Pisa* (Bollettino Storico, Pisano, 1936).

CHAPTER 2: RELIGION'S GRIP
1. J. M. Heberle, ed. J. Strange, *Caedite eos. Novit enim Dominus qui sunt eis.* Caesarius of Heisterbach, Caesarius Heiserbacencis monachi ordinis Cisterciensis, Dialogus miraculorum, Cologne, 1851, vol 2, 296–8.
2. J-P Migne (ed.), *Patrologia Latinae cursus completus*, series Latina, 221 vols. (Paris, 1844–64), vol. 216: col 139.
3. Frederick Engels, *Dialectics of Nature*, p. 21.

4. *Gendercide and Genocide*, ed. Adam Jones (Vanderbilt University Press, USA, 2004).

CHAPTER 3: SCIENCE BEFORE GALILEO
1. B. L. van der Waerden, 'Euclid', *The Encyclopedia Britannica*, 2006 edn.
2. Charles Singer (ed.) *Studies in the History of Science* (Oxford University Press, 1917), p. 240.
3. W. C. Dampier, *A History of Science and its Relations with Philosophy and Religion* (Cambridge University Press, 1984), p. 35.
4. Lucretius, 'The Persistence of Atoms', in *On the Nature of Things* (*c.*60 BC).
5. W. C. Dampier, *A History of Science and its Relations with Philosophy and Religion* (Cambridge University Press, 1984), p. 28.
6. Ibid., p. 25.
7. Leonardo da Vinci, *Codex Atlanticus*, 109v-a., Ambrosiana Library, Milan.
8. Ibid., 182 v-c.
9. Leonardo da Vinci, *Trattato della pittura* (*Treatise on Painting*), ed. A. P. McMahon (Princeton University Press, 1956), p. 686.
10. G. J. Toomer, Biography in *Dictionary of Scientific Biography* (New York, 1970–90).
11. Nicolaus Copernicus, *De Revolutionibus Orbium Coelestium* (*On the Revolutions of the Heavenly Spheres*), bk 1, ch. 10.

CHAPTER 4: REBEL WITH A CAUSE
1. *Le Opere di Galileo Galilei*, vol. XVIII (Barbera, Firenze, 1968), p. 145.
2. Del Monte to Galileo, 30 December 1588, *Opere di Galileo Galilei*, vol. X (Barbera, Firenze, 1968), p. 39.
3. *Le Opere di Galileo Galilei*, vol. IX (Barbera, Firenze, 1968), p. 7.

CHAPTER 5: DEBUNKING ARISTOTLE
1. Galileo, '*De Motu*' (1590).
2. Galileo, *Le Opere di Galileo Galilei*, ed. Antonio Favaro (Florence, 1890–1910), IX, p. 213.
3. Galileo, *Two New Sciences* (University of Wisconsin Library, Madison, USA), p. 68.
4. Galileo, *Le Opere di Galileo Galilei*, ed. Antonio Favaro (Florence, 1890–1910), III, 187.
5. Leonardo da Vinci, Ms. F, 33v, Institut de France, Paris.
6. Galileo, '*De Motu*', 1590 (written in the margin of original manuscript).
7. Galileo, *Le Opere di Galileo Galilei*, vol. XIX (Barbera, Firenze, 1971), p. 111.

CHAPTER 6: A FRESH START
1. Jeffrey Richards, *Sex, Dissidence and Damnation: Minority Groups in the Middle Ages* (Routledge, New York, 1994), p. 150.
2. Galileo, *Le Opere di Galileo Galilei*, ed. Antonio Favaro (Florence, 1890–1910), vol. II, p. 45.
3. Ibid., vol. X, p. 102.

4. Ibid., vol. II, p. 101.
5. Ibid., vol. XIV, p. 126.
6. Galileo Galilei, *Operations of the Geometric and Military Compass*, trans. Stillman Drake (Smithsonian Institute Press, Washington, 1978), p. 39.

CHAPTER 7: CONFLICT
1. J. J. Fahie, *Galileo: His Life and Work* (London, John Murray, 1903), p. 68.
2. Ibid., p. 69.
3. Ibid.
4. Ibid., p. 71.
5. Galileo Galilei to Johannes Kepler, *Opere di Galileo Galilei*, vol. X (Barbera, Firenze, 1968), p. 69.
6. Ibid., p. 116.
7. Ibid., pp. 275–85.
8. Luigi Barzini, *The Italians* (Atheneum, New York, 1964), p. 319.

CHAPTER 8: THE CRYSTAL MOON
1. 'Thomas Harriot', in *Oxford Figures: 800 Years of the Mathematical Sciences*, ed. J. Fauvel, R. Flodd and R. Wilson (Oxford University Press, 2000), pp. 56–9.
2. Ms. F, 25r., Institut de France, Paris.
3. Ms. A, 12v., Institut de France, Paris.
4. Gaetano Cozzi, *Paolo Sarpi ra Venezia e L'Europa* (Einaudi, Turin, 1979), p. 180.
5. Galileo Galilei, *The Starry Messenger*, trans. Stillman Drake, in *Telescopes, Tides and Tactics* (Chicago University Press, 1983), p. 19.
6. Galileo Galilei, *Il Saggiatore* (1623), *Opere di Galileo*, vol. VI, p. 259.
7. Galileo Galilei, *The Assayer*, p. 57.
8. *Telescopes in Space*, Zdenek Kopal (Hart Publishing Company, 1970), p. 15.
9. *Le Opere di Galileo Galilei*, vol. X (Barbera, Firenze, 1968), pp. 250–1.
10. Ibid.
11. Galileo Galilei, *The Starry Messenger*, trans. Stillman Drake, in *Telescopes, Tides and Tactics* (Chicago University Press, 1983), p. 15.
12. Ibid., p. 24.
13. *Le Opere di Galileo Galilei*, vol. X (Barbera, Firenze, 1968), p. 283.
14. Galileo Galilei, *The Starry Messenger*, trans. Stillman Drake, in *Telescopes, Tides and Tactics* (Chicago University Press, 1983), p. 56.
15. Ibid., pp. 88–9.
16. Niccolo Machiavelli, *The Prince*, chapter XXV.
17. *Telescopes in Space*, Zdenek Kopal (Hart Publishing Company, 1970), p. 15.
18. *Le Opere di Galileo Galilei*, vol. X (Barbera, Firenze, 1968), p. 287.
19. *Life and Letters of Sir Henry Wotton*, ed. Logon Pearsall Smith (Oxford, 1907), vol. I, pp. 486–8.
20. Galileo Galilei, *The Starry Messenger*, trans. Albert Van Helden (Chicago University Press, 1989), p. 94.
21. *Le Opere di Galileo Galilei*, vol. X (Barbera, Firenze, 1968), p. 348.

References

CHAPTER 9: PAPAL SECRETS, HOLY INTRIGUES

1. *Le Opere di Galileo Galilei*, vol. XI (Barbera, Firenze, 1968), pp. 170–2.
2. *Galileo's Florentine Residences*, Righini Bonelli, Maria Luisa and William R. Shea (Instituto di Storia della Scienza, Florence, 1979), p. 19.
3. *Creative Women in Medieval and Early Modern Italy: A Religious and Artistic Renaissance*, E. Ann Matter and John Coakley (University of Pennsylvania Press, Philadelphia, 1994), p. 205.
4. *Le Opere di Galileo Galilei*, vol. XI (Barbera, Firenze, 1968), p. 119.
5. Francesco Sizzi, *Dianoia Astronomica, Optica et Physica* (Venice, 1611).
6. *Le Opere di Galileo Galilei*, vol. XI (Barbera, Firenze, 1968), pp. 170–2.
7. Ibid., p. 71.
8. Ibid., p. 60.
9. Ibid., p. 79.
10. 'Galileo's Visits to Rome', J. Walter and S. J. Miller, *Sky and Telescope*, vol. 11, 1952.
11. Christopher Clavius, (commentary on the *Sphere* of Sacrobosco for his collected works) in *Opera Mathematica* (Bamberg, 1611), trans. James M. Lattis, *Between Copernicus and Galileo* (University of Chicago Press, 1995), p. 161.
12. *Le Opere di Galileo Galilei*, vol. XI (Barbera, Firenze, 1968), p. 143.
13. Ibid., pp. 79–80.
14. Ibid., p. 89.
15. Ibid., vol. XII, p. 172.
16. *Galileo, Courtier*, Mario Biagioli (Chicago University Press, Chicago, 1993), p. 253.
17. *Robert Bellarmine, Saint and Scholar*, James Brodrick (Newman Press, USA, 1961), p. 176.
18. *Le Opere di Galileo Galilei*, vol. XII (Barbera, Firenze, 1968), pp. 206–7.
19. *Discoveries and Opinions of Galileo*, Stillman Drake (Anchor, New York, 1957), p. 189.
20. Andrew Dickson White, *A History of the Warfare of Science with Theology* (Macmillan, London, 1900), p. 145.
21. *Le Opere di Galileo Galilei*, vol. XI (Barbera, Firenze, 1968), p. 102.
22. Ibid., p. 103.
23. Andrew Dickson White, *A History of the Warfare of Science with Theology* (Macmillan, London, 1900), p. 148.
24. *Le Opere di Galileo Galilei*, vol. XI (Barbera, Firenze, 1972), p. 427.
25. Ibid., vol. XX, p. 422.
26. Ibid., vol. XI, p. 247.
27. *Discoveries and Opinions of Galileo*, Stillman Drake (Anchor, New York, 1957), p. 100.
28. *Le Opere di Galileo Galilei*, vol. XX (Barbera, Firenze, 1972), p. 422.
29. Ibid., vol. XI, pp. 326ff.
30. Galileo Galilei, *The Assayer*, p. 50.
31. *Galileo: His Life and Work*, J. J. Fahie (John Murray, London, 1903), p. 130ff.

CHAPTER 10: THE FIGHT BEGINS

1. *Le Opere di Galileo Galilei*, vol. XI (Barbera, Firenze, 1969), p. 605.
2. Ibid.
3. Ibid., vol. X, pp. 502–3.
4. Galileo Galilei, *Contributi alla storia della Academia dei Lincei* (Biblioteca dei Lincei, Rome, 1989), p. 966.
5. *Galileo Galilei e fra Tommaso Caccini*, Antonio Ricci-Riccardi (Successori le Monnier, Florence 1902), p. 68.
6. Ibid., p. 70.
7. *The Crime of Galileo*, Giorgio de Santillana (University of Chicago Press, Chicago, 1955), p. 36.
8. 'Galileo in Acquasparta', Giuseppi Gabrieli, *Atti della Reale Academia d' Italia* (Memoria della Classe di Scienze Morale e Storiche, Rome, 1943), p. 45.
9. *Le Opere di Galileo Galilei*, vol. XII (Barbera, Firenze, 1970), p. 146.
10. *The Crime of Galileo*, Giorgio de Santillana (University of Chicago Press, 1955), p. 117.
11. *Le Opere di Galileo Galilei*, vol. XII (Barbera, Firenze, 1970), p. 183.
12. Ibid., p. 181.
13. Ibid., p. 205.
14. Ibid., p. 206.
15. Galileo Galilei, *Dialogue Concerning the Two Chief Systems, Ptolemaic and Copernican*, trans. Stillman Drake (University of California Press, Berkeley, 1953), p. 67.
16. *Le Opere di Galileo Galilei*, vol. XII (Barbera, Firenze, 1970), p. 226.
17. Ibid., p. 227.
18. Ibid., p. 228.
19. Ibid., p. 238.
20. *Le Opere di Galileo Galilei*, vol. XIX (Barbera, Firenze, 1972), p. 320.
21. *The Galileo Affair: A Documentary History*, ed. Maurice A. Finocchiaro (University of California Press, Berkeley, 1989), p. 174.
22. *Le Opere di Galileo Galilei*, vol. XIX (Barbera, Firenze, 1972), p. 278.
23. Ibid., vol. XV, p. 122.
24. Ibid., vol. XII, p. 248.
25. *Documenti sul barocco in Roma*, ed. J. A. F. Orbaan (Societa Romana di Storia Patria, Rome, 1920), p. 134.
26. Ibid., vol. XII, p. 241.

CHAPTER 11: THE CALM BEFORE THE STORM

1. *Le Opere di Galileo Galilei*, vol. XII (Barbera, Firenze, 1970), p. 443.
2. Ibid., vol. XIII, p. 24.
3. Ibid., p. 25.
4. Ibid.
5. Galileo Galilei, *The Assayer*, p. 154.
6. *Le Opere di Galileo Galilei*, vol. XI (Barbera, Firenze, 1970), p. 257.
7. Ibid., p. 324.

8. *Le Opere di Galileo Galilei*, vol. XIII (Barbera, Firenze, 1970), p. 135.

9. Ibid., p. 140.

10. *Le Opere di Galileo Galilei*, vol. XIII (Barbera, Firenze, 1970), pp. 208–9.

11. Ibid., p. 160.

12. Ibid., p. 145.

13. Ibid., p. 234.

14. Kepler to Herwart von Hohenberg, 26 March 1598, *Gesammelte Werke*, XIII, pp. 192–3.

15. *Le Opere di Galileo Galilei*, vol. III (Barbera, Firenze, 1968), pp. 119–33.

16. Taken from the pope's inauguration, Vatican Library.

17. *The Crime of Galileo*, Giorgio de Santillana (University of Chicago Press, 1955), p. 161.

CHAPTER 12: UNHOLY INTRIGUE

1. *Le Opere di Galileo Galilei*, vol. XVI (Barbera, Firenze, 1971), p. 117.

2. Ibid., vol. XI, p. 232.

3. Ibid., vol. XIV, pp. 359ff.

4. Ibid., vol. XIII, pp. 225–7.

5. Ibid., p. 370.

6. Ibid., vol. XV, pp. 25–6.

7. Ibid., vol. XI, p. 117.

8. Ibid., vol. XIII, p. 186.

9. Ibid., p. 340.

10. *The Galileo Affair: A Documentary History*, ed. Maurice A. Finocchiaro (University of California Press, Berkeley, 1989), p. 214.

11. Ibid., p. 231.

12. St Augustine, *Liber sententiarum*, VIII, book IV, Dist. 2, in G. Lecordier, *La doctrine de l'Eucharistie chez Saint Augustin* (Paris, 1930).

13. Pietro Redondi, *Galileo Heretic*, trans. Raymond Rosenthal (Princeton University Press, Princeton, 1983), p. 208.

14. Ibid., p. 196.

15. Stillman Drake, *Discoveries and Opinions of Galileo* (Doubleday, New York, 1974), p. 274.

16. Ibid., p. 253.

17. *Catechism of the Council of Trent Pt 2*, chapter IV Q XLIII.

18. Historical Archive of the Superior General Curia of the Society of Jesus (Rome), *Fondo gesuitico 657*, p. 183., cited in *Baliani e gesuiti* (C. Constantini, Florence, 1969), p. 59.

19. Archive of the Sacred Congregation for the Doctrine of the Faith, Vatican Archive, Rome, Series ADEE, fols. 292r, 292v and 293r.

20. *Le Opere di Galileo Galilei*, vol. XIII (Barbera, Firenze, 1970), p. 365.

21. Archive of the Sacred Congregation for the Doctrine of the Faith, Vatican Archive, Rome, Series ACDF, EE, f.291r-v, trans. Professor Rafael Martinez, from *Revisiting Galileo's Troubles with the Church: A Short Essay by Mariano Artigas and William Shea* (www.metanexus.net/metanexus_online/printer_friendly.asp?2673).

CHAPTER 13: THE STRONG ARM OF THE CHURCH

1. *Galileo Galilei: A Biography and Inquiry into His Philosophy of Science*, Ludovico Geymonat (McGraw-Hill, 1965), p. 140.
2. *Le Opere di Galileo Galilei*, vol. XV (Barbera, Firenze, 1971), p. 68.
3. *The Galileo Affair: A Documentary History*, ed. Maurice A. Finocchiaro (University of California Press, Berkeley, 1989), p. 240.
4. *Le Opere di Galileo Galilei*, vol. XV (Barbera, Firenze, 1971), p. 34.
5. Ibid., p. 85.
6. This and all subsequent references quoting from the records of the trial are to be found in A. Favaro, *Galileo and the Inquisition*, Florence, 1907.
7. Ibid., p. 98.
8. Giuseppe Galli, *O.P., Il Card. Vincenzo Maculano al processo di Galileo* (Estratto dalla rivista memorie domenicane, 1965), p. 123.
9. *Galileo Galilei and the Roman Curia*, Karl von Gebler (Richwood Publishing Company, Merrick, New York, 1977), p. 263.
10. *Le Opere di Galileo Galilei*, vol. XV (Barbera, Firenze, 1971), p. 106.

CHAPTER 14: GAGGED

1. *Galileo Galilei and the Roman Curia*, Karl von Gebler (Richwood Publishing Company, Merrick, New York, 1977), p. 269.
2. Ibid., p. 271.
3. Andrew Dickson White, *A History of the Warfare of Science with Theology* (Macmillan, London, 1900), p. 245.
4. *Le Opere di Galileo Galilei*, vol. XVIII (Barbera, Firenze, 1971), p. 127.
5. Ibid., p. 223.
6. Ibid., p. 224.
7. Ibid., p. 226.
8. Ibid., vol. XIX, p. 393.
9. Ibid., p. 324.
10. *The Private Life of Galileo*, Mary Allan-Olney (Macmillan, London, 1870), p. 334.
11. *Galileo at Work: His Scientific Biography*, Stillman Drake (University of Chicago Press, Chicago, 1978), p. 360.
12. Galileo Galilei, *The Discourses on the Two New Sciences*, trans. Stillman Drake (Madison, USA, 1974), p. 129.
13. *The Crime of Galileo*, Giorgio de Santillana (University of Chicago Press, 1955), p. 324.
14. *Da Galileo alle Stelle*, Francesco Bertola (Biblos, Padua, 1992), p. 101.
15. *The Crime of Galileo*, Giorgio de Santillana (University of Chicago Press, 1955), p. 397.
16. *Le Opere di Galileo Galilei*, vol. XVIII (Barbera, Firenze, 1971), p. 232.
17. Ibid., p. 245.
18. *Galileo's Mistake: A New Look at the Epic Confrontation between Galileo and the Church*, Wade Rowland (Arcade Publishing, New York, 2001), chapter 25.

References

19. *Galileo at Work: His Scientific Biography*, Stillman Drake (University of Chicago Press, 1978), p. 436.

CHAPTER 15: PHOENIX RISING

1. *Le Opere di Galileo Galilei*, vol. XVIII (Barbera, Firenze, 1971), p. 378.
2. Translation from *A Philosophical Dictionary*, from the French of M. de Voltaire with Additional Notes, Abner Kneeland (Boston, 1835), p. 172.
3. 'Neue Gesichtspunkte zum Galilei-prozess', Zdenko Solle, *Geschichte der Mathematik, Naturwissenschaften und Medizin*, vol. 24 (Vienna, 1980), p. 58.
4. *The Evolution of Physics*, Albert Einstein and Leopold Infeld (Simon and Schuster, New York, 1938), p. 7.
5. *Le Opere di Galileo Galilei*, vol. XIX (Barbera, Firenze, 1971), p. 393.

CHAPTER 16: TWENTY-FIRST-CENTURY WITCHCRAFT

1. *Paschini e la Roma ecclesiastica*, 49–93 in *Atti del convegno di studio su Pio Paschini nel centenario della nascita: 1878–1978*, Monsignor Michele Maccarrone (Pubblicazioni della Deputazione di Storia Patria del Friuli Udine, 1980).
2. *Corriere della Sera*, 30 March 1990.
3. 'Speech of His Holiness John Paul II', in *Einstein Galileo*, Brenno Bucciarelli (Libreria Editrice Vaticana, Vatican City State, 1980), p. 79.
4. 'Discourse to the Pontifical Academy of Sciences', John Paul II, *Origins* 22, 12 November 1992.
5. *Galileo*, Bertholt Brecht, English version by Charles Laughton (Grove Press, New York, 1966), p. 84.
6. 'Discourse to the Pontifical Academy of Sciences', John Paul II, *Origins* 22, 12 November 1992.
7. *Galilei und die Kirche oder Das Recht auf Irrtum*, Walter Brandmüller, (Pustet, Regensburg, 1982).
8. Cardinal Joseph Ratzinger, taken from the text of a speech delivered to a Eucharist Congress in Benevento, Italy, 25 May–2 June 2002, entitled 'Eucharist, Communion and Solidarity'.

Bibliography

Allan-Olney, Mary, *The Private Life of Galileo* (Macmillan, London, 1870).

Aristotle, *The Works of Aristotle* (Great Books, Chicago, 1952).

Biagioli, Mario, *Galileo Courtier* (University of Chicago Press, Chicago, 1993).

Bonelli, Righini, Maria Luisa and William R. Shea, *Galileo's Florentine Residences* (Instituto di Storia della Scienza, Florence, 1979).

Brecht, Bertholt, *Galileo*, English version by Charles Laughton (Grove Press, New York, 1966).

Brodrick, James, *Galileo: The Man, His Work, His misfortunes* (Latimer & Trade, Plymouth, 1964).

——, *Robert Bellarmine, Saint and Scholar* (Newman Press, USA, 1961).

Brooke, John Hedley, *Science and Religion* (Cambridge University Press, Cambridge, 1991).

Campanella, T., *A Defense of Galileo, the Mathematician from Florence* (Notre Dame, 1994).

Cohen, I. Bernard, *The Birth of a New Physics* (Penguin Books, London, 1992).

——, *Revolution in Science* (Cambridge, MA, Belknap Press, 2001).

Copernicus, Nicolaus, *De Revolutionibus Orbium Coelestium* (Great Books, Chicago, 1953).

De Santillana, Giorgio, *The Crime of Galileo* (Heinemann, London, 1958).

Dijksterhuis, E. J., *The Mechanization of the World Picture* (Oxford University Press, Oxford, 1969).

Drake, Stillman, *Essays on Galileo and the History and Philosophy of Science*, 3 volumes (University of Toronto Press, Toronto, 1999).

——, *Galileo* (Oxford University Press, Oxford, 2001).

——, *Discoveries and Opinions of Galileo* (Doubleday, 1957).

——, *Galileo: Pioneer Scientist* (University of Toronto Press, Toronto, 1990).

——, *Galileo at Work: His Scientific Biography* (University of Chicago Press, Chicago, 1981).

Draper, John William, *History of the Conflict Between Religion and Science*, International Scientific Series (D. Appleton and Company, New York, 1957).

Eamon, William, *Court, Patronage and Institutions: Science, Technology and Medicine at the European Court, 1500–1700* (Boydell Press, Woodbridge, 1991).

Bibliography

Fahie, John J., *Galileo, His Life and Work* (1903).

Fantoli, A., *Galileo: For Copernicanism and for the Church* (Vatican City, 1994).

Fernand, Hayward, *A History of the Popes* (Dutton & Co., New York, 1931).

Feyerabend, Paul K., *Farewell to Reason* (Verso, London, 2002).

——, *Against Method* (Verso, London 1993).

Finocchiaro, Maurice A., *The Galileo Affair: A Documentary History* (University of California Press, Berkeley, 1989).

——, *Galileo on the World Systems* (University of California Press, Berkeley, 1997).

——, *Galileo and the Art of Reasoning: Rhetorical Foundations of Logic and Scientific Method* (Dordrecht, Boston, MA, 1980).

Freedberg, David, *The Eye of the Lynx: Galileo, His Friends, and the Beginnings of Modern Natural History* (University of Chicago Press, Chicago, 2002).

Galilei, Galileo, *Le Opere di Galileo Galilei*, ed. Antonio Favaro, 20 volumes (Barbera, Firenze, 1968).

——, *Sidereus Nuncius* (1610).

——, *Dialogue Concerning the Two Chief World Systems*, trans. Stillman Drake (University of California Press, Berkeley, 1953).

Ganss, George (trans.), *The Constitutions of the Society of Jesus* (Institute of Jesuit Sources, St Louis, 1970).

Geymonat, Ludovico, *Galileo Galilei: A Biography and Inquiry into His Philosophy of Science* (McGraw-Hill, New York, 1965).

Holton, Gerald, *Thematic Origins of Scientific Thought* (Harvard University Press, Cambridge, MA, 1988).

Howell, Kenneth, *God's Two Books* (Notre Dame, 2002).

James, Jamie, *The Music of the Spheres* (Abacus, London, 1994).

Jammer, Max, *Concepts of Space* (Dover, New York, 1993).

Koestler, Arthur, *The Sleepwalkers* (Hutchinson & Co., London, 1959).

Koyré, A., *Galileo Studies* (Atlantic Highlands, New Jersey, 1978).

Kuhn, Thomas S., *The Copernican Revolution* (Harvard University Press, Cambridge, MA, 1971).

Langford, Jerome J., *Galileo, Science and the Church* (University of Michigan Press, Ann Arbor, 1966).

Machamer, Peter (ed.), *The Cambridge Companion to Galileo* (Cambridge University Press, 1998).

Matter, E. Ann, and Coakley, John, *Creative Women in Medieval and Early Modern Italy: A Religious and Artistic Renaissance* (University of Pennsylvania Press, Philadelphia, 1994).

Musgrave, Alan, *Beyond Reason* (Kluwer, Dordrecht, 1991).

Norwich, John Julius, *A History of Venice* (Penguin, London, 1982).

Paschini, Pio, *Vita e Opere di Galileo Galilei* (Herder, Rome, 1965).

Poupard, Paul Cardinal (ed.), *Galileo Galilei: Toward a Resolution of 350 Years of Debate, 1633–1983*, trans. Ian Campbell (1987).

Redondi, Pietro, *Galileo: Heretic* (Princeton University Press, 1987).

Reston, James, Jr, *Galileo: A Life* (Cassell, 1994).

Richards, Jeffrey, *Sex, Dissidence and Damnation: Minority Groups in the Middle Ages* (Routledge, New York, 1994).

Rowland, Wade, *Galileo's Mistake* (Arcade Publishing, New York, 2003).

Russell, Colin A. and Goodman, David, *The Rise of Scientific Europe 1500–1800* (Open University Press, Milton Keynes, 1991).

Sharratt, M., *Galileo: Decisive Innovator* (Cambridge, 1994).

Shea, Steven William R. and Artigas, Mariano, *Galileo in Rome* (Oxford University Press, Oxford, 2003).

——, *Galileo's Intellectual Revolution. Middle Period, 1610–1632* (New York, 1977).

Singer, Charles (ed.), *Studies in the History of Science* (Oxford University Press, 1917).

Sobel, Dava, *Galileo's Daughter* (Penguin, 2000).

Stukeley, William, *Memoirs of Sir Isaac Newton's Life*, ed. A. Hastings White (Taylor and Francis, London, 1936).

Walker, D. P., *Studies in Musical Science in the Late Renaissance* (London, 1978).

Westfall, R. S., *Essays on the Trial of Galileo* (Vatican City, 1989).

White, Andrew Dickson, *A History of the Warfare of Science with Theology in Christendom*, 2 volumes (Yale University Press, 1955).

White, Michael, *Machiavelli: A Man Misunderstood*, Little, Brown, 2005.

——, *Leonardo: The First Scientist* (Little, Brown, 2000).

Index